First World War
and Army of Occupation
War Diary
France, Belgium and Germany

28 DIVISION
Headquarters, Branches and Services
Adjutant and Quarter-Master General
16 November 1914 - 25 October 1915

WO95/2269/1

The Naval & Military Press Ltd
www.nmarchive.com
Published in association with The National Archives

Published by

The Naval & Military Press Ltd

Unit 10 Ridgewood Industrial Park,

Uckfield, East Sussex,

TN22 5QE England

Tel: +44 (0) 1825 749494

www.naval-military-press.com

www.nmarchive.com

This diary has been reprinted in facsimile from the original. Any imperfections are inevitably reproduced and the quality may fall short of modern type and cartographic standards.

© Crown Copyright

Images reproduced by permission of The National Archives, London, England, 2015.

Contents

Document type	Place/Title	Date From	Date To
Heading	28 Div Commander Royal Artillery		
Heading	28th Division Divl Artillery C. R. A. Dec 1914-Oct 1915		
Heading	Headqrs. R.A. 28th Division Vol I 16.11.14-31.1.15		
War Diary	Winchester	16/11/1914	21/01/1915
War Diary	Pradelles	21/01/1915	31/01/1915
Miscellaneous	28th Divisional Artillery. Appendix "A" Nominal Roll of Officer Appendix "A"	28/01/1915	28/01/1915
Heading	Headquarters (Intelligence) 28th Division Vol I 22-30.1.15 121/4327		
War Diary	G.H.Q. Summary Pradelles	22/01/1915	30/01/1915
Heading	Headquarters: R.A. 28th Division Vol II 1-28.2.15 121/4636		
War Diary	Chateau S.W. of Ypres (Sq H 23 b)	01/02/1915	05/02/1915
War Diary	Farm House In Square H.11.d.7.7.	06/02/1915	09/02/1915
War Diary	Chateau Vidal	09/02/1915	28/02/1915
Miscellaneous	Order To Bataille Appendix B		
Miscellaneous	28th Divisional Arty Appendix C		
Miscellaneous	113th Heavy Battery Royal Parrison Artillery Nominal Roll Of Officers Appendix D		
Miscellaneous	Heavy Brigade Royal Garrison Artillery 28th Division. Nominal Roll of Officers. Appendix E		
Miscellaneous	28th Divisional Arty Appendix F		
Miscellaneous	B.M./181 Appendix "G"	26/02/1915	26/02/1915
Heading	28th Divisional Arty Vol III 1-31.3.15		
Heading	A.G. The Base Herewith War Diary 28th Divisional Artillery For March 1915		
War Diary	Chateau Vidal	01/03/1915	31/03/1915
Miscellaneous	Roll of Officers Who Have Joined 28th Divisional Artillery Appendix H	00/03/1915	00/03/1915
Miscellaneous	B.M./197. Appendix J	04/03/1915	04/03/1915
Miscellaneous			
Miscellaneous	Roll of Officers Who Have Joined 28th Divisional Artillery Appendix L	00/03/1915	00/03/1915
Heading	Headqrs R.A. 28th Division Vol IV 1-30.4.15		
War Diary	Chateau Vidal	01/04/1915	10/04/1915
War Diary	Rue De Dixmude Ypres	11/04/1915	12/04/1915
War Diary	Ypres	13/04/1915	21/04/1915
War Diary	Chateau North of Vlamertinghe	22/04/1915	22/04/1915
War Diary	Vlamertinghe	22/04/1915	30/04/1915
War Diary	Diary of The 28th Divisional Artillery During The Second Battle of Ypres From 22nd April To The 14th May. 1915	22/04/1915	14/05/1915
Heading	Hd. Qrs. R.A. 28th Division Vol V 1-31.5.15		
War Diary	Vlamertinghe	01/05/1915	04/05/1915
War Diary	Farm H.7.C.50	05/05/1915	05/05/1915
War Diary	H 7 C 50	05/05/1915	06/05/1915
War Diary	Brandhoek	06/05/1915	12/05/1915
War Diary	Inn H11b20	13/05/1915	13/05/1915
War Diary	Inn H11b	13/05/1915	21/05/1915

War Diary	Farm H.7c 81	22/05/1915	22/05/1915
War Diary	Brandhoek	23/05/1915	31/05/1915
Heading	28th Division H.Q. R.A. 28th Division Vol VI 1-30.6.15		
War Diary	Watou	01/06/1915	17/06/1915
War Diary	Westoutre	18/06/1915	27/06/1915
Miscellaneous	A/49th Battery R.F.A. (Howitzer)		
Heading	28th Division Hd.Qrs. RA. 28th Division Vol VII 1-31-7-15		
War Diary	Westoutre	01/07/1915	22/07/1915
War Diary	Locre Chateau	23/07/1915	31/07/1915
Miscellaneous	Brigade Major R.A. 28th Division.	07/07/1915	07/07/1915
Miscellaneous	Items of Interest	15/07/1915	15/07/1915
Miscellaneous	A.A. G.H.Q./280/2 (C) 2nd Corps Q.C. 619/7 28th Divn. 2209/7 R.A. 28th Divn. 1952	11/07/1915	11/07/1915
Miscellaneous	Target Reports And Progress Reports	20/07/1915	20/07/1915
Miscellaneous	Items of Interest	21/07/1915	21/07/1915
Miscellaneous	Items of Interest	22/07/1915	22/07/1915
Miscellaneous	Items of Interest	26/07/1915	26/07/1915
Miscellaneous	Items of Interest	29/07/1915	29/07/1915
Miscellaneous	2nd Army 2nd Corps, 28th Divn 28th R.A.	29/07/1915	29/07/1915
Miscellaneous	Items of Interest	30/07/1915	30/07/1915
Miscellaneous	28th Divisional Artillery Routine Orders	31/07/1915	31/07/1915
Miscellaneous	Items of Interest	31/07/1915	31/07/1915
Miscellaneous	28th Div. G. 353	31/07/1915	31/07/1915
Miscellaneous	10th Heavy Brigade R.G.A.		
Heading	28th Division Hd Qrs. R. A. 28th Division Vol VIII From 1-31.8.15		
War Diary	Locre Chateau	01/08/1915	31/08/1915
Miscellaneous	Items of Interest For 24 Hours Ending 3.0 p.m. 1st August 1915		
Miscellaneous	Items of Interest For 24 Hours Ending 3.0 p.m. 2nd August 1915		
Miscellaneous	Items of Interest For 24 Hours Ending 3.0 p.m 3rd August 1915		
Miscellaneous	Items of Interest For 24 Hours Ending 6.0 p.m 5th August 1915		
Miscellaneous	Items of Interest For 24 Hours Ending 6.0 p.m 6th August 1915		
Miscellaneous	28th Divisional Artillery Items of Interest For 24 Hours Ending 6.0 p.m 7th August 1915		
Miscellaneous	28th Divisional Artillery Items of Interest For 24 Hours Ending 6.0 p.m 9th August 1915		
Miscellaneous	28th Divisional Artillery Items of Interest For 24 Hours Ending 6.0 p.m 10th August 1915		
Miscellaneous	Brigade Test	13/08/1915	13/08/1915
Miscellaneous	28th Divisional Artillery Items of Interest For 24 Hours Ending 6.0 p.m 14th August 1915		
Miscellaneous	Hd Qrs No. 2220 14-8-15 28th Div Artillery	15/08/1915	15/08/1915
Miscellaneous	28th Divisional Artillery Items of Interest for 24 Hours Ending 6.0 p.m 15th August 1915		
Miscellaneous	28th Divisional Artillery Practice. Carried Out Sunday 15th August 1915		
Miscellaneous	28th Divisional Artillery Items of Interest For 24 Hours Ending 6.0 p.m 16th August 1915		

Miscellaneous	28th Divisional Artillery Items of Interest For 24 Hours Ending 6.0 p.m 17th August 1915		
Miscellaneous	28th Divisional Artillery Items of Interest For 24 Hours Ending 6.0 p.m 18th August 1915		
Miscellaneous	O.C. 69th Battery R.F.A.	18/08/1915	18/08/1915
Miscellaneous	Registration By Squares		
Miscellaneous	28th Divisional Artillery Items of Interest For 24 Hours Ending 6.0 p.m 19th August 1915		
Miscellaneous	28th Divisional Artillery Items of Interest For 24 Hours Ending 6.0 p.m 20th August 1915		
Miscellaneous	69th Battery B/680		
Miscellaneous	Items of Interest	20/07/1915	20/07/1915
Miscellaneous	28th Divisional Artillery Items of Interest For 24 Hours Ending 6.0 p.m 22nd August 1915		
Miscellaneous	28th Divisional Artillery Items of Interest For 24 Hours Ending 6.0 p.m 23rd August 1915		
Miscellaneous	28th Divisional Artillery Items of Interest For 24 Hours Ending 6.0 p.m 24th August 1915		
Miscellaneous	69th B/763		
Miscellaneous	28th Divisional Artillery Items of Interest For 24 Hours Ending 6.0 p.m 25th August 1915		
Miscellaneous	69th		
Miscellaneous			
Miscellaneous	Officer Commanding, 3 146 Brigade R.F.A.	26/08/1915	26/08/1915
Miscellaneous	28th Divisional Artillery Items of Interest For 24 Hours Ending 6.0 p.m 26th August 1915		
Miscellaneous	28th Divisional Artillery Items of Interest For 24 Hours Ending 6.0 p.m 27th August 1915		
Miscellaneous	69 C/5		
Miscellaneous	28th Divisional Artillery Items of Interest For 24 Hours Ending 6.0 p.m 28th August 1915	27/08/1915	27/08/1915
Miscellaneous	69		
Miscellaneous	28th Divisional Artillery Items of Interest For 24 Hours Ending 6.0 p.m 29th August 1915		
Miscellaneous	2nd Army Corps Summary of Information	29/08/1915	29/08/1915
Diagram etc	Sketch Map Showing Route (marked By Arrows)		
Miscellaneous	31st Brigade Test	29/08/1915	29/08/1915
Miscellaneous	28th Divisional Artillery Items of Interest For 24 Hours Ending 6.0 p.m 30th August 1915		
Miscellaneous	28th Divisional Artillery Routine Orders	30/08/1915	30/08/1915
Miscellaneous			
Miscellaneous	28th Divisional Artillery Items of Interest For 24 Hours Ending 6.0 p.m 31st August 1915		
Miscellaneous	Nominal Roll of Officers Headquarters, 28th Divisional Artillery		
Miscellaneous	3rd Brigade R.F.A.		
Miscellaneous	31st Brigade R.F.A.		
Miscellaneous	146th Brigade R.F.A.		
Miscellaneous	A/73rd Battery		
Miscellaneous	B/89th Howitzer Battery		
Miscellaneous	A/49th Howitzer Battery		
Miscellaneous	28th Divisional Ammunition Column		
Miscellaneous	Trench Howitzer Battery		
Miscellaneous	9th Anti Aircraft Section		
Miscellaneous	12th Anti Aircraft Section		

Heading	28th Division Hd Qrs. R.A. 28th Division Vol IX Sept 15		
War Diary	Locre Chateau	01/09/1915	22/09/1915
War Diary	Merris	23/09/1915	26/09/1915
War Diary	Bethune	27/09/1915	30/09/1915
Miscellaneous	28th Divisional Artillery Items of Interest For 24 Hours Ending 6.0 p.m 2nd September 1915		
Miscellaneous	28th Divisional Artillery Items of Interest For 24 Hours Ending 6.0 p.m 3rd September 1915		
Miscellaneous	28th Divisional Artillery Items of Interest For 24 Hours Ending 6.0 p.m 4th September 1915		
Miscellaneous	28th Divisional Artillery Items of Interest For 24 Hours Ending 6.0 p.m 5th September 1915		
Miscellaneous	28th Divisional Artillery Items of Interest For 24 Hours Ending 6.0 p.m 6th September 1915		
Miscellaneous	28th Divisional Artillery Items of Interest For 24 Hours Ending 6.0 p.m 7th September 1915		
Miscellaneous	28th Divisional Artillery Items of Interest For 24 Hours Ending 6.0 p.m 8th September 1915		
Miscellaneous	28th Divisional Artillery Items of Interest For 24 Hours Ending 6.0 p.m 10th September 1915		
Miscellaneous	28th Divisional Artillery Items of Interest For 24 Hours Ending 6.0 p.m 17th September 1915		
Miscellaneous	28th Divisional Artillery Items of Interest For 24 Hours Ending 6.0 p.m 19th September 1915		
Operation(al) Order(s)	28th Division Operation Order No. 53 Appendix 20	26/09/1915	26/09/1915
Miscellaneous			
Miscellaneous	A Form. Messages And Signals		
Operation(al) Order(s)	28th Division Operation Order No. 34 Appendix 21	27/09/1915	27/09/1915
Heading	28th Division Hd.Qrs. R.A. 28th Division Vol X October 15		
War Diary	Chateau Des Pres Sailly La Bourse	01/10/1915	01/10/1915
War Diary	Sailly La Bourse	02/10/1915	19/10/1915
War Diary	Bethune	20/10/1915	20/10/1915
War Diary	On Train	21/10/1915	22/10/1915
War Diary	Marseilles	23/10/1915	25/10/1915
Heading	Hd.Qrs. R.A. 28th Division Completion Of Vol X Oct 15		
Miscellaneous			
Miscellaneous	Appendix 127	20/10/1915	20/10/1915
Miscellaneous	28th Division Programme of Entraining Fouquereuil Station		
Miscellaneous	28th Division. Programme of Entraining Lillers Station		
Miscellaneous	O.C. Seige Group Appendix 123	01/10/1915	01/10/1915
Miscellaneous	BM482 Appendix 124	01/10/1915	01/10/1915
Operation(al) Order(s)	28th Divl Arty O.O. No. 50	03/10/1915	03/10/1915
Miscellaneous	A Form. Messages And Signals		
Map	Appendix 126	14/10/1915	14/10/1915
Miscellaneous	The Following Table Shows Rates of Fire To Be Employed In Carrying Out The Programme On The 13th Instant.	11/10/1915	11/10/1915
Operation(al) Order(s)	28th Divisional Artillery Operation Order No. 51	09/10/1915	09/10/1915
Miscellaneous	Amendment To Tables of Rates And Distribution of Fire Appendix 125	12/10/1915	12/10/1915
Miscellaneous			
Miscellaneous	Distribution of Fire Of 28th Divisional Artillery		

Map	1st Phase
Map	2nd Phase
Map	3rd Phase

28 DIV

COMMANDER ROYAL ARTILLERY

28TH DIVISION
DIVL ARTILLERY

C. R. A.
DEC 1914-OCT 1915

121/4210

Head Qrt: R.A. 2nd Division.

Vol I. 16.11.14 — 31.1.15

WAR DIARY 28th Divisional Artillery

INTELLIGENCE SUMMARY.

(Erase heading not required.)

Army Form C. 2118.

Hour, Date, Place	Summary of Events and Information	Remarks and references to Appendices
1914 WINCHESTER. 16th Novr.	The batteries forming the 28th Divisional Artillery landed in England from India. They consisted of the 3rd Brigade composed of the 18th, 62nd & 75th Batteries, also the 100th & 103rd.	
19th Novr.	Batteries reached WINCHESTER & here encamped on MAGDALEN HILL. Here they were attached to the 27th Divisional Artillery — to which half of the 100th Battery was transferred. The batteries were ordered to complete up to war establishment but many officers, men, horses & much equipment however were taken to complete the 27th Divisional batteries in WINCHESTER.	
17th Decr.	Owing to inclement weather batteries moved into billets in WINCHESTER.	

22nd "	Orders given for the batteries to divide in order to form four gun batteries. Each battery thus formed had 3 guns only the personnel & horses of the parent battery. The 18th became the 18th & 365th.
	      " 62nd " 62nd & 366th
	      " 75th " 75th & 367th
	      " 103rd " 103rd & 69th
	The 100th Battery — having already only half a battery — did not again divide. The batteries were brigaded as follows:—
	 3rd Brigade 18th, 62nd, 365th.
	 31st " 69th, 100th, 103rd.
	 146th " 75th, 366th, 367th.
	Officers & personnel were posted, horses drawn from the Remount Dept.	

28th Divl Artillery

WAR DIARY
or
INTELLIGENCE SUMMARY.
(Erase heading not required.)

Army Form C. 2118.

Hour, Date, Place	Summary of Events and Information	Remarks and references to Appendices
1914 WINCHESTER. 22nd Decr.	In WINCHESTER; deficiencies in technical equipment, vehicles, & ammunn were made up from the Ordnance Deptt. 146th Bde went into billets on line HEADBOURNE WORTHY — ITCHEN ABBAS, the 3rd Bde A.C. at WEEKE, the 31st Bde on line TWYFORD – COLDEN COMMON & COMPTON (except HQ & 100th A. Battn which remained in WINCHESTER). This to make room for 84th Bde in the town. W.E.	
29th Decr.	Co-operation between guns & aeroplanes practised on SALISBURY PLAIN. Brig Genl A.W. GAY A.S.C. assumed command of the 28 Divnl Arty, which had been temporarily commanded by Lt Col A.L.WALKER. Orders issued for formation of Divisional Ammn Column at SLOUGH W.E.	Appendix A.
1915 5th Jany 12th Jany 14th Jany.	Co-operation with aeroplanes again practised on SALISBURY PLAIN. W.E. The division was inspected by H.M. the King. W.E. After many changes having to ardurs [?] either the cavalry, the divisional artillery was ordered to embark to SOUTHAMPTON on the 15th & following days. Each brigade accompanying an infantry brigade. Nominal roll of officers who accompanied HQ, Bdes, & Div A.C. is shewn in Appendix A. W.E.	
15th Jany 16th " 16th " (18th) "	3rd Bde left for SOUTHAMPTON by route march. W.E. do " " " W.E. HQRA & 146th Bde left for SOUTHAMPTON W.E. Divl A.C. left SLOUGH by rail for SOUTHAMPTON The [...] 123rd Heavy Battery – which were shewn in	

28th Divnl Artillery

Army Form C. 2118.

WAR DIARY
or
INTELLIGENCE SUMMARY.
(Erase heading not required.)

Instructions regarding War Diaries and Intelligence Summaries are contained in F.S. Regs., Part II. and the Staff Manual respectively. Title pages will be prepared in manuscript.

Hour, Date, Place	Summary of Events and Information	Remarks and references to Appendices
1915		
19th Jan-	As last 4th the Divisional Artillery did not in the end accompany it abroad.	
31st -	3rd Bde - was complete in its billets N. of PRADELLES. Inf.	
	31st Bde having been kept all day outside LE HAVRE was complete with billets about STRAZEELE. Iwas attached to the 84th Infy Bde - Spherical HQ was at STRAZEELE. Inf.	
21st Jany	HQ 2.8th Divn R.A. reached PRADELLES, where it went into billets Inf.	
22" "	146 Bde. went into billets at Hamn N. of BORRE was attached to 85th - 87th Bde Inf.	
23rd "	Its HQ opened up at CAESTRE Inf.	
25th "	Divl Ammn Column was complete in billets S. & S.W. of BORRE. Inf.	
29th "	Brig Genl accompanied Brig Genl R.A. Vth Corps to YPRES & inspected the French batteries of the 31st - Division Inf.	
	Bde Commanders with Battery Commanders observing Officers went out to YPRES & spent the day reconnoitring the approaches to gun positions & observing the approaches at which the French guns were firing. The highest was also apart.	
30th "	Studying the French methods & Officers returned in 30th. Inf.	
	A. Q & U Batteries under Lt Col Rouse, having been posted on loan to the Divn the R.A. Comdr. B.C. Comdr & Observation Officers went out with Brig Genl R.A. to YPRES & examined the French positions they were to take over & reconnoitred forward areas. 88th Heritage Bty from VII Division was transferred to 28 Divn instead to join on the line of march on Tuesday coming under 28 C.D. Inf the orders when it the 28 Divn Question Mbrs Not received durably & move to YPRES. of Inf Fibry. Inf. Column. 28 Div - moved into BORRE.	
31st "	The 3 R.H.A. batteries - on loan from 2nd Cav Divn - moved into BORRE. The 2 R.H.A. batteries about STRAZEELE. Ams Cols. at BORRE. Arrwr. Battns positions again reconnoitred by Lt Col Rouse. Ofters in charge M.2 received YPRE's position from details of French batteries. Inf. Evry man details infantry taking over of French batteries. Inf.	

PRADELLES

28TH DIVISIONAL ARTILLERY.
NOMINAL ROLL OF OFFICERS

28th January 1915.

Rank	and Name		Unit.	Remarks.
Br. Gen.	Gay	A.W., D.S.O.	Hd.Qrs. 28th Divn.Arty.	Commanding
Major	Fergusson	V.M.	" " " " "	Brigade Major
Capt.	Burkhardt	V.R.	" " " " "	Staff Captain
2/Lieut	Gay	A.B.	" " " " "	Aide-de-camp
Lt-Col	Walker	A.L.	Hd.Qrs. 3rd Bdge. R.F.A.	Commanding
2/Lieut	Whitehead	J.L.	"	Adjutant
Major	Manley	W.G.H.	18th Battery R.F.A.	
Lieut	MacGregor	J.St.C.	"	
2/Lieut	Maxwell	J.E.	"	
2/Lieut	Macdonald	J.E.	"	
Major	Drake	H.M.	62nd Battery R.F.A.	
2/Lieut	Ethelston	S.	"	
2/Lieut	Paterson	A.	"	
2/Lieut	Harris	W.G.	"	
Capt.	Bower	H.G.L.	365th Battery R.F.A.	
2/Lieut	Pierce	H.L.	"	
2/Lieut	Strickland	R.G.	"	
2/Lieut	Collingwood	A.H.	"	
Capt.	Clarken	G.	A.C. 3rd Brigade R.F.A.	
2/Lieut	Franey	J.S.	"	
2/Lieut	Creesky	R.L.	"	
2/Lieut	Culpin	H.	"	
Lt-Col	Kelly	H.T.S.	Hd.Qrs. 31st Brigade R.F.A.	Commanding
Lieut	Ireland	K.G.M.		Adjutant
Major	Bedwell	E.P.	69th Battery R.F.A.	
Lieut	VanStraubenzee	A.B.	"	
2/Lieut	Brown	J.G.L.	"	
2/Lieut	Swain	G.A.	"	
Major	Ramsden	R.E.	100th Battery R.F.A.	
2/Lieut	Mallalieu	W.	"	
2/Lieut.	Lomax	R.H.W.	"	
2/Lieut	Hawkins	A.E.	"	
Major	Hope	J.R.	103rd Battery R.F.A.	
2/Lieut	Kennedy	A.C.	"	
2/Lieut	Cumming	C.E.	"	
2/Lieut	Gretton	W.	"	
Major	Cape	J.S.	A.C. 31st Brigade R.F.A.	
2/Lieut	McKenzie	D.R.	"	
2/Lieut	Benham	J.R.	"	
2/Lieut	Johnson	P.E.	"	
Bt-Col	Rundle	G.B.T.	Hd.Qrs. 146th Brigade R.F.A.	Commanding
Lieut	Graham	S.D.		Adjutant
Major	Jervis	N.J.M.	75th Battery R.F.A.	
2/Lieut	Benny	G.R.	"	
2/Lieut	Coad	E.H.	"	
2/Lieut	Hosack	P.J.O'F.	"	
Major	Wickham, D.S.O.	T.E.P.	366th Battery R.F.A.	
2/Lieut	Hay Webb	C.R.A.	"	
2/Lieut	Balcombe Brown	W.E.	"	
2/Lieut	Cooley	H.J.	"	

Appendix "A"

Nominal Roll of Officers (Continued)

Rank	and	Name		Unit	Remarks
Capt.	Macdona		B.V.	367th Battery R.F.A.	
2/Lieut	Tuite Dalton		G.	" " "	
2/Lieut	Johnstone		F.J.C	" " "	
2/Lieut	Stansfield		E.J.	" " "	
Capt	Hinds		C.W.	A.C. 146th Brigade R.F.A.	
2/Lieut	Stoyle		E.G.	" " " "	
2/Lieut	Russell		G.C.	" " " "	
2/Lieut	Hayes		L.F.	" " " "	
Lt-Col	Kerrich		W.E.	Hd.Qrs. 28th Divn. Ammn. Col.	Commanding
Capt.	Allen		J.T.	" " " " "	Adjutant
Capt	Stevens		H.	No. 1 Section Divn. Ammn. Col.	
Capt	Mitcheson		H.G.S.	" " " " "	
2/Lieut	Schuster		E.H.J.	" " " " "	
Capt	Warner		C.	No. 2 " " " "	
Lieut	King		E.T.	" " " " "	
2/Lieut	Foster		A.C.	" " " " "	
Major	Hoare		G.S.	No. 3 " " " "	
2/Lieut	Brooke		J.R.I.	" " " " "	
2/Lieut	Maitland		A.	" " " " "	
2/Lieut	Hoare		A.H.	No. 4 " " " "	
2/Lieut	Vanderbyl		P.B.	i/c Base Details.	

Brigadier General
Commanding 28th Divisional Artillery.

121/4327

Head Quarters (Artillery) 28th Division.

Vol I. 22 — 30.1.15
N.d.

Army Form C. 2118.

Instructions regarding War Diaries and Intelligence
Summaries are contained in F.S. Regs., Part II.
and the Staff Manual respectively. Title pages
will be prepared in manuscript.

WAR DIARY
INTELLIGENCE SUMMARY.
(Erase heading not required.)

1915.   28th Division.

Hour, Date, Place	Summary of Events and Information	Remarks and references to Appendices
G.H.Q. Summary. 22.Jan. PRADELLES FRUGES	Absence of special train movement in rear of German line. Roads in and LILLE-TOURCOING-ROUBAIX clear of large bodies at 10.30.a.m. River LYS in flood and many bridges cannot be used.	(Air report.
6. p.m. "	FRELINGHIEN and vicinity clear of movement.	Tel.
6. p.m. "	Airmen report motor transport all round PERENCHIES and 40 motor vehicles towards LOMPRET (N.W. of LILLE). Total vehicles 150.	Tel. G.98.
1. p.m. "	G.H.Q. agents report considerable concentration of German Corps at LILLE and MENIN.	Tel. G.95.
4. p.m. "	Concentration at MENIN confirmed by French Mission.	Tel. G.96. E. Major
G.H.Q. Summary. 23.Jan. "	No sign of movement in rear of German line. Roads round LILLE - TOURCOING - MENIN clear at 11.30.a.m.	Air report. E. Major
G.H.Q. Summary. 25.Jan. "	Enemy attacked in force on line GIVENCHY - CUINCHY. Enemy, after 5 attacks, gained footing in GIVENCHY but was driven out and 24 th. (Germans) R'gts taken by I Corps. 51 prisoners of 56 th.	G.H.Q. Summary and Tel. G.137.
G.H.Q. Summary 25.Jan "	A German Battn. attacked at 9. a.m. at BROODSEINDE (E. of ZONNEBEKE) but was repulsed with 300 casualties to enemy.	E. Major
" 26. Jan "	At BROODSEINDE on 25 Jan., the attack was by 7 battalions, instead of only 1 b. - Area ST. ELOI, HOLLEBEKE, YPRES-COMINES Canal, HOUTHEM, GAREE in trenches, MESSINES-WYTSCHAETE, DIEU, MESSINES reported clear of movement at 4.10 pm. Our enemy seen in morning.	Air report. E. Major

Army Form C. 2118.

WAR DIARY
INTELLIGENCE SUMMARY.
(Erase heading not required.)

Hour, Date, Place	Summary of Events and Information	Remarks and references to Appendices
1915 G.H.Q. Summary 29.Jan. PRADELLES	Two battalions seen moving into MOORSLEDE at 11.50 a.m. 28th Jan. — Otherwise roads of approach were generally clear. Park of 250 motor vehicles seen about COURTRAI; of 80 at ROLLEGHEMCAPPELLE; of 60 near BISSEGHEM. The area LILLE-DOUAI-LENS reported normal.	Air report. E. Major.
30. Jan. "	Transport parks one mile long near COURTRAI in the forenoon. Two steam engines (? for heavy gun) seen on COURTRAI-MENIN road.	Air report.
" "	Column of 1500 men seen at 9.30 a.m. marching from LILLE to PERENCHIES. No transport observed with it.	Tel. G. 2113. E. Major. G.S.O. III.

121/4636

121/4636

Head Qrs: R.A. 28th Division

Vol II. 1 — 28.2.15

WAR DIARY
INTELLIGENCE SUMMARY

Army Form C. 2118.

28th DA

Hour, Date, Place	Summary of Events and Information	Remarks and references to Appendices
Chateau S.W. of Ypres. (Sq H 23 b). 1st February 1915	In accordance with 28th Divnl Operation Orders Nos 1 + 2 the Divnl Artillery marched to area South of VLAMERTINGHE. On arrival at each Battery wagon lines of this date with Brigade + Battery Headquarters + Inspection of Ammn Column by Capt A.B.E. R.H.A., 1st which 2 sections moved. The Brigade went into billets in areas allotted at 6.40 P.M. the guns covered the railway line S. of VLAMERTINGHE moved to their ammo positions. On arrival they relieved No section of the French artillery. Then in action with exception of L U Battery which took up a field position. One section of R.H.A. on each flank was told off for aeroplanes. The relief was conducted without any hitch by 10.50 P.M. on night 1/2 of Feb. Horses were allotted to Brigades for the Artillery — at an ythinic 3 mm before next day. Teams returned to billeting area before dawn.	A
2nd February	During the day B's registered, but owing to phone wires being continually cut + to the difficulty of finding suitable observing places otter than the Observation Post any observation has not completed by dusk. The French guns arranged to remain another night. The remainder of the B's ton + Ammn Column marched from PARADELLES this same procedure was carried out and whilst the guns were not put into position — except in the case of U Battery on the French lines remained. Communication was established during this day, with 83 & 84 cnfs Battery. + establish themselves ready to open fire at any moment with 2 B's + 146 B infantry — them midnight all R.H.A B'to, 31st B'ty + the guns they had in action; 3rd B'ty had not been able to find communication during day + the battery in 146 B.s had men under terrifically before dawn.	

WAR DIARY

INTELLIGENCE SUMMARY

Army Form C. 2118.

28/5-3A.

5

Hour, Date, Place	Summary of Events and Information	Remarks and references to Appendices
3rd February.	At 5 P.M. the remaining French guns were withdrawn & their place was taken at night fall by the remaining section of the Divisional Artillery. The night was concluded without casualties or difficulties of any sort. During day Registration shoots were concluded. 56 Howitzer Battery arrived & was billeted in reserve Sn. C.O. ammunition reluctantly a portion. Arrangements made for an aeroplane from V Corps to assist in registration of target for howitzers tomorrow, at 5:15 P.M. report from 83rd Bde that it was being shelled from SW on to trench in I 34 C. French heavy guns under onlookers had arrived but out & that direction. Any howmover it was also to short where hostile detachments at Forme. He fired however at enemy battalions in Squares 0.5 & 9.1, 0.11 & 6.8 + P 12 & 8.2. The last which had been indicated by A.B.55 Observing Officer as a probable direction of enemy position. W.F.	
4. February.	Div HQ reports as a result of enemy hyng some four Trenches lost as French heavy guns asked to open on same ground as yesterday. At 8:40 A.M. fire opened at 11.20 information received from 83rd Bdy that enemy fire slackened & heavy gun fire was effective. Obtained at what hour 83 B.R. were shelled yesterday & they upon looked Arty VCorps to turn heavy guns on to hostile battery near OOSTAVERNE at 3.30 P.M. result not known. 146th & 31st Bdes reported at 10.50 A.M. that they were asked to support the 84th Bdy but that our own fill of hostile aircraft. Asked Div HQ for assistance from own Flying Corps + announcements were made to send over a fighting aeroplane. Antiair craft guns manned all Bdy employed under instructions from 2nd Bdes which they were ordered, at 11:55 P.M. 84th Bdy report Arty fire very effective & that German shelled Trench Sq. I.35. at 3.50 P.M. report received from A"B"Observing Officer that 83rd Bdy patrol marked enemy massing in trench Sq. I 34 C & in O 4 A for an attack. A battery at once fired on trench in Sq. 04 & 3.5. An attack ordered by Div HQ + 5. P.M +

Army Form C. 2118.

28th DA

6.

WAR DIARY
INTELLIGENCE SUMMARY.
(Erase heading not required.)

Instructions regarding War Diaries and Intelligence Summaries are contained in F.S.Regs., Part II and the Staff Manual respectively. Title pages will be prepared in manuscript.

Hour, Date, Place	Summary of Events and Information	Remarks and references to Appendices
4th (Continued)	afterwards postponed. At 9.5P.M report from Div HQ that 83rd Bde would attack along the canal at 9.30 P.M. French Heavy Artillery asked to shell bridge in Sq O4.b.3.5 whilst 88th How By shelled bridge Sq O5.b.7.5. The 3rd Bde were left at the disposal of 83rd Bde, 146th By Cmdr + the communication with 31st Bde + Q.B5 being temporarily cut, the fire of 146th Bde was ordered to shell communication Sq I.34.d.7.0 + the two bridges mentioned above. Communication with 31st Bde being re-established, Q.B5 was returned to open on the road running S.W. from bridge O4.b.3.5 to O4.c.4.3. Whilst 31st Bde was covered road I.34.d.7.0. The 141st Bde was taken off + put to its original line. A steady fire at irregular intervals was ordered at 10.45 P.M. No report received as to effect of fire, which died down when the moon rose. Antiaircraft fire did not come in.	WWE Smg
5th February.	Morning passed uneventfully. News received about 3.50 P.M. of an attack by 83rd Bde + February. to take place at 9.0 P.M. from German trenches in square I.34.d. - N.W. A Gunner Officer O'R.Hn was ordered to proceed to most Sq I.34 + at 8.55 P.M to open notify fire for ten minutes on hostile trenches then to withdraw. The exact position to be selected by Co in communication with BOC 83rd B.A. at 7.30 P.M. this order was cancelled by 83rd B.A. Cmdr. At 4.25 return were received to report R.F.A. to put a belt of fire on German supports in trees notwithstanding that 9.0 P.M. previously, the direction of the fire to be controlled by fire of 83rd By.- Batteries opened fire at hour ordered but the 83rd Bde Cmdr being in the trenches shown no 'phone was cut- but communication with HQ + the supporting guns. Shortly after + what burst of rifle fire a steady fire of shrapnel intervals was kept up. This intensity from died down. OC.3 Bde received a call for a searching fire on Sq I.34.d about midnight, communication between 83rd Bde Cmdr thinking himself being main re-established but during the day aeroplane located Trench 5 in Square D.26.a + I.36 a.9.9. The 86th How.Bn were to employ anything the Shell into HOLLEBEKE Chateau during the afternoon shelled the part of Some hostile heavy from	WWE

Army Form C. 2118.

WAR DIARY
INTELLIGENCE SUMMARY.
(Erase heading not required.)

28th D.A.

Hour, Date, Place	Summary of Events and Information	Remarks and references to Appendices
Farmhouse in Square H 11 d 7.7		28th DA will in future be at CHATEAU VIDAZ in future.
6th February	The day passed uneventfully. A wireless installation arrived and was sent to work with 86th How Battery. Weather cloudy but on the whole bright. In the morning an anti-aircraft gun was sent to HAZE-BROUCK by II Army. Orders from Div received for the removal of the HA 28th Division — 2 hours after its arrival it was ordered back to HAZE-BROUCK by II Army. Orders from Div received for the removal of the HA anti-aircraft section. In the afternoon a flight of No 6 Sqdn RFC came over with his observer with them in opening up wireless targets for registration with 86th How Bty. Night passed uneventfully. WF	
7th February	Day cloudy. Howitzers practically registered another target. Capt COGAN came in morning & registered with OC 18th Bty about target 5 for registration tomorrow. Div Air Columns reported & from BORRE to HILLS S of POPERINGHE. 22nd, 118th Batteries RFD marched ABEELE, where they are to remain until the howitzer Bty formation of 3 four gun batteries is complete. Conference at V Corps Hd about the use to be made of BELGIAN Batteries which are to come into HILLS S of POPERINGHE shortly. He be attached to 28th Div A.F. WF	
8th February	Day passed uneventfully. First bad attempt to register Howitzer proved a failure. Targets acted for registration by 18th Bty were at X area. So OC 103rd Bty sent for to arrange with Capt Cogan regarding registration of target T35 a 8.8 6A.95 which about 500 yards from hostile trenches who a night at 7.30 am obtained — shrapnel found to contain bullets of nearly metal of lead. WF	
9th February	Belgian Artillery Commander this Coy visited farmhouse & conferred with CRA arranged the details attendance of the RFA Batteries on action at a time, commencing on the 15th & finishing on the 11th. Belgian Cos then accompanied RFA BCs & inspected the proposition. It was decided that 2 gun to 3 batteries. 2/WE	

Army Form C. 2118.

28 DA

WAR DIARY
or
INTELLIGENCE SUMMARY.
(Erase heading not required.)

8

Hour, Date, Place	Summary of Events and Information	Remarks and references to Appendices
CHATEAU VIDAL 9th February.	One battery should be kept in reserve whilst two went into the gun positions of the 1st Sept "A/18" completed g/the 97, 9 B & 19th B.batteries the first should remain in reserve the other should replace "Q" B.5 & "A" B.5 as instructed. The 2nd Bout "A/19" completed g/the 100, 101 & 102 4 Batteries, the last should be in reserve, the 100th Should replace "U" Battery which should however a new position about I 17. Information received after expected arrival on the 12th of the 37th Howitzer B.5 the 113th Heavy Battery (4.7") to replace part of french Heavy Artillery on the night of 12th 13th. An anti aircraft Gun on a motor reported for duty with the 28th Division. Nominal roll of Belgian Officers shown in Appendix B. The following officers reported for duty on loan from Batteries noted. Captain Pardoey Extra – attached Adjt 146th Bde R.F.A) Captain Lawson " " " 3rd " ") 6th Feb. 15. 3rd Bde R.F.A Lt BATES from "A" to 62nd Lt A. PATERSON to "A" temporarily. Lt BEVIR " " X " 18th Lt R.L. CREASEY " X " Lt BRYANS " " X " 365th 2/Lt A.H. COLLINGWOOD " K " 31st Bde R.F.A Lt G.R. SIMPSON " "Q" to 69th 2/Lt J.L. BROWN " Q " Lt L.G. LUTYENS " "G" " 100th Lt F.R. BENHAM " G " Lt A.G. HESS " "N" " 103rd 2/Lt A.C. KENNEDY " N " 146th Bde R.F.A Lt P INCHBALD " "L" to 367th 2/Lt E.S. STANSFIELD to U " Lt K.E. WINGFIELD " "V" " 75th 2/Lt P.M. HOSACK " V " DIGBY Lts MASON & C. HTOWN from 27th Divnl Arty posted to 18th By & 31st Bde A.C. respectively.	Appendix B.

Army Form C. 2118.

WAR DIARY
or
INTELLIGENCE SUMMARY.
(Erase heading not required.)

28th D.A.

Hour, Date, Place	Summary of Events and Information	Remarks and references to Appendices
CHATEAU VIDAL 10th February.	103rd Battery succeeded in registering two targets with the assistance of aeroplanes. 8. A.M. 25th Lnfy Bde. asked for fire from "A" Bn. on Little Zinckes: fire was accordingly opened. Both "A" + "U" shelled during the day. 1.30 P.M. 103rd + 115th asked to fire on Square D4a by 85th Bde. Cmdr. complied + have informed fire was effective. 75th B.B. engaged on aviatik. The zones of fire of 17th Bty altered in order to bring fire of Belgian Battaires on A + U positions on to the region of EIKHOF + that of U + W to the West portion known as Z on 5 the other flank, namely Squares I 29 d 5 to I 30 d 3.7. The Belgian wiring commenced at 6. P.M. was completed without difficulty by 10. P.M.	
11th February	Aeroplane worked with 103rd Battery. Belgian section transferred to vis-à-vis the their Zone. "A" + "Q" Batteries ordered to leave their Telephone wire down as the Belgian Batteries are unquiet. The relay of the remaining RHA sections proceeded satisfactorily & was completed by 10 P.M. + the retired section proceeded to their billeting area. Capt BRIDGE. RHA appointed liaison officer to Belgian Artillery Commander. It has been decided that the battery being formed from the 22nd + 118th shall be called 22A as a temporary measure. Moves and spheres in these batteries shown in Appendix C. About 5 P.M. 3rd Cav. Div. applied for assistance from guns. The 21st + 146th Bdes were ordered to shell battleing about KLEIN ZILLEBEKE Sq. I 35 + I 30 d. While the French Heavy guns engaged hostile batteries about HOLLEBEKE. Cavalry reported immediate cessation of hostile fire. ref.	Appendix C
12th February	RHA Battaires marched to ABEELE to rejoin 1st Indian Cavalry Div. The 29th Bde + 113rd Heavy Battaries reached POPERINGHE + two left the 28th Division.	

(73989) W.14141—463. 400,000. 9/14. H.&J.Ltd. Form/C. 2118/10.

WAR DIARY / INTELLIGENCE SUMMARY

Army Form C. 2118.

No. 28 D.A.

Hour, Date, Place	Summary of Events and Information	Remarks and references to Appendices
CHATEAU VIDAL 12th (continued)	Went into billets. The Cor. Major NEWMAN KELLY inspected, informed with C.R.A. & reconnoitred position. Nominal roll of officers shown in Appendix D. At about 11.45 AM the 83rd Bde asked for assistance. The 3rd Bde were ordered to fire on line bridle O4d NE to I34d, while the 31st Bde engaged from road junction I35a 40 SW to limit of their zone. While French heavy guns shelled German farms about HOLLEBEKE. The 3rd Bde were shortly after ordered to cleanse zone in their range in order to approach the German trenches. Hostile fire ceased. At 4.30 P.M. 85th Bde reported hostile fire in trenches from direction of O4. Reported 3rd + 85th to open on German trenches - a few rounds were fired + the 96th Howitzer Bde was turned on to German Hostile battery known to be in S2, O10d. Hostile fire ceased.	Appendix D.
13th February	Dull rainy day. No aeroplane observation possible. The 37th Howitzer + 113th Heavy Batteries got into position in the morning. During the morning a German sap was reported to be in course of being driven in S2 I34C. Gun support was asked for by 24th + 25th Bdes. About 8.15 P.M. 85th Howitzer Bde Comdr announced he was to dig a new trench running from 3rd + 31st Bde + A Battery of Belgian Arty a drew notice of him to distract the enemy attention. A slow rate of fire was commenced across entire sentinel with a short pause now & all night.	
14 February	Fire has continued by 3rd Bde & Belgian A Battery till about 5 AM at 7 AM a trench was reported to have been made by the Germans about 10.30 AM fire was opened by 3rd + 31st Bde + A Belgian Battery on enemy new line moving NE from there. 86 Howitzer Bde opened on hostile battalion in O4 while French heavy guns fired on enemy area. The fire was stopped by order of 85th Bde Cmdr. who asked guns to stand by. An attack by region. The 3rd Bde + A Belgian Bde were ordered to region trenches for 2 P.M.	

WAR DIARY
INTELLIGENCE SUMMARY
(Erase heading not required.)

Army Form C. 2118.

28th D.A.

Hour, Date, Place	Summary of Events and Information	Remarks and references to Appendices
CHATEAU VIDAL 14th (continued)	ordered to fire on the same line - expecting into the wood were small to try to catch German batteries, which are known to be there about. The 86th Howitzers opened on Germans about HOLLEBEKE CHATEAU with fuses being given again & fired fire. An intermittent fire was kept on up to 7.45 P.M. Complete surprise & communication between drawing officers & brigades seemed & it was impossible to ascertain how the attack was progressing. At 7.45 Batts: were ordered to stop firing but to remain on the alert all night in case a resumption of fire was required at short notice. About 8 P.M. it was notified by Division that a furious had started an attack was imminent. The whole artillery were ordered to attack in readiness to open at a moment's notice - each battery its own zone. The 31st RFA named HOLLEBEKE Chateau was allotted to the 86th Howitzers as an objective, whilst the French Heavy Arty. Commander was asked to prepare to open upon German Gun Emplts which he knows to be the most important line. At 3.30 AM information received that infantry attack had failed will fires were to open fire at dawn. By 3.40 AM all guns Patrick French Belgium had been warned. By 6.30 AM all had fused fire. The 31st Bty opened at 5.45 AM but were stopped by order of RA at 7.45 AM all batteries were actually firing except 5th Bde at 9.15 AM only one battalion of 3rd Bde continued firing on line centre 58 O.3d NE + one dugout either side. At 11 A.M. one 3.7-in Hd defeated He was in trench with 85 half, B^{ty} HB fired burn ordered to open fire with height, fire afterwards with the same another 58 + NE for 150 yards. after 4½ hour later the note being returned to observer by order of Div Comder who also ordered initial fire. A horse 31st B^{y} battery was ordered to emplace on same area as common observation but had meanwhile a suitable problem on the saved back. The 3rd Rd returned to enfilade on the lost French Sq.03460. The 86th Howitzers ranged on German main trench & also did the Belgian A battery, this firm being observed by the 86th Bty observer on the Belgium gunners was assisted by B.I.A. patrolers while on the way to his observing post. Orders were issued for fire to be opened on German trench at 8.30 P.M. for two minutes at 8.55 P.M. the range was to be increased by 150 f. The frontage to be divided by giving to line of fire of the	
15th February		

WAR DIARY
or
INTELLIGENCE SUMMARY.

(Erase heading not required.)

Army Form C. 2118.

28th DA

Hour, Date, Place	Summary of Events and Information	Remarks and references to Appendices
CHATEAU V IDAL 15th (continued)	German asked to take firer on for 10 minutes. At 9.15 the fire was to stop. The trench to be evacuated at 9.0 P.M. at 8.0 P.M. the Div. Gnl. decided it would be futile not to engage the German trench as orders were given for fire on the outposts from the 2nd 35th Bde, fire commenced punctually at 8.50 renewed at 9.5 P.M. 2. 35th Bde. the Belgian A Battn. reported later that the 85th Bde. had asked for more fire to cover the advance of reinforcements going up to the recovered trench. This was accorded.	
16th February.	V Corps commander wired his congratulations to the 85th - 2nd Bn., 1st Bn. Artillery. Through the 28th Division. 27th Div also wired congratulations to 28th. Cmdr 85th + 5th Bde. Attribute successes to Buffs + Artillery. Aeroplane came over to work with 113rd H.A.B. but went to recce the trench to Poperinghe. Skynewal arrived at 16.30 + obtained from heavy battery intended to Poperinghe at 9 A.M. 63rd Bty ordered 146 FE to stand by all day making the action impossible. 31st were also moved. expected an attack at any moment. About 8.00 A.M. an attack was repulsed so a few mi. known was met across the front at the Division for a few minutes. At 9.10 P.M. at guns of 83rd Bty 15th Bn., 2nd Bty opened on I.24.d.5.1 + I.35.a.7.7. After later it was reported that all was quiet so fire was stopped. Orders were received that the 85th B. intended to attack positions trenches O + P at 2.0 A.M. night 16th/17th. Orders were passed on to 3rd B5 + 86th brigades & Battery Batteries to be ready to support the Middle the French Heavy guns were asked to be ready to open on the Granis O10 1020. at 3.0 P.M. the 84th Bde were ordered to 3rd Bde to fire in his support. This was done.	
17th February	About 3.20 AM orders were received to make arrangements to open fire after daylight on trenches O + P (which had not been recaptured in the night). Men were firm accordingly by Bd. 3rd B, 4th, 86th B5 + A R Belgian Battn. The proximity of trenches R + S (still in our possession) from pts out to Hd 86th Battery had allotted P trench while A + B Belgian restricted O trench. There was great delay in opening fire as the observing officers telephone wire was	

WAR DIARY or INTELLIGENCE SUMMARY

Army Form C. 2118.

28th D.A.

Hour, Date, Place	Summary of Events and Information	Remarks and references to Appendices
CHATEAU VISART^R (continued)	Carried away by shell fire. The 3rd B. therefore opened at 9 AM & commenced to reply to "P" trench. About 10 AM the 66 & B5 communication was reestablished & fire was commenced. Owing to the high wind, however, airshell fell deep enough the trench R. as the battery cease firing unspotted. In this line of fire the 3rd B. were moved 2 degrees to the right. The 3rd B. observers reported many rifle land flats the 26th observers reported several direct hits, but a shrapnel had been substituted for the army to explode in air. Its effect was not so great as it might have been. At 9.20 PM 146th B.d. reported having been ordered to shell Zwartebeen. Its work expected to cover an attack by the 83rd B.d. & U Belgian batteries also (part of) About 2:15 am attack was reported coming up through I 34 d. So the 31 R.d. as battery of the 3rd (in whose area it was) + 2 Belgian batteries were ordered to open fire. Anything of this which was reported in I 34 d. but the trench was soon retaken. The prisoners then moved further west & the battery of 3rd B. was ordered to increase its rate of fire. Meanwhile A Belgian battery acquired trench with 5' observing wheel reported on trench "O". About 3:44 STPM it was reported R. hussars were moving behind hill 60 Sq I 29 C.9.1. The 146th B4 were ordered to search behind the hill with our battery. During this time our guns have were worried by fire from thirsters as from time to time French heavy guns were asked to open fire on their position in 010 d. Decided by division that 8th should dig into trench in the night. In cases for assistance required the night was tell off at about Shiver shell ... 115 2, 255 + 5 AM manage. The full ohoo were allotted to 18th B5 + 85 Hangs. She arrived to A. Belgian B.H., + 62 u. The night have all tomato conducted at their different places here were placed. The 115-Texas Batteries ordered back to Hollen Cab the 71 H.Q. H.B. to limited to the Division United HQ. Heary Bde & Nollyn/31 Battery wombat Forcepangeme Forms/C. 2118/10. hut	

Army Form C. 2118.

WAR DIARY
or
INTELLIGENCE SUMMARY.
(Erase heading not required.)

28 D.A.

Hour, Date, Place	Summary of Events and Information	Remarks and references to Appendices
CHATEAU VIDAL 18th February	O.C. Heavy Bd. reconnitred positions. Remainder of 122nd Battery reached POPER-INGHE through IPRES. Advise given for 1 Section 9/121st Battery to relieve the B.H. Battery, for which permission applied for to march straight to POPER-INGHE escorting the Indian Corps. Lt. C.A.L. BROWNLOW posted to 5/28th from 31st Div + Lt. T.H. BRIDE from 5th Bn. He is posted to 37/146 Bty respectively. During the morning 62nd Battery heard shelled but without any casualties. Throughout the afternoon the trenches about B/C shelled by 8 mm trench mortars 31/B5 replied to hun. Some hostile gun positions. I35.C.77 + I33.d.6.7 were also fired at. Rumour trench. I46.7B.7 (reported I29.8.1) the reputed position of howitzers-hostile fire opened. At 8.35 P.M. machine-guns were issued for the support of the infantry working party which was digging a trench. The night was undisturbed on the front ...spelle, the same batteries allotted to the shell. In addition the 37th howitzer Battery + the French 7mm Artillery were warned to be ready to support any German gun trying which might be allotted to them in the night. It was found unnecessary, however, for the guns to open fire. The 121st Heavy Battery was to have maintained its position which the 113th R.5 located earlier in the evening. The first gun however got firmly embedded in the mud + could not be shifted. 9th R.5 R.F.A. relieves 85th R.5. in the Division line.	Minimal Roll Heavy Bd - Appendix E.
19th February.	Cloudy day meant edge fire work with aeroplanes. Dr 7th battery performed positions for his howitzer. Registration on Rumour trench. On S9.03 d. 10 + a canal out by 37 + I46 Howitzers + 3 Brigade admit life in howitzer gun. Scored by the first named. During the day the French Heavy Artillery were ordered to for an enemy Heavy gun which was shelling the trenches. Dimming the noon an indication to its position but throughout the night no sufficient was required from the artillery. By 7.30 P.M. 3 guns of 121st Heavy Bn were in position. During the afternoon 16 HE shells were fired at 2 Belgian Batteries which were blinded. A sketch of the formed in O4.a. I03.a Taken by 37th Battery O'Brien office from D.C's station in I33.d. was brought in explained to VC.A.G.	

WAR DIARY or INTELLIGENCE SUMMARY

Army Form C. 2118.

28th D.A.

Hour, Date, Place	Summary of Events and Information	Remarks and references to Appendices
CHATEAU VIDAL 20th February	Commander. Diffian? function was interrupted by a search-light from the German trenches. Fire however was not opened by the Artillery.	
21st February	Registration left of the canal bank carried out by 3rd B.ty. "O" trench enfiladed by 37th Battery & through this drawn of 86th Battery also. Report from S/L in trench fixing "D" that fire on afternoon of 19th very effective on that trench. 31st Bde scored 6 direct hits on known S.I.34/6.2 which was supposed to contain a minenwerfer. Orders received for 88th & 87th Battery to be relieved by 65th on 21st at return to "TETE DE Cant?". At 4:30 P.M. it was reported that a German advance was pushing across I 34 d.1. The fire of our batteries, aided by 3rd + 31st B.des was brought on to the square. The Belgian battery also firing. It was reported that trench Y had been lost near effort was to be made at 9.0 P.M. to retake it. There was again ordered to S/L at the attack. At 12:30 P.M. when received to open fire at 12:45 A.M. to cover fresh attack on salient Y+2 (letter reported in hand of German). The battery east of 3rd + 31st B.des opened after firing for 15 minutes were stopped by order of Divl Comdr. No news was received from the infantry, they have been heard about 10 P.M. from the Left of the 28th Divl area. French artillery commander informed O.C.H.6 Bde that it was an attack on left of 3rd Cav Divn that was causing loss refund. About 7 A.M. a probable attack was ordered on Y + Z + was enfiladed by the 3rd + 31st Bde batteries in that area. The infantry being refused the trenches in question vacated the was turned by opponent into known in I.34 c 9.8 & 86th Battery on heavy German fire was coming from the Glencairn opened a rapid shell falling about the known when hid it from view 37th Battery shelled trench D doing asked by infantry to shift fire	

WAR DIARY or INTELLIGENCE SUMMARY

Army Form C. 2118.

28th D.A.

Hour, Date, Place	Summary of Events and Information	Remarks and references to Appendices
CHATEAU VIDAN, 21st (continued)	Fire 150° to 300° to the West. Having opened on infantry who were falling about, but were stopped. The H. Battery had been 3 g—in action ready to fire when the H.Q & (How) B[de] reported at 2 p.m. during the morning U Belgian Battery had 10 shells fired at it, which half were French (shrapnel 155 m/m). In the afternoon the 3rd B[de] reported on Red House-containing snipers – in Sq. I.34 c 9.8 received several direct hits. They occupied some time as a mist hid the house for several hours. It was then too dark to get the howitzers into po[sitio]n, so they shelled trench O on their original line scored some hits. The relief of the night action by the 9th Inf B[de] was carried out without necessity for support was concluded by 1.20 am. The 86th Battalion was relieved by the 75th (on action at daw[n] during the night & left in the morning for ERQUINGHEM BRIDGE. Orders received to hunt Belgian shirks and wanderers. H.F. bns which, as unable to cope with aeroplane. 3rd Battery ordered to fire at infantry in trenches on O'Driscoll... bearing of part A.N. Trig for observation common? between inf[antry] H.H.Q before till 3 P.M. when useful information was obtained. On shell hit up No farmhouse from O Trench about 3.30 P.M. firing & putting three shells into Red House as the next had cleared. On shell fell on trench that cut up one of infantry who killed 6 of ours. Three direct hits seemed a house with 9 civili[an]s seen firing from therein. On our left in early morning in the afternoon 31st Battery had occasional rounds during the night at the request of the inf[antr]y to keep down rifle fire. H.F.	Nominal roll & H[ow]/B Replies Appendix F
22nd February		

Army Form C. 2118.

WAR DIARY
or
INTELLIGENCE SUMMARY.
(Erase heading not required.)

28^A DA

Hour, Date, Place	Summary of Events and Information	Remarks and references to Appendices
CHATEAU VIDAL 23rd February.	5.15 A.M. Div HQ informed CRA that tonight 2nd Bde proposed to attack Y trench held by the Germans & asked that artillery might be ready to support. 9th Bde Cmdr had been similar orders to infantry brigade.	
8.10 AM	Div HQ inquired if 9th Bde required support of the artillery. CRA Belgian battery 31st Bde told to stand by for orders.	
10.30 AM	27th Bde ordered to fire on enemies trenches should trade it, under orders of Div HQ.	
11.50 AM	31st Bde open on the S.W. of Canal by order of 9 Bde Cmdr.	
4.0 PM	Infantry about ZWARTELEEN reported casualties from own fire. The batteries of 31st & 46th Bde opened on their Ramur feld sile & French there. Artillery into O.I.O.d.	
	The night passed without incident. H.W.F.	
24th February.	Orders given for redistribution of guns. If fire were used on to shelling of Belgian Communion.	
	3rd B.Bty hw Edn from night line to I 34 c 9.7. 31st Bde Hd to midway (incl) will 146 Bde Take from Railway (incl) to left of line (I 30 (central)). Belgian Bde. remain. A. aviation of B to cover.	
	4 + 2 - " - " - " - " 1.46 n "	
	" - 31 " - "	
	n. Heavy rifle firing at Bridge B5 to trenches infantry Bde section	
	A minenwerfer about ZWARTELEEN caused much trouble to trenches 3, 4t, 4a 5. was searched for by the 146th Bde. The position was not located but when battery was firing the minenwerfer stopped.	
12.20 PM	HE Shell 13 - 6 4th 4th Bde trenches. Doctor being shelled with light field gun & recovered 31st Bde reported be was dealing with field gun. Fabriek Henry artillery turned in I 35 d & 2 where known German guns were there.	

Army Form C. 2118.

WAR DIARY
or
INTELLIGENCE SUMMARY.
(Erase heading not required.)

28th DA

Place	Hour, Date	Summary of Events and Information	Remarks and references to Appendices
CHATEAU VIDAL (continued)	24th 3.23 PM	13th Bty B.A. report troops in H.4 & H.5 trenches have been bombed out & that it is expected that fire should be maintained down in front to check any concentration for attack. 146th R.B. of no man trenches. QUARTEREEN + Command Tpg T.7.0. 31st Bde take up line to west of Q & 2 Belgian battalion any occasional rounds into German trench in this area. 12th B5 fired 5 rounds of 4.7" mm with remainder have this line in a perfectly normal manner. Must prevent EIKHOF from being further registered.	
	4.30 PM	31st Bde report many heavy shelled from South French heavy Arty put into O15a & to Several casualties to O10d 4.2 & O22 & 6.9. Lieut HOPE-JOHNSTONE inflicted. Lt A.G.HESS R.H.A. (attached) killed. Maj. HOPE + GWYNN wounded. The latter mortally. A Lieutenant killed. June 13th B5 B.S.Major wounded.	
	7.30 PM	order sent to 118th Battery to come up & rejoin the already allotted (partially prepared) position. Night passed quietly.	
25th February		During the night the 103rd Battery was withdrawn. The 118th occupied its new position. O.C. 31st Bde reconnoitred new positions for his batteries. Z Belgian battery having been shelled in the 24th + had a 6" in the Spur dug out also moved. Occupied fresh position from which it proceeded to shell the German trenches in its zone. The 146th R.B. not being able to shoot on German trenches offered to T.490.5D 2 Howrs proceeded to register. This with infantry observation.	
	9.40 AM	31st Bde again shelled French Heavies turned on the batteries O21 B 2.6	
	12.Noon	D22 A No.6 & O15 & 9.1.6 reported by French aeroplane reconnaissance. 31st B.de asked to shell chateaux farm in I.35c.7.7. Had no rounds of fuzes	

Army Form C. 2118.

WAR DIARY
or
INTELLIGENCE SUMMARY.
(Erase heading not required.)

28th DA

19

Hour, Date, Place	Summary of Events and Information	Remarks and references to Appendices

CHATEAU VIDAL 25th (continued).

For them it was again heavily shelled. The French heavy guns refused at once or the same objection. Their shells after shifted. Infantry complained from some dropping shells into our own trenches. R.O.S. at 3 P.M. all guns stopped firing by order of G.O.C., at 3.20 mm dull fire into trenches seemed, having they were German shells – probably from an unusual direction. During the morning the 75's B5 were ranged upon German rating. Smoke shells evidently to get the line. There have not before been observed in this area.

26th February

Heavily shelled almost midnight until 4 a.m. A prisoner had stated an attack was coming at midnight. All ArtIIIry in that zone ordered to stand by. 115th Brigade informed. B'= R'st Cmdr considered attack not coming. That gun need stand by no longer. Day cloudy but cleared up in afternoon. Aeroplanes observed for 37/65 Howitzers & reported two targets. Series made difficult by another battery (probably French) shooting at same time. Programme arranged for both heavies + fr/heavy light with the heavy brigade.

1 P.M.

Strong artillery activity for both heavy batteries + HOLLEBEKE Chateau replying by 1st during registration. Some damage done to German entanglement + working parties. 65th How registered fortuno of German trench dropped a couple shells right into our ___ for a medium destruction of the artillery of the Division in order

Army Form C. 2118.

WAR DIARY
or
INTELLIGENCE SUMMARY.
(Erase heading not required.)

28th D.A.

Hour, Date, Place	Summary of Events and Information	Remarks and references to Appendices
CHATEAU VIDAL 10.30 P.M. 27th February.	to make co-operation with infantry still more intimate. The letters are allotted as shown in appendix. The 13th Bgde was relieved without incident by the 83rd Brigade. 2/Lt 37th Bty had to report to 9 R. Dub. Fus. Capt Simpson & 2 men knocked out. Lt Simpson (Q R.W.S.) attached to 13 Bty was wounded while observing fire.	Appendix G
LT 28th February 10 A.M.	a conference of Lt Col was held & a memorandum of future work taken in accordance with G.H.Q. secret No 250. 3/15 How. registered one target with howitzers one plane in morning. 37th registered on farm & Somme trench SW (cant in afternoon). 31 H.B. 37 H.B. & 5 shot under direct orders of Inft Brigadiers commanding in their sections. Night passed quietly. W.E.	
9 A.M.	Another day of shelling closes continued at aerodrome. This clear morning enabled planes to work with 71st 37 H.B. had major trouble had to go back. Very light mg at work with 37 & H.B.5, had to return towards W. in her broke down returned also but registered 3 targets with Huntz Brigade. Field Artillery worked under orders of Inf. Bde commander. Two calls for fire made by 9th Inf.Bde to C.R.A. trench was in the 37th Bty Rifleman on field gun in I 34.d. Huntzen also fired to stop fire of a machinegun. Night passed quietly.	

Signed [signature]

Appendix B.

Ordre de Bataille

Régiment d'Artillerie

Commandant du Régiment : Lieut.-Colonel Agent d'état Major Dujardin

Officiers Adjoints : Lieut. Paul Teclinden

18.e Brigade

Cond.t de Groupe : Cap.t Agent d'état Major Vansombrugge
Officiers Adjoints : Cap.ne en 2.d Boels
Sous-Lieut.t Rolin

19.e Brigade

Cond.t de Groupe : Major Pichier
Officiers Adjoints : Lieut.t Honnon
Sous-Lieut.t Sassage

	97.e	98.e	99.e	100.e	101.e	102.e
Cond.t de B.ie	Sextraete	Longean	Tahon	Van Waldeghm	Scheid	Cumont
Lieut.t	Bigault	Nicaise Van Ockroy		Hermans		Boels
Sous-Lieut.t	Vanderhaaghen		Linth	Kees	Van Spranq Servais	Trimmermans

28th Divisional Arty Appendix C

List of Officers belonging to fourth Batteries of 18 pr Brigades.

Rank and Name		Unit	Remarks
Major	Stewart D	22nd Bty	22nd By.
Captn	Farrant M	"	
Lieut	Bather E.J.	"	
2nd Lieut	McQueen G	"	
Major	Hudson A.R.	118th Bty	118th By
2nd Lieut	Arbuthnot R.Wm	"	
"	Russell G.R.	"	
Captain	Ellis R.S.	149th Bty	22A until renumbered by W.O. (now 149th By)
2nd Lieut	Russell G.C.	"	
"	Game H.J.	"	
"	Coles J.W.	"	

Appendix D

113th Heavy Battery. Royal Garrison Artillery.

Nominal Roll of Officers.

Rank	Name	Remarks
Major	Kelly. C.R.	
Major	Robinson. J.A.P.	
Capt.	Sidebottom. A.L.	
Lieut.	Harman R.E.	
Capt.	Eaton Hall. R. (T-F)	Divn Ammn. Pk. and column.

37th Howitzer Battery R.F.A.

Nominal Roll of Officers

Rank	Name	Remarks
Major	Harding-Newman. E.	
Captain	Hutchison H.O.	
Lieutenant	Bellingham. R.	
2nd Lieut	Bishop C.B.	
2nd Lieut	Morgan W.D.	

HEAVY BRIGADE? ROYAL GARRISON ARTILLERY.   Appendix E.

28th DIVISION.

NOMINAL ROLL OF OFFICERS.

Rank and Name.			Battery	Remarks.
Lt-Col	Burney	P de S	Hd. Qrs.	
Capt.	Carson	R	" "	
Capt	Wyatt	C.J.	" "	Medical Officer.
Lieut	Tufts	S.R.	" "	Veterinary Officer
Major	Barne	W.G.B.	71st Bty	
Capt.	Pask	I.A.J.	" "	
Lieut	Prickett	L.	" "	
2/Lt.	Henry	W.T.	" "	
"	Weir	J.G.D.	" "	
Lieut	Boys	E.J.E.	A.C. 71st Bty	
Major	Owen	C.H.W.	121st Bty	
Capt.	Adams	H.R.	" "	
2/Lt.	Goodman	E.W.	" "	
"	Foster	J.	" "	
"	Street	A.	" "	
Lieut	Whittingham	H.	A.C. 121st Bty.	

28th Divisional Arty. Appendix F

List of Officers belonging to 8th Howitzer Brigade R.F.A.

Rank & Name			Unit	Remarks
Col	Duffus C.B.	E.J.	H.Qrs	
Captn	Yorke	P.G.	"	
Lieut	Ardagh	R.W.	"	
Captn	Fyrth	W.	"	A.V.C. (T.F.)
Lieut	Work	A.W.	"	R.A.M.C.
Major	Harding Newman	E.	37th By	
Captn	Hutchison	H.O.	37th By	
Lieut	Bedingham	R.W.	37th By	
2nd Lieut	Bishop	C.E.J.	37th By	
"	Morgan	W.D.	37th By	
Major	Blois	D.G.	65th By	
Captn	Corbally	L.	65th By	
Lieut	Palmer	G.A.	65th By	
2nd Lieut	Lyogme	R.E.C.	65th By	
"	McLernon	R.W.	65th By	
"	Stacey	T.J.	65th By	
Captn	Wall	R.R.B.	Amn Col	
2nd Lieut	Johnston	C.J.	Amn Col	

B.M./181   Appendix "G"
                                   ―――――――
                                    26-2-1915.

In order that co-operation between the Infantry and the Guns may become yet more intimate the Brigadier General R.A. has now decided to redistribute the Divisional Artillery as follows :-

(1). Under orders of Infantry Brigade Commanders

    (a) GROUPED with the RIGHT Infantry Brigade

        3rd Brigade R.F.A.

        One Howitzer Battery R.F.A.

    This right group to be commanded by Lieut-Colonel A.L. WALKER.

    (b) GROUPED with the LEFT Infantry Brigade

        31st Brigade R.F.A.

        146th Brigade R.F.A.

        One Howitzer Battery R.F.A.

    This left group to be commanded by Lieut-Colonel E.J. DUFFUS C.B.

(2) Under the direct orders of the Brigadier General R.A.

        Heavy Brigade R.G.A.

        2 Groups Belgian Artillery.

(3). O.C. 8th (Howitzer) Brigade will allot his batteries to the two sections as early as possible, informing Lieut-Colonel Walker.

(4). When all arrangements are complete for bringing this redistribution into effect Group commanders will furnish a report.

(5) Acknowledge.

6.45 P.M.   Major.
                              Brigade Major R.A. 28th Divn.

28th Divisional Arty:

Vol III 1 - 31.3.16

AQ. The Base

Herewith War Diary 28th Divisional Artillery
for
March 1915

McTiernan
Maj Brener

1/4/15

Army Form C. 2118.

28th D.A.

WAR DIARY
or
INTELLIGENCE SUMMARY.
(Erase heading not required.)

Hour, Date, Place	Summary of Events and Information	Remarks and references to Appendices
CHATEAU VIDAL 1st March 9.17 AM	Captain Mansfield RFA attached to French Batteries, interviewed CRA with a view to working with 28th Divl Batteries. A list of targets was allotted. Fire was opened at 9.17 AM by 31st Bde on Ferm in I.34.d.9.0 r I.35.c.7.7 at request of 9th Infy Brigade Commander.	
11.10 AM	9th Bde report being shelled by French mortars from wood N of Canal 04.9.9.9 & 3rd FA Bde ordered to turn on the 37th (Hny) Bty. how trench with 9h 84 howitzer machine light aerodrome had to return to repair howitzer which carried away. Very light machine caught fire also. but to return to POPERINGHE. 118th Bn Battery shelled with high positive french heavy guns turned on D.20 & 21. No damage done to hostile shelling eased shortly after. While 31st Bde was withdrawn to fresh positions. Belgian Artillery claim to have destroyed three German observing station yesterday.	
3.30 P.M	Conference at Corps Headquarters.	
6.30 P.M	Relief of Left Section Afternoon by 13th RFA Brigade.	
11.30 P.M	31st Bde shelled in new position. BM/181 Redistribution Batteries carried into effect.	
2nd March 12.30 AM	31st B again shelled, 4 men wounded, french heavy batteries opened on 0.21 & 0.22.	
1.15 AM	on receipt of report at 1.10 PM 62nd Battery opened on trench Sq. O.21 in order to see what damage to entanglement could be done by shrapnel amount. Sergt. acted significantly. Fire stopped another front for attack allotted. Light failed so shot was [illeg]	

Army Form C. 2118.

WAR DIARY
or
INTELLIGENCE SUMMARY.
(Erase heading not required.)

28th D.A.

Hour, Date, Place	Summary of Events and Information	Remarks and references to Appendices
CHATEAU VIDAL. 2nd (Continued) 12 Noon	No registration carried out with aeroplane, weather too cloudy. About 12.30 the 37th Battery reported that their observers saw Germans massing in 04.d.08. O.C. 9th R.A. gave orders to 191st & one battalion 4th B.I.F. heavy battery were ordered to fire on the spot by H.Q. Germans dispersed Heavy battery now quiet.	
6.0 P.M.	Div H.Q. informed C.R.A. of a place of trench No 23 to be occupied by 27th Division. 3rd Bty warned to keep extra close touch with 4th Brigade 7th Belgian battery. Guns kept on German trench opposite 23 in case they were required in the night. No request for fire support was made during the night. H.F.	
3rd March		
9.15 A.M.	3rd Bde continue the wire entanglement cutting experiment. 266th Battery shelled - two guns while broken 191st H.Battery shelled at same time. Trench heavily shelled. Turned on to J.2.5.d.4.2.	
2.45 P.M.		
4.0 P.M.	2nd Brigade report being heavily shelled from direction 020. Trench heavy artillery ordered to fire on O.15.c, O.20.c, J.022.a.2.8.	
4.45 P.M.	German heavy battery started shelling.	
6.0 P.M.	Secret G.X.319 from VCorps received. Col Duffus & Dr Jardin sent for to talk matters over. Report sent in at 9.45 P.M.	
11.30 P.M.	Report received of casualty to Lt Groom of 65th Battery - wounded by shrapnel on road - both legs broken. Bomb who accompanied him had night leg broken. Heavy firing during night from North of MENIN Road. Lt Bellingham. 37th Bty - died during night while with wagon line. No returns yet to hand.	

Army Form C. 2118.

WAR DIARY
or
INTELLIGENCE SUMMARY
(Erase heading not required.)

28th D.A.

23.

Hour, Date, Place	Summary of Events and Information	Remarks and references to Appendices
CHATEAU VIDAL 3rd (continued)	During the day seven young officers joined for duty with 28th D.A.C. No work done with aeroplanes - weather too cloudy.	Appendices H. Shewing how they were posted.
4th March	3rd Bde reports portion of German main trench S.W. of canal. Report on wire cutting hits ammunition factory. Enemy bursting very practically - some parts of wire cutting in front right in air. Two length 9/20 x wire cut in one place now length 9/10 x in another. Impossible to see actual damage to wire itself. Range 4300.	
10.10 AM	Right Sect. ordered to open fire on all German trenches South of canal (to keep down bombing at night fire) by 9th left B. Conln. Trench 23.6 reported flown in by own fire + communication cut with 24-26. 9th B. take	
10.30 AM	Left of Sec'n. Fire. French heavy artillery fired on O 15 a 7b. At Belgium battery turned onto main trench opposite O, the 71 - onto E1 K H F trenches. Shelly after 31st Bde shelled after own heavy artillery had turned	
10.40 AM	German shelling of 21st Bde ceased after own heavy artillery had turned	
11.30 AM	on by O1	
12.45 PM	36st Bt shelled + French heavy fire on O10d42 stopped it.	
	During afternoon infantry reported our shells falling near our own trenches on the right. This was found to be the 7th 27th Division. 118th Battery shelled + French heavy artillery were turned onto O15d at the request of the 21st Bde Comdr.	
7.15 PM	During the night the 15th Bde relieved the 9 & 11 B.Bdes in the Right Sector. No request was made for artillery support.	

Army Form C. 2118.

WAR DIARY
or
INTELLIGENCE SUMMARY.
(Erase heading not required.)

2nd D.A.

24.

Hour, Date, Place	Summary of Events and Information	Remarks and references to Appendices
CHATEAU VIDAL 4th (continued)	In accordance with orders received from Div HQ each battery ordered to have an observing station, from which guns served by the battery is visible. Battery to be connected by phone to this observing post at night. Guns from B.C. to remain out of control fire & keep communication. 366-B.C. observing station made untenable, partly destroyed. 31st B.C. shelled at intervals throughout the night.	BM/197. Appendix J.
5th March.	Heavy firing from 7.30 to 8 am North of YPRES. 366-B.C. shelled. 146 B.C. Enemy fired on apparent position of German Aircraft with his other two batteries. During the morning the 71st Battery registered on redoubt near EIKHOF & 121st on trench in front of Chateau of HOLLEBEKE, 312 B.C. shelled at intervals throughout the morning. Several Heavy Artillery 4.7 Guns opened in various German emplacements in Squares O.15, 17, 20, 21, r.22. A number of shells dropped into YPRES - and lately dropping some on HOOTTIAM - HOLLEBEKE TZANDVOORDE.	
2.30 P.M.	German battery searched for French team near 3rd Bde, no damage done to either. 4.7 Guns turned onto O.14.b.2.9.	
6.0 P.M.	Conference between D.C. R.A., D.G. Art Condr at DICKEBUSH. Permission obtained from 9th French Corps for 2nd B.C. to put battery N of MENIN Road. Belgium ordered to reconnoitre an observing station for A battery in road where German trenches E of St ELOI are visible. It to be ready to open on those trenches at 12 noon on the 6th.	

Army Form C. 2118.

WAR DIARY
or
INTELLIGENCE SUMMARY.
(Erase heading not required.)

28th Div Arty

Instructions regarding War Diaries and Intelligence Summaries are contained in F.S. Regs., Part II. and the Staff Manual respectively. Title pages will be prepared in manuscript.

Hour, Date, Place	Summary of Events and Information	Remarks and references to Appendices
CHATEAU VIDAL 6th March	Very heavy firing to N of YPRES from about 4 AM to 7.30 AM. Probably French 20th Corps.	
11.15 AM	News from 27th Div that STEEN being shelled. 37 MKS turned onto O7oC 4.3 7½" on O15.5.2. 17.4C 2.7.	
11.45 AM	No diminution of shell fire. Returned heavy battery turned on O2oC 8.8. R.I. 12" on O15.8.8. + artillery Fresh battery on O2oC 7.2.	
12.45 PM	German fire intensify. Canal anew started again. All batteries stopped firing.	
1 PM	While 27th Div in cap[tured] S system a Belgian battery fired on German main trench.	
2 PM	Belgian reported 6" Howr shelling main German trench with good results. Informed Pom Ex 27th for fleuriel, from Belgian description, position of German trench. 27th Div Cmdr sent his Bde to Belgian Artillery for further information.	
4.30 PM	"A" battery ceased firing. Shells dropped S + E of YPRES during the day + two German positions were engaged. Firing ceased. Hostile aeroplane Cmdr captured with Co about half a mile out of [?] inshirkent in YPRES being used by spies. See 71 MKS instrument. Told Ctr to listen + extra operators sent down tonight. Cloudy day, no exp[ected] location done.	

(73989) W4141—463. 400,000. 9/14. H.&J.Ltd. Forms/C. 2118/10.

Army Form C. 2118.

WAR DIARY
or
INTELLIGENCE SUMMARY.
(Erase heading not required.)

Instructions regarding War Diaries and Intelligence Summaries are contained in F.S. Regs., Part II. and the Staff Manual respectively. Title pages will be prepared in manuscript.

28th D.A.5

Hour, Date, Place	Summary of Events and Information	Remarks and references to Appendices
CHATEAU VIDAL 7th March	Cloudy — no reconnoissance or registration by aeroplane. Heavy Battery fired on redoubt O3d 9.8. & infantry reported that so much damage was done that Germans were too busy repairing parapet in night 7/8 to have time for rifle firing. 121st Battery engaged trench infront of HOLLEBEKE Chateau reporting much damage. Applied made by 27th Divl Arty to open fire on German trenches which made SW of DICKEBUSCH. Sined heavy Artillery fired on shelling camps round O15b99 + O2ia/8. Allowance ammn increased and to prepare programme of work for Heavy Artillery or B5tp for the week. Programme shewn in appendix K. Copies sent to Infantry Brigades. Night passed without event.	Appendix K.
8th March	Programme commenced. 71st Battery unable to commence in morning as 9ft wire to trenches been cut in the night after division tire repaired before fire commenced. 146th B. called on to shell short range guns by Infantry twice before 8 AM were themselves shelled by 6" German How.
2.40 PM 146 "B" again shelled French heavy Batteries turned on to J26 b 80. J26 d 66 + J25 d 42. Shells coud.
6.00 PM Reports received that enemy dug by heavy batteries. In all 10 direct hits were Sared by German trenches on Hill 60 & opposite HOLLEBEKE Chateau. CRA went to DICKE BUSH to confer with CRA 27th Div about Tomorrows Shoot.
7.30 PM Orders received for continuation. Targets allotted for French, heavy	

(73989) W4141—463. 400,000. 9/14. H.&J.Ltd. Forms/C. 2113/10.

WAR DIARY
or
INTELLIGENCE SUMMARY.
(Erase heading not required.)

Army Form C. 2118.

Remarks and references to Appendices: 28th Div Art.

27

Hour, Date, Place	Summary of Events and Information
CHATEAU VIDAL 9th March	Heavy firing 6.30 AM to 7.0 AM North of YPRES.
At 7.0 AM	27th Div commenced shelling German trenches opposite ST ELOI at same time 71st, 121st Heavy & 37th How Battery ordered to commence their programme. 65th How Programme altered to kill 60 at input of Infantry & time fixing postponed till 10.45 AM to suit their plan. 37th Howitzers did damage done to trenches S/S and to breastwork to North of German shelled corner of YPRES Road entrance to Chateau Vidal. General Heavy fire put into Ch. 2.9.
10.5 AM	
10.40 AM	Left group under report 75th B.G. shelled for 20 minutes from direction of KLEIN ZILLEBEKE French Heavy Turret in I.26 Centre. During afternoon a second series fired by Heavy Batteries & 37th Howitzers but effect reported both by observers & Infantry in trenches. Problem summarised by 22nd Battery pre-casualties Tonight, from which Chine has been brought into use intact. Major Wickham wounded while reconnoitring Overseeing Station at VERBRANDEN MOLEN partially destroyed by shell. An target partially adjusted by 31st Hy Heavy Battery with wireless, but 4 of ment of 7 guns motored.
7.0 P.M	Intelligence. Belgian & French Artillery cooperated with O.R.A. Final programme drawn up for tomorrow. Gen. Right front ordered to send a section to VOORMEZEELE as well as to Noir Jamel to entrain tomorrow.

V.M.F.

Army Form C. 2118.

WAR DIARY
or
INTELLIGENCE SUMMARY.
(Erase heading not required.)

28.   28th Divl Arty

Hour, Date, Place	Summary of Events and Information	Remarks and references to Appendices
CHATEAU VIDAL 10th March	At day light Sect 22"85 North of Canal fired 10 rounds at diverange at aeroplane reported 30' opposite trench appeared to be destroyed.	
9.0 A.M.	Reports of 1st series received. Howitzers blew away 20' of trench immediately North of Canal. Heavy Battery did considerable damage to parapet north South - shells alight to the trench.	
10 P.M	2nd series with T.S. reported very effective. Aeroplane Battery obtained good effect on trench O. Howitzers shown not.	
12.30 P.M	3rd series reported. Howitzers had blown away 50' of parapet. Heavy Battery made several large breaches. Four MEZERES Section 22"85 destroyed wire entanglement in two places - each 50' wide.	
3.15 P.M	4. series reports show T.S. series effective. Effort to rejoin Co with aeroplane unsuccessful. Clouds. Some rounds misfired.	
11th March	Cos issue orders for tomorrow. Employer of Lieutenant Colt A Scott Tinned Dial Art in return to 266th Battery - was highly excellent. Day started misty + parapets for shooting arranged by Sec Capts had to be improved several hours. Registration was completed by 2.30 P.M. at which hour programme was due to commence. Enemy damages reported to be done to the parapet in the through being engaged have entanglement reported to have been totally destroyed in several places.	

WAR DIARY or INTELLIGENCE SUMMARY

Army Form C. 2118.

28th D.A.K.

Hour, Date, Place	Summary of Events and Information	Remarks and references to Appendices
CHATEAU VIDAL 11th (Continued)	Very light of hostile summer ranged an attempt to take on with the 127th Battery. No registration carried out. No firing during the night. V Corps orders for tomorrow received for gun programme. Sw. SPEL01 at HOLLANDSCHUUR FARM. Reconnaissance by 71st & 65th Batteries.	Inds.
12th March.	Morning misty. Guns unable to commence registration at 7.30am as arranged. Orders received to carry on when lifted enough. Adjut. Hour for commencement of programme postponed from 8 Am until 2.45 P.M.	
3.5 P.M	Registration was much delayed by mist but was completed by 2.30 p.m. The 71st Heavy Battery at 3.15 P.M. At 3.30 the 71st Heavy Battery opened on line O.P. & 65th Howitzer Battery on Sw. charged to HOLLAND SCHESHUUR FARM. Reports state that fire was very effective & much damage was done both to trenches & to farm buildings.	
4.0 P.M	Fire ceased. During the day the Belgian Artillery shelled two observing stations & silenced a Minenwerfer. The 121st Heavy battery did considerable damage to redoubt O 3.d. Said batteries & 37th Howitzer fire were ordered by 2nd FA Comdr. An aeroplane passed over & dropped bombs billets in POPERINGHE & YPRES during the afternoon. 40 yards of French trench was blown up by Germans about 35.T.40. Inspection of FA batteries & howitzers under command of 2nd FA Brigade, 2 Belgian batteries were laid on that section of the front. Orders issued for a line to be run direct from FB3.U.HR to HQ of 14th FA Brigade. W.J.F.	

(73989) W.4141—463. 400,000. 9/14. H.&J.Ltd. Forms/C. 2118/10.

WAR DIARY or INTELLIGENCE SUMMARY

Army Form C. 2118.

30. 28th Div Arty

Hour, Date, Place	Summary of Events and Information	Remarks and references to Appendices
CHATEAU VIDAL 13th March	Light March & Smith. Got orders for the day received at 11.30 A.M.	
7.30 AM	Aeroplane came over but found it too misty to air instrument.	
	Shell dropped in YPRES.	
11.45 AM	7.19" Heavy in HOUTHEM by enemy artillery. French Heavies turned on ZANDVOORDE + HOLLEBEKE. Aeroplane endeavoured to bomb hospital at Lunatic Asylum but missed it by 20 ft. Remainder of day Lieut Smith.	init.
14th March	Enemy morning. Some registration been done with aeroplane. Field batteries that so worked under orders of DAC of Div. Centre. Two miniewerfers were silenced, one by Belgian one by the 35th Howitzers. Other batteries engaged targets allotted by CRA.	
5.00 PM	Violent fusilade commenced from ST ELOI. Right Bde called on 3" Fr Bty to fire on all French Saute of Canal. A Belgian Battery was added. 2 Battery fired on ZWARTELEEN SALIENT.	
5.35 PM	27th Divn in infant attack on trenches 16, 17 + 18 trenches. "A" B Bty + 61st Bty so turned on to meet leading to ST ELOI from South. Heavy batteries	
5.45 PM	engaged redoubt from targets. 3rd A Bty shelled trench area turned on to other German gun positions.	
5.50 PM	Fire was stopped. No news yet of the attack was met.	
1 AM	Information received. German intended counter attack by 27th Division for which the following disposition was made 3" RBy + 37 (forming Right Comp) were informed of the hostilities 11 & 22 & warned to watch the

WAR DIARY
or
INTELLIGENCE SUMMARY.

Army Form C. 2118.

28© Div Arty

Hour, Date, Place	Summary of Events and Information	Remarks and references to Appendices
CHATEAU VIDAL (night 14/15)	the right flank of the Divn in its ask for orders from Right Inf'y Bde Cmdr. Belgians were ordered to be in the ready to fire during the night on German trenches opposite O3c, I24 end & I29d, French heavies on O14 c 3.8 - O15a † D10d, while the Heavy B'y layed on Point C & searched STEEN - OOSTAVERNE Road. attack postponed till 2.0 A.M.	
15th March.	Our trench kept all night with B? 27th Division.	
2.0 A.M.	Fire opened under - A'Ballin trench opposite trench 23. Pt Point C	
2.20 A.M.	French heavies opened on O14c 38. O15a † D10d - but attack party of 27th Bn were stopped by O20b 28 - O20a 86. O15c 66. (Germans firing positions)	
2.45 A.M.	The section 71st turned on O8 d 19. now of 121 on O20c 26 (both from positions)	
3.20 A.M.	Heavy Bty ordered to fire moderate target to save ammn. 3 mg's continued firing by ours. About same time 27th Div Arty reported that attack was held up temporarily	
5.55 A.M.	27th Div mounted attack about 5.0 & heavies from arty't asked for	
6.0 A.M.	French heavies turned on O10b 16. O20b 63. O20c 73. O21b 18. Pts Heavy	
7.30 A.M.	Battries O15a 36. O15b 66. O74 c 27. O74 b 99. Now received that the shelling about †15 L †† he practically ceased so fire was stopped.	
8.30 A.M.	27th Div'l Artillery informed of intended attack ordered for confirm'n in keeping down hostile gun fire. Arrangement made to do so.	

Army Form C. 2118.

WAR DIARY
or
INTELLIGENCE SUMMARY.

(Erase heading not required.)

32.

2/8th Div Ark.

Hour, Date, Place	Summary of Events and Information	Remarks and references to Appendices
CHATEAU VIDAL (15th Continued)	Orders from Capt Mr John received to bring fire of our many guns as possible on + East of the hamlet at ST ELOI. Both heavy batteries put into hand coming S + S.E. from that place, one howitzer battery put on to the hamlet itself, blowing station found where hamlet visible + were observed. Several direct hits attended.	
12.248 P.M.	Several heavy hits on to 3 german gun positions to stop fire on 146 - R.M.	
1.0 P.M.	65th How Siege Battery ordered to fire on hamlet. The 37 Division between	
1.30 P.M.	3rd + 4th heavy shelled h.5.9's + French battery turned on to 070 d 6.2.	
2. P.M.	Field batteries worked methodically to infantry positions.	
	Down of the men 146 th by heavy shelled.	
4.30 P.M.	A Battery report heavy hostile shells for some time shifting two counties.	
	French heavies turned into 074 6.99. 015 a 4.5. d0 9.4.18	
5.10 P.M.	37th battery shelled. French firm 0104 18 + 079 a 00 - new position located by aeroplane	
	from hostile in the afternoon.	
6.3 P.M.	Orders from 27th Division for batteries to cease fire at 6.30 P.M. forward our infantry would then attack the hamlet. Orders sent out by an officer a cyclist by phone.	
6.18 P.M. 6.25 P.M	Orders from 27 Division that infantry were not ready fire was to be continued a phone message was being sent orders came for original orders to stand fast.	

Army Form C. 2118.

WAR DIARY
or
INTELLIGENCE SUMMARY.
(Erase heading not required.)

28th Div Arty

33

Hour, Date, Place	Summary of Events and Information	Remarks and references to Appendices
CHATEAU VISTA 16th March	Field Batteries fired under orders of Left Brigade Cmdr. – Heavy Attack. Batteries remained with Arm. Lyddite on the Mound 15 rjt., in case of resumption of the offensive. Belgian batteries engaged close north from trench mortars, also shelled German Sap Head opposite Trench 35. In cloudy for work with aeroplane. 10.55 P.M. to 11.5 P.M. very heavy gun fire [unreadable] on the Left.	
17th March	Howitzers & Heavies layed on roads & trenches S. of the MOUND at ST ELOI – ready to open fire if required. Orders given to batteries to fire in support sections if required by R.A. Cmdrs. all ready to register with aeroplane. Belgians to fire on trench mortars retaliating from when not employed to German layed on Trench S. of Mound. Trenches I & 3 d, in each side of ZWARTELEEN Salient. Field Batteries under Left Brig de Cmdr. during the morning the Belgian batt⁹ "A" shot at German aeroplane head effort at Church. 3.5. + dropped several shell into it.
4.15 PM 27th D	was reported that DICKEBUSCH Church was being shelled from line about I 56. French opened on Left in S aeroplane in J 31 & 20.r P 1 a 3.1. Order regarding ammun. if hostilities renewed. No retaliation carried out with aeroplane. Day too cloudy. Though an effort was made in the morning to register it was found impossible. Night passed quietly.	

Army Form C. 2118.

WAR DIARY
or
INTELLIGENCE SUMMARY.
(Erase heading not required.)

28th Divl Art.
34.

Hour, Date, Place	Summary of Events and Information	Remarks and references to Appendices

CHATEAU VIDAL

18th March. Gentlhuile, Brown & Short accompanied CRA around the artillery of the Division during the morning. Arrangements made for dealing with aeroplane which was opened fire. Aeroplane programme made for working with 121st & 71st Battery. No registration.

19 March. Milling to mend. Arrangements made to bring up field gun in known times in Try with V Belgian Battery & 12th Heavy. Programme arranged for 108th to work with heavy aeroplane. No registration carried out.

20th March.
9.50 AM — Divl Cmdr & CRA inspected Divl Ammn Column. Short range from Ypres and Armoured batteries shelled most in which it was thought to line. Explode shoot has apparently by the wire being cut as heavy & field fire did not synchronise on subject of the trenches.

1.30 PM — 15th Battery heavily shelled & French batteries opened in the most probable German gun positions.

1.30 — Shortrange from Ypres area again opened.
During the morning 101st Battery shelled. Sorrel, Ypres myfield, 2lts Arnber & Fuch ffomed pointed to 8th & 3rd Bde respected.
German aeroplane up from an early hour — 71st & 121st shelled. Smoke ball dropped.

21st March. S. of KRUISSTRAAT, registration of heavy batteries delayed first actual observation of German gun on trades & or Ypres. Several targets registered in afternoon in batteries. Armd registration in afternoon by wireless. Lively machine gun betwn in direction of HOUTHEM.

WAR DIARY or INTELLIGENCE SUMMARY

Army Form C. 2118.

28th Divl Arty

35

Hour, Date, Place	Summary of Events and Information	Remarks and references to Appendices
CHATEAU VIDAL 22nd March	Less activity on part of enemy artillery, but men on part of Trench Mortars & machine guns. 37 RB5 & 3rd RB fired several short serenades to knock down int. 2 to Stefan batteries were fully silenced enemy in Trenches D 28 with enfilade fire. 4 Tay S retaliated by heavy Batteries & 5 by field batteries with aeroplane. Balloon observer wounded by shrapnel from the N.of YPRES also no retaliation could be done with balloon. Stuvenfeld but only slightly wounded. Rifle fire from direction YSTELOI. Two howitzer battery layed on to St Mourns & Kruin Battn in woods leading S. from the village.	
9.0 PM		
23rd March 4.20 AM	heavy Germ rifle firing from the direction of 27th Division, but firing had started from 3rd Divn in. Division asked if assistance was required. All replied quiet in 27th area firing died down.	
4.40 PM		
10.0 PM	German heavy Germ shelled French battery. This French batteries opened on position in O9. With 71st — fired at O9 D4. Firing ceased.	
11.40 AM	French battery again shelled. The French batteries & 71st replied & 27th divisn asked to take on same in O9 D9.5.	
	4 Tay S retaliated by aeroplane. During the entire part of the night rifle firing was heavier than usual. Summons from shelled Trenches to 146. doing no harm a shell was worth one. 30k R 6th Can Br obtained 146 E Rd to fire a few rounds into German trench opposite Three boys at 9 PM. Major Hannan posted 6178 Buttery, R kn, Scarlett 6782.	
9 PM		

Army Form C. 2118.

WAR DIARY
or
INTELLIGENCE SUMMARY.
(Erase heading not required.)

28th Div Arty

36

Hour, Date, Place	Summary of Events and Information	Remarks and references to Appendices
CHATEAU VIDAL 24th March	Cloudy morning, clear in afternoon but no observation could be carried out. Aero-planes made several ascents to England to adjust at W.O. Day + night passed quietly. An enemy registration impossible to carry out. Tomorrow a programme was made at request by Divnl Commander for trying to draw back the German batteries which air reconnaissance above have moved in to closer range. 27th Div. R.A. closed down at DICKEBUSCH + 3rd Div. opened.	
25th March	Several target which had previously been adjusted were engaged by the Heavy Batteries during the day. The 75th Battery was heavily shelled in the afternoon the Heavy Battery Armrd battery position but no damage done. HOOGEMEERE Chateau, being seen to contain an enemy fire 9.4.7 Battery was turned on. Several direct hits were made. 65th Howitzer Battery adjusted 9M.H.R turned fire onto German trenches opposite 49+50 trenches. Several shell fell into German trenches. Humans Sh.W VLAMERTINGHE + the OUDERDOM road from the N.N.W.	
8.0 P.M.	Night passed quietly in this area, though there was some heavy rifle fire from the North of YPRES, also much activity amongst the Germs. 75th Battery changed its position. Col. Drake Brooks left for England.	

Army Form C. 2118.

WAR DIARY
or
INTELLIGENCE SUMMARY.
(Erase heading not required.)

37.   28 Div Arty

Hour, Date, Place	Summary of Events and Information	Remarks and references to Appendices
CHATEAU VIDAL 26th March	3 targets were registered by the heavy howitzers in the afternoon. An attempt was made to shoot one to pieces of hostile trenches, later this shot + Q Battery two tried shelled. Some were wounded. 37th Bty fired 4 rounds of Lyddite on enemy parapet & did considerable damage. Special ammunition: S/Lt S. Lyddite made to infiltrate after line for a Shrapnel hunter. Registration called for from Right front a & from the ammunition should be expended both directions top. YPRES–VLAMERTINGHE road shelled between 1 PM & 2 PM. No damage done. Troops and convoys with troops. Night heavy smith.	
27th March	Some aeroplane surprise. Q battery of field arty + a wh bde dropped. An plane flew over battery for some little time though bombs were not fd. Retaliation programme allowed to allow 2.0 Batteries to shoot instead. Smoke shell dropped in neighbourhood of MOORMEZEELE. 37th had direct hit in human parapet received much damage. Heavy batteries registered targets, of which two were actually firing at the time. Some targets were but is to happen in but advantage was taken after the opportunity which offered in. At LOVEROCK found 46th Brigade both temporaries changing came up the convoy to reinforce with batteries commander. Night heavy smith. MW F	
7.45 PM		

Army Form C. 2118.

WAR DIARY
or
INTELLIGENCE SUMMARY.
(Erase heading not required.)

38.   28th Divn Arty.

Hour, Date, Place	Summary of Events and Information	Remarks and references to Appendices
CHATEAU VIDAL 28th March	Two targets registered by aeroplane with wireless. Other batteries unsuited for this fashion were unregistered. Wireless machine installed with 2 Battery heavy Battery. Received orders to open a careful slow time which caused front munition. (Shots from enemy Ruhr I.3.Q.C. till about 9 a.m. also air 37th wheatfield opposite trench 29. Several targets engaged during the day which were too hazy to French + most of artillery Bdes demanded by V.Corps. Night Quiet.	
29th March	Germans shelled Menin Road in early morning. Enemy trench mortar in front of 367th Battery. Fired over heavy batteries. Stood to Wied. Germans batteries. Two targets were registered by aeroplane in afternoon. About 5 P.M. German stated shelling YPRES - VLAMERTINGHE Road & registered HE almost 65th Battery ad fresh horses + ten heavies put onto info Ford from machine. Fire ceased. Enemy also fired on German trenches opposite 29 + 30 & through down fire of French mortars. Retaliation fire was also fired at staffed Germs. Major CARLYON posted to 367 Battery vice Captain B.W. MACDONA sick. During the night 6th Bty Battery remained new position + registered at daylight.	W.F.

WAR DIARY
or
INTELLIGENCE SUMMARY.
(Erase heading not required.)

Army Form C. 2118.

28th Div'l Arty

39

Hour, Date, Place	Summary of Events and Information	Remarks and references to Appendices
CHATEAU VIDAL 30th March	Several targets registered with aeroplane by Heavy Batteries Pilcken (5th + 3rd) Batteries were shelled during the day as also was the MENIN Road. The YPRES – VLAMERTINGHE Road. Heavy Batteries fired. Heavy Artillery replied. Shelling ceased. But	
31st March	Several targets registered by Heavy Batteries. During registration a human was struck below up. A battery which was observed firing was engaged + four hits were scored.	
9.50 P.M.	During the night two rockets were fired + according to the arrangement made the F.Bde. in the area at once opened fire. It was found that the rocket did not originate in British trenches, so fire was stopped. Staff officers went round damage done by fire to machine gun silenced. Wilfrquam my Pompa 11.30 AM 1.4.15	Appendix L. Flag Officers We have fired during month.

WAR DIARY.   Appendix

Roll of Officers who have joined 28th Divisional Artillery.

March 1915.

RANK	NAME	DATE OF JOINING	UNIT WITH WHICH SERVING.
Lieut	Broadhurst G.H.	3.3.15.	103rd Battery R.F.A.
2/Lieut	Backhouse H.W.	3.3.15.	22nd Battery R.F.A.
"	Mollindinia A.W.	3.3.15.	69th Battery R.F.A.
"	Hollwey J.B.	3.3.15.	103rd Battery R.F.A.
"	Brink J.H.	3.3.15.	103rd Battery R.F.A.
"	Killkelly E.C.R.	3.3.15.	118th Battery R.F.A.

Appendix H

APPENDIX J.

B.M./197.   4th March 1915.

(1). The 15th Infty Bde will relieve the 9th Infty Bde in the Right
    Section tonight. Extra vigilence is, therefore, enjoined on the
    Right Group Commander.

(2). The Heavy Batteries will lay their guns tonight on the same
    German gun positions as were selected for last night.

(3). Each Battery is to arrange, without delay, for a separate observ
    ing station, from which the zone covered by the battery is visib
    le and which is to be connected to the battery by telephone,

(4). The officer in the observing station will be the Battery command
    er for fire purposes and will fight the battery.

(5). Group Commanders, Heavy Brigade and Belgian Artillery will report
    without delay their requirements in wire telephone instruments, an
    and operators to effect this object.

(6). At night one officer per Brigade will remain out for controlling
    fire and keeping communication with the trenches.

(7). Acknowledge.

                                            Major BMRA. 28th Divn

Appendix K.

UNIT.	SUNDAY	MONDAY	TUESDAY	WEDNESDAY	THURSDAY	FRIDAY	SATURDAY	REMARKS.
71st Heavy	Concentrate on redoubt in O3d9.8 fire 3 series	Concentrate on main trench in front of chateau in O4a4.2 & fire 3 series	as for Sunday	Chateau O4d 2.8 & outbuildings 1 series LIKHOF farm 1 series Trench in front of LIKHOF farm 1 series	as for Monday	Guns O 14b 1.9.2 series	HOLLEBEKE chateau & outbuildings 1 series LIKHOF farm 1 series Trench in front of LIKHOF farm 1 series	Each series for 4.7" will consist of 30 rounds. The first two during the day with H.E. the third, when shooting at a parapet will be fired after dark with Time Shrapnel.
121st Heavy	Concentrate on redoubt in O3d9.8 & fire 3 series	Concentrate on main trench in front of chateau in O4a 42 & fire 3 series	as for Sunday	Guns 136 (centre) 2 series Guns 135c 7.8 1 series	Hill 60 I 29 o 3L 3 series	as for Sunday	Gun centre of I 36 1 series KLEINZILLE-BEKE 1 series	
37th Howr.	Shell O trench	New German trenches & communications immediately N of canal O 4 o	as for Sunday	Search O4 for guns	Machine gun emplacements 6" howrs	Gun O.14b19	Road and railway O 6o77	Each series 4.5" will consist of 10 rounds fired at irregular intervals when firing at the parapet first 2 will be fired during the day with H.E. The third after dark with Time Shrapnel.
65th Howr.	Search for battery centered I 36 and one in I 35 a 7.8	Guns I 30 b 25. 2 series I 35 o.9.7 3 series.	on redoubt German I 30c36 3 series	German trench opposite our No 37 3 series	Hill 60 3 series	Redoubt I 30c36 3 series	Hill 60 3 series.	

The French Heavy Artillery will be used as counter batteries and for firing at guns and distant targets when other French guns and howitzer batteries are firing with aeroplanes. They will fire a few rounds daily at the cross roads in the German lines and at the villages of the ZANDVOORDE & HOLLEBEKE.

Appendix L

WAR DIARY

Roll of Officers who have joined 28th Divisional Artillery.

March 1915.

Rank	Name		Date of joining	Unit with which serving	Remarks
Major	Lewin	L.O.	23.3.15.	18th Battery R.F.A.	
"	Scarlett	J.	23.3.15.	62nd Battery R.F.A.	
"	Carlyon	T.	31.3.15.	367th Battery R.F.A.	
Capt.	Scott	C.A.R.	11.3.15.	366th Battery R.F.A.	
2/Lieut.	Gamblin	J.L.	6.3.15.	365th Battery R.F.A.	
"	Clarke	J.A.	10.3.15.	37th (Howr) Bty. R.F.A.	
"	Kenoe	J.T.	10.3.15.	65th (Howr) Bty. R.F.A.	
"	Greenfield	H.	11.3.15.	A.C. 146th Brigade R.F.A.	
"	Cooper Smith	L.J.	27.3.15.	149th Battery R.F.A.	
"	Loverock	G.	28.3.15.	367th Battery R.F.A.	
"	Finch	W.R.	19.3.15	O.C. 3rd Brigade R.F.A.	

121/5195

Head Qrs. R.A. 28th Division

Vol IV. 1 — 30.4.15.

Army Form C. 2118.

28th Div Arty.

40.

WAR DIARY
or
INTELLIGENCE SUMMARY.
(Erase heading not required.)

Hour, Date, Place	Summary of Events and Information	Remarks and references to Appendices
CHATEAU VIDAL 1st April	Some targets were reported by Heavy Battery & Belgian Artillery. In the afternoon a hostile exposed trench S.E. from the N.E. - a new place. 37th Howr Left battery 3" 13 fired in enfilade opposite & the 103rd Battery engaged hostile battery. In evening 3rd Div asked for assistance against battery which was shelling SHELON. Several German gun positions engaged & shelling ceased. Night passed quietly. V/Kent Scout No 8 secured. W.F.	
2nd April	Germans shelled MENIN Road about 11:30 a.m Platts turned their fire into 75th Battery causing much walls. Germans soon in O.9 m engaged but fire continued. 75th with 3rd Artillery ceased to annoy 75th Battery again shelled but fire in J.31 r stopped it. Aeroplane appeared for effort a movement from the lines in J.31 r O.9 had to be attended to as it was too cloudy for aeroplane observation. Brigade Major W/T.5th Divisional Artillery came over & interviewed the Brigade Commander. Night passed uneventfully. W.F.	
3rd April	MENIN Road shelled about 7.30 am 131st Battery put into 131 Street. French into MENIN Road beyond GHELUVELT shelling ceased. Several targets reported by aeroplane. CRA visited French artillery Commander & 3rd Division.	

WAR DIARY
or
INTELLIGENCE SUMMARY.
(Erase heading not required.)

Army Form C. 2118.

28th Divl Art.

41

Hour, Date, Place	Summary of Events and Information	Remarks and references to Appendices
CHATEAU VIDAL 4 April	Trench 39 shelled during the day & the trench opposite was heavily shelled by 1 Howitzer, 1 Heavy & 1 Field Battery. Several trench mortars engaged on either side after 11ve & their fire stopped. During afternoon 2 series of shots fired by Heavy Batteries with aeroplane observation. Result unknown. Good.	
8.10 PM	VLAMERTINGHE shelled from the N.N.E. About 8 shells dropped but no damage. It appeared between the town & the huts to the South.	
10.0 PM	A ZEPPELIN reported to have passed over by OC French Heavy Artillery. It appears coming from direction of CASSEL	
10.15 PM	YPRES shelled from the East - about 15 shells fell in town. damage not known. Enemy fire is to Jas engaged by 101st HTS French Heavy Artillery.	
	Un disturbed night - enterior Proprise to North tir about 8.0 AM	WF
5th April 11 AM	Trench 35 was bombed by trench mortar + 3" Fd Arty fired on 5 points before writing it at 9.35 a.m.	
3 PM	Bomb throwing again commenced - The hous in observation position again engaged & shots made upon it. B.Try I35C 9 was ropped at the Some torge 6' it not reported to be firing.	

Army Form C. 2118.

WAR DIARY
or
INTELLIGENCE SUMMARY.
(Erase heading not required.)

42.   28th Div Arty

Hour, Date, Place	Summary of Events and Information	Remarks and references to Appendices
CHATEAU VIDAL (5th Continued)		
6th April	Turned 32 mm howitzer twice during the day on enemy's ox's in a trench. Battery to fire battery engaged trench opposite 32. + firing stopped about immediately. Night passed quiet. During the morning trench mortar again bombed trenches 35.c.34. 9mm located in a.26.c.m.a.t. of Stone house. The 3rd A Bde engaged trench in I 35.a.75. The 65th Howitzers fired on the house opposite with shrapnel while 65th Howitzers fired on the house. O heavy battery was laid on arrangements made for an aeroplane reconnaissance trip to J.P. Target was registered with afternoon, + the trenches opposite were subjected to heavy fire from heavy guns, Belgians + our own field + howitzers. Ambrigrand. WMF	
7th April	8.15 AM 20 shells dropped into YPRES, which is crowded with 27 Div. Considerable damage done. Spencer Sgn + O.P. were at tree engaged by Heavy guns while French Heavies were also turned on to known German positions in these squares. Shelling ceased about 8.35 AM. Day passed quiet. North Midland Heavy Battery came under CRA in morning turned 29 shells of 9.2mm + all calibre opened trench opposite. Shelling ceased. Have received from eligible 3rd Div arty to commence my 6 p/m 8/9. Preliminary orders issued. WMF	

WAR DIARY
or
INTELLIGENCE SUMMARY.

(Erase heading not required.)

Army Form C. 2118.

43.   28th Div Arty

Hour, Date, Place	Summary of Events and Information	Remarks and references to Appendices
CHATEAU VIDA 8th April	Orders as to meeting of 5th Div arty by Guides & also to relief of our section issued.	
8.45 PM	YPRES-VLAMERTINGHE Road shelled by Field guns + several Heavy Artillery turned into shrapnel 079 + 70.	
	North Midland Heavy Battery Commander reported arrival. Battery now under Cmd VIII Corps BATEMAN RHA; Heavy Artillery in Corps troops.	
9.30 PM	Guide from each battery met incoming section of 5th Divn Arty	
6.11 PM	to take them to Battery positions.	Nominal Roll of
	Heavy Commander from the Front. Night first met.	Officers.
9th April 2 AM	Relief of first section completed without difficulty.	
	Incoming 5th Divn section minted	
1.45 PM	YPRES shelled. Three batteries turned into shrapnel from positions.	
	Major Linton of batteries withdrawn to W. of POPERINGHE	
	BA. Column announced ready for 27 Divn to have anything in that area that they have recently new positions.	
9.30 PM	Remaining section of 5th Divn incoming artillery met by Guides	
11 PM	& led them to battery positions.	
	Commander of Troops - had too heavy a lot my C.T. but Divr issued for replacement of our French Section on night 11/12 & for registration on 12th -	

Army Form C. 2118.

WAR DIARY
or
INTELLIGENCE SUMMARY.
(Erase heading not required.)

44. 28th Div Art.

Instructions regarding War Diaries and Intelligence Summaries are contained in F.S. Regs., Part II. and the Staff Manual respectively. Title pages will be prepared in manuscript.

Hour, Date, Place	Summary of Events and Information	Remarks and references to Appendices
CHATEAU VIDAL 10th April 12.45 AM	Relief of second section by 28th Division completed without difficulty and relieved section moved to rest area W of POPERINGHE at this hour command of the Artillery on the front passed to CRA 5th Divn.	Address will be shown here after as YPRES.
10. AM	HQ RA 28th Divn moved to 57 Rue de DIXMUDE YPRES	
	In afternoon CRA visited the batteries in the rest area.	
Rue de DIXMUDE 11th April	CRA moved out to join Divnl Cmdr at POTIJZE Chateau.	
	In the evening 11/12 the first section of 28th Divl Arty Bettenes relieved the section of the French 3rd Division Brigade grpts were met by guides at POTIJZE Cross Roads at 8.30 P.M. that half hour intervals.	
8.30 – 10 P.M	The troops occupied new positions.	
12.45 P.M	The relief was completed without difficulty.	
12th April	Registration was carried out by the first section & 13th Cmdr being satisfied with the result — the remaining sections came in the evening. Guides met the sections at Isanne Plus and the 11th + 12th 1.45 P.M the relief was completed the the French guns had withdrawn.	
	Report line was established in new area EAST of YPRES	
	A ZEPPELIN passed over during the evening moving Eastwards. Some bombs were dropped on VLAMERTINGHE during the evening from Enemy Counter fire caused chiefly amongst the Civil Population. Additional ammn allowed for registering.	

(73989) W4141—463. 400,000. 9/14. H.&J.Ltd. Forms/C. 2118/10.

Army Form C. 2118.

WAR DIARY
or
INTELLIGENCE SUMMARY.
(Erase heading not required.)

45.   28th Div Arty

Hour, Date, Place	Summary of Events and Information	Remarks and references to Appendices
YPRES. 13th April.	Registration continued. However trench mortar fire was trouble in trenches. Our trench howitzer battery arrived. Enemy aeroplane much in evidence - reported to Divn in turn. Anti aircraft guns were not about 1.0 P.M. W.F.	
14th April	O/C Commander went for visit to Brigade Commanders tomorrow. New sector allotted to 28th Division on the left. CRA went out & saw Brigade Commanders regarding readjustment of front. RA of French division on left warned of arrival of Col Rendle & reconnaissance of this portion. Great difficulty locating trench howtzer. Several hit in enemy reply by trench gun & howitzer stopped turnpound. Few rounds actually fired intermittently heavy. W.F.	
15th April	O/C Commander visited Brigaders. At 1 P.M. 2 Howitzers & 2 Field batteries shelled trench howtzer were suffered etc. Later 37th Bn put men down said to be the next off it we fired from. Several howtzers nt. Otherwise usual reporting an attack which is refuted with Salient tonight. Battln all horses returned by first ltt.	

Army Form C. 2118.

WAR DIARY
or
INTELLIGENCE SUMMARY.
(Erase heading not required.)

29th Div Arty

Hour, Date, Place	Summary of Events and Information	Remarks and references to Appendices
YPRES 16th April	Night passed quietly.	
	Aeroplanes reported position of wire weft for Emplacement & registered 37th Battery on them. Several aircraft fired during the day on hour & other hostile approaches to entrain the trench howitzer. As fire was stopped from time to time but it always began again. Considerable damage done to our trench. Hail been excessive caused. An extra allowance of Amm't or Ammn allowed to enable this battery to be complied with. Programme prepared. Aeroplane observer arm sent out to confer with O.C. 37 How Battery. 146 "B" expended a large number of rounds answering the expected call from the left for fire support. The relation 37 R.R.A relieved during night by R.R.A Steel hand reported to proceed to Command 2 London & North Midland Heavy Brtyrs. Several targets registered by Aeroplane.	WIE WIE WIE
17th April	Numerous positions & emplacement taken on by 37. Howitzer battery with Aeroplane observation. firing stopped but commenced again at intervals. Retaliation. by firing lyddite of German trench offsite succeeded in stopping bombing at times also. but trench howitzer was not actually located. Eight targets were registered by aeroplane during the day. In the afternoon O.C. 146 R.B. had shelled out of his billet but no casualties were caused. Enemy This HQ attachment.	

Army Form C. 2118.

28th Div Art

WAR DIARY
or
INTELLIGENCE SUMMARY.
(Erase heading not required.)

Hour, Date, Place	Summary of Events and Information	Remarks and references to Appendices

YPRES 17th (continued).

In the evening the 37th Battery otherwise succeeded in locating an M/Gun which was firing. It put his gun on & after a direct hit him. M/Gun ceased firing but other m/g continued. Orders received for a demonstration by 28th Div's to assist 5th Div in its attack on Hill 60.

7.30 P.M. 3rd Bde fired on men capt. trenches opposite our trenches 11.12. Fire continued till 7.40 P.M.

7.40 P.M. The N. Midland & 122 Army Batteries fired for 10 minutes on turn S trks of BECELAERE. 1 Section 146th Bty relieved 1 Section F11th D.A. being hung having from Army M/S Div'n in all night. Enemy siezed our trench at BROODSEINDE in counter attack at midnight. Later.

18th April

3.30 A.M. at 3.30 A.M. another counter attack on captured trench was partially successful.

6.30 P.M. Another attack was ordered & field batteries covering the area were ordered to shoot. Supported by 37 How Battery. Since the cessation of heavy battery in East Bde— shoot been in position one night to two have unfortunately the My's trenches opposite our own not completed. The M/G battn of the 146th Brigade has left to cover area of BROODSEINDE Cross Road.

Heavy Battery was told N/ as another battery & a list N/possible thoughts communicated to

Army Form C. 2118.

WAR DIARY
or
INTELLIGENCE SUMMARY.
(Erase heading not required.)

48.   28th Div Art

Instructions regarding War Diaries and Intelligence Summaries are contained in F. S. Regs., Part II. and the Staff Manual respectively. Title pages will be prepared in manuscript.

Hour, Date, Place	Summary of Events and Information	Remarks and references to Appendices
YPRES. 18th (continued)	Attack was further reinforced & came up after 8. A.m. 6 & 1 P.M. the 37th Howitzer Battery cooperated in locating large trench Howitzer gun silencing it with 4 shells. Standing of gun fire again on this day. Some trench were up visited by Aeroplane, by both 65th = How. 122nd How & by 37 B.d. Sorry shell put into YPRES in evening 2 Hydrs H. Battery moved into wood C.10 shelled by VII Corps.	
19th April	YPRES shelled intermittently all morning. Shooting commenced in the evening, when the aeroplanes went down. Some information brought out by North Midland H.A. Battery, the 3rd Pozlgele W.M. aeroplanes. 65th Battery registered upon the most important target in 37 area. 3.45 P.M. Ammunition again opened fire & 37th H. Battery turned on it stones Blowing up & rightling a house in the immediate vicinity & its position human unable use alarmed. During the evening some 17 inch shell were but into YPRES attn there were shortly shelled by 9mm. & another Calibre. considerable damage was done to houses & some casualties caused amongst the troops. Some registration carried out by aeroplane. M.F. D.B.	

Army Form C. 2118.

WAR DIARY
or
INTELLIGENCE SUMMARY.
(Erase heading not required.)

28th Div Arty

Instructions regarding War Diaries and Intelligence Summaries are contained in F. S. Regs., Part II. and the Staff Manual respectively. Title pages will be prepared in manuscript.

Hour, Date, Place	Summary of Events and Information	Remarks and references to Appendices
YPRES 20th April	Orders issued for reconnaissance of positions for fourth batteries with a view to early occupation. YPRES heavily shelled both by 17 inch & smaller calibres. Enemy mortar remained silent all day. Some ay(?) ration carried out. H.Q. moved back to VLAMERTINGHE during afternoon. YPRES shelled during the night. Troops moved out with WF	
YPRES 21st April	Intermittent trench fire during the afternoon now searched for by 37 – How(?)itz(?) & Battery. RA HQ moved back to Divnl. H.Q.	WF
CHATEAU NORTH OF VLAMERTINGHE 22nd April 5:0 P.M.	Germans opened fire with big howitzers & damaged trench about BOESSENDE. Reports of enemy massing for attack came in. Curtis(?) kept stood by with one heavy & one extra Howitzer Battery. No attack came Some ay(?) ration carried out. Very heavy bombardment commenced to North – on left of Canadians – & also of YPRES. RFC observes reported that all enemy German lines advance Cloud of smoke driving over the French lines. Later _	

(73989) W4141—463. 400,000. 9/14. H.&J.Ltd. Forms/C. 2:18/10.

Army Form C. 2118.

27th Div AK

50

WAR DIARY
or
INTELLIGENCE SUMMARY.
(Erase heading not required.)

Hour, Date, Place	Summary of Events and Information	Remarks and references to Appendices

VLAMERTINGHE

7.30 PM — After a heavy cannonade, musketry & rifle was directed painful to the right & making them wait. Report received that Germans had broken through the French lines & turned the left flank of the Canadians. Ammunition Columns ordered to stand by ready to send up ammunition. Div Am Col. + Park also warned. All communication with Brigade cut, but eventually by Div visitors route.

Col HIND — N. Midland Heavy Battery reported at ??? that the detachment had withdrawn from the guns that they left them in position My WIELTJE. On account of heavy shrapnel & machine gun fire in that area. Shortly afterwards an Officer of the 4th London H. Battery arrived to report to Captain ??? by the ??? This reported officially by the adjutant.

VLAMERTINGHE 23rd April

9.30 PM — Message from Canadian Division reported Heavy Battery in C.22.d

Still firing recommended its withdrawal. Officer sent with land still firing recommended with them. There were instructed though it would be difficult not with them. There were instructed though it to join Col HIND officer halting & LtCol Harris his adjutant two miles hitherto turned out to take up positions common

POPERINGHE.

2.45 AM — Later when it was found BOESINGHE still in French possession

118 Batty
365

WAR DIARY or INTELLIGENCE SUMMARY

Army Form C. 2118.

2nd Div Arty

51

Hour, Date, Place	Summary of Events and Information	Remarks and references to Appendices
VLAMERTINGHE (23rd cont)		
4.10 A.M.	The 365th Battery were put into position to cover toward in C.10.d. The 118th Battery was left in reserve. The other French Blocks having been thrown away, also hut in to position.	
	Asked to cooperate in counter attack at 4.45 P.M. Objectives allotted to 365th & N Midlands, who synced him.	
11.15 A.M.	Reconnaissance made by West Brook [Col?] with a view to selection of gun positions for recent him. Ballium fire continual.	
	French reported held up on line C13c – C22a. 363rd Battery put into common him line & N Midland Heavy By into Road Junction C3a d.3d. 365th Battery ordered to put in touch with French Commander at Mnar B18b. 118th Battery ordered up to cooperate with his fire on left – from C14 Central to C14 a 55.	
1.15 P.M.	Orders received that the 13th Bgd Brigade would support attack at 2.30. that by the field batteries the N.M. Heavy Position would cooperate.	
2.15 P.M.	The Artillery Officers got in touch with Bry ade Commander three worked direct under his orders.	
	Attack postponed till 3.45 P.M.	
3.45 P.M.	Attack commenced. Advance was slower blocks were prevented from 5th Div Batteries to lit up the N Midland after this time.	

Army Form C. 2118.

WAR DIARY
or
INTELLIGENCE SUMMARY.
(Erase heading not required.)

52   28th Divl. Artillery

Hour, Date, Place	Summary of Events and Information	Remarks and references to Appendices
VLAMERTINGHE (23rd cont)		
24th April	Heavy firing died far into the night	
8.15 AM	Reports from FABs showed that on Centre & Right Front everything had Quiet. No report from 146 Bty. 75th Battery which was lent to the 5th Division was called back - Major JERVIS ordered to bring as many guns as possible - his Battery being split up - West of Canal - Lieut Col DUFFUS CB whose batteries were temporarily handed over with other FABs was called in with his staff.	
9.10 AM	North Midland HQ. turned on to forming in C8d10.2 & C+d104 which aeroplane reports being full of Germans. Lets Battn. was put into Cross Roads about PILCKEM.	
11.45 AM	Lt Col DUFFUS reported men sent to TRENS TOURS to get the guns of two Canadian Batteries as possible to support French counter attack.	
12.30 PM	Major JERVIS reported with two guns more moved at Col DUFFUS' disposal. Major now V'craft artillery reports the 122nd HB being withdrawn to W of Canal + attached to 28th Divisional Artillery.	

Army Form C. 2118.

WAR DIARY
or
INTELLIGENCE SUMMARY.
(Erase heading not required.)

53.   28th Div a/g

Hour, Date, Place	Summary of Events and Information	Remarks and references to Appendices
VLAMERTINGHE (24th Cnt)		
7.40 P.M.	In order to assist support the French Counter attack the battery has just made Lt Col Duffy's who was ordered to find a position for it N. or N.W. of ELVERDINGHE. The Front Commander was informed of this intention, through the Canadian Div. HQ. Owing to hostile attacks S. JULIEN having rendered it for 6TH with orders have issued to the 149 Bde to withdraw on a certain east of X 866 + 867 Battries to position N of VERLORENHOEK to support the attack which is to be delivered on that line. Canadian A.A. informed. Maneuvered from Cnt that 2nd Belgian batteries were placed at 18"S in support. Orders from the item for their action somewhere N of LA BRIQUE to support attack on S. JULIEN tomorrow. Oc hdq Battery reported having retired which caused from WIELTJE having left our guns which knocked them Nw with the team killed. Co. heavy arrangement kept Pounuart. Batty remained in action till all ammunition was exhausted.	
11 P.M.	Report from TCnt Artillery that battery of brks is out 67m. Distributed at sam time Belgium B.C. reports it was found that their batteries were too few in men & to make it impossible to put them in for up to LA BRIQUE. They were there from [illegible] in the night of the three Brit. Batteries west of the canal.	108 HS ?

hnE

WAR DIARY or INTELLIGENCE SUMMARY

Army Form C. 2118.

54.   **28th Div Arty**

Hour, Date, Place	Summary of Events and Information	Remarks and references to Appendices
VLAMERTINGHE 25th April 4.15 P.M.	N. Midland Bde directed on Cross Roads C.3.b.74 French objective from there this time, including Railway at PILKEM at 5:30 P.M. & South Un Lt of LANGEMARCK at 6 P.M.	
6.45 P.M.	OR 118 ordered to sent forward an Anover with a telephone to ascertain how the French attack was progressing & to put in batten into support of objectives. The 365th & 75th to take their orders from him.	
6.55 P.M.	Report received from 146th Bde that two sections would be placed in Diq B from which attack on ST JULIEN would be supported.	Batten ?
8.0 P.M.	Capt ___ artillery telephoned that 60pr Battery would be kept under Corps Placed near 9.2 Bm in wood A.30. Orders issued to batteries W. of Canal for support of French attack timed for 1.0 P.M.	
1.0 P.M.	Attack postponed till 1.15 P.M.	
3.15 P.M.	OR 365th Battery reported having shelled German support, enemy artillery delivered, that the batteries had no attack was being delivered, that batteries to be ready to open fire if there was the least sign of movement. Report received from 31st Bde that in addition to 2 batteries of 146 Bde — an intense fire was starting at Advance German in squares 57 & 8 with 1 section of each.	
5.30 P.M.	Col Duffus informed CRA of postponement of French attack to attack at 9 P.M. without previous artillery preparation. Batteries warned to stand by at	

WAR DIARY
or
INTELLIGENCE SUMMARY.
(Erase heading not required.)

Army Form C. 2118.

28th Divl Arty

Hour, Date, Place	Summary of Events and Information	Remarks and references to Appendices
VLAMERTINGHE (25th Contd)	That however stated ready to fire if asked for assistance. 85th Battery ordered to send an officer to French Commander's position at 8 P.M. but latest information. Col. Duffus sent for to interview C of S. Artillery.	
5.20 P.M	Officer sent with confidential instructions. 458th Cmdr conveyed the information necessary for the occupation of M.R.2. French attack ordered for 9.0 P.M. & bayonet charge without previous gun preparation being the idea. Guns were allotted to divisions & objectives given French guns.	
8.30 P.M.	Attack postponed till 2 A.M. Same orders to hold good.	
4.0 A.M.	Attack delivered, reached German trenches but failed. Batteries ordered to open fire which they did.	
7.0 A.M.	365th Battery reported German massing in C.9.C. in farm buildings. Col. Duffus wounded. French reported five Tons stopped a few min aft	
8.15 P.M	lttr. this was done.	
8.20 A.M	2 Section. at farm & given to Mr Midlands. Information by phone received from 7th Cnfs. Artillery that our charges were to take place. All 18 pdr batteries both Canadian & 28th Divn which are East of Canal are placed under Col. DUFFUS. C.B. with 122nd 143, 459 Can How & N. Mid. Seige Battery placed under Col. MARSH.	
12 Noon	AdjGenl Borris rushed 28th D and AO & placed 18 pdr batteries of 28th Divn & British batteries under CRA 28th Divn. Batteries ordered to fire on German main trenches at T.20 &

WAR DIARY or INTELLIGENCE SUMMARY

Army Form C. 2118.

57.   28th Div Arty.

Hour, Date, Place	Summary of Events and Information	Remarks and references to Appendices
VLAMERTINGHE (26th Cont)		
1.12 P.M	Maintain a steady rate of fire till 2.0 P.M. From 2 to 2.5 minuted fire per gun commenced at increased rate of support. OC 365th Reported that enemy breach of B – B said to be fleeing by fire at 1.20 would start his next attack.	
1.20 P.M	Batts. refused to cap. artillery orders given for fire the commenced at hour ordered by Gnl Pommé. This was done. Repts received that French had been forced to fall back in the centre after attack moving to asphyxiating gas, that LAHORE Div was also held up. Later repts stated the French were making progress to the North, hurrying up the French, which they ended by storming German main trench between points Cross-Road C.14a SE to C.14 & 10.10.	
3.30 P.M	18hr Battn was ordered to engage German main trench between points Cross-Road C.14a SE to C.14 & 10.10.	
4.0 P.M	Air cleared between bursts. Fire stopped.	
6.45 P.M	Heavy firing from North from French guns heard flatter, never received of German counter-attack in C.15. Three batteries turned on to shoot at North end of C.15 a to.	
27th April		
2.20 A.M	Wire from 84th Infy Bde saying that owing to artillery having to shoot by map this assistance was not very effective. Asks that for continuation of attack, artillery support should be from especially against houses and buildings along MOSSELMARKT - FORTUIN Road.	
2.30 P.M	CRA 27th Divn adjusts to get his supporting battery commanders in touch	

WAR DIARY / INTELLIGENCE SUMMARY

Army Form C. 2118.

57.   **28th Div Arty**

Hour, Date, Place	Summary of Events and Information	Remarks and references to Appendices
VLAMERTINGHE (26th Cont?)		
7.30 AM	In touch with O.C. 85th Spft Bty & with O.C. 146th FA Bny de at VERLORENHOEK. Col Kelly – Bombd with 84th Bde – informed question taken. Wire from 85th Spft Bde – asking for more guns as Germans had brought up some guns close to trenches.	
9.0 AM	Orders at once out to O.C. 146th Battery to take his battery forward to support the Brigade, reporting himself at B.H.Q. Liaison Officer with 27th Div wired to ask if he desired 27th Div Guns to move forward in close support & asking for any known Gun positions of the enemy. Replied indicating C.29 as a area from which close support could be attempted and asking that close touch might be maintained with 85th Bde – Order this sent artillery Cmdr Col RUNDLE.	
11.25 AM	Orders, concerning attack by Indian Division received; Batteries warned & 3 more arranged to cover ground fired on by 149th Battery.	
11.55 PM	Orders received from Cdg Artillery & asking orders sent out to cover where to Batteries my anticipated knew for Theses fort. 12.30 to 1.15 PM preliminary bomb. – ordered. Assault at 1.15 must however [?] range.	
1.20 PM	French Cmdr ordered supporting batteries to avoid shooting into an angle formed by line between M. trees C.7 & C.8, thus thence to dividing line between figures C.14 & C.15. Batteries therefore ceased firing.	
2.30 PM	French refused held up in C.15.c & losing heavily. 18pr Batteries in general ordered kept into attack with French Cmdr with a view to supporting him.	

Army Form C. 2118.

WAR DIARY
or
INTELLIGENCE SUMMARY.
(Erase heading not required.)

58   28th Divnl Arty

Instructions regarding War Diaries and Intelligence Summaries are contained in F. S. Regs., Part II. and the Staff Manual respectively. Title pages will be prepared in manuscript.

Hour, Date, Place	Summary of Events and Information	Remarks and references to Appendices
VLAMERTINGHE (27th Cont). 3.10 PM 4.55 PM	French 75 cm firing on German main trench but French Comdr asks Brittain to send to try order to tr fire. Orders for bombardment to commence at 5.15 P.M. by 18 pr Btys are coming French advance. Btys ordered to cooperate with French Comdr who did not wish to open fire.	
28th April. 10.20 AM	Orders received transferring to CRA 28th Divn Control of Canadian r. 28th Divn Batteries W. of Canal. This gives 4 Canadian Batteries - 3 Field Batteries Brit. J. - 2 Belgians - 2. 47" one 60 pr and one 9.2 in. to 2nd Gen. to command. French announce intention of attacking at 2.0 P.M. and Cmdr Artilly advises intended them firm to cooperate in own way. Division approached to General Cure's Headquarters thought took the Hyuict the heavy guns might shoot at Langemarck Station the Bixschoot Ears Road Junction. These did that first which was well out of range now to burn at sit of the guns which are shooting 1000 below map range. 365th Battery from 418th Batteries in intimate touch with 2nd JOFFRE with when they are working. Col. DUFFUS ordered 85th in touch with French Commander also.	

Army Form C. 2118.

WAR DIARY
or
INTELLIGENCE SUMMARY.
(Erase heading not required.)

59   28th Divnl Arty

Instructions regarding War Diaries and Intelligence Summaries are contained in F.S. Regs., Part II. and the Staff Manual respectively. Title pages will be prepared in manuscript.

Hour, Date, Place	Summary of Events and Information	Remarks and references to Appendices
VLAMERTINGHE (28th Cont.)	Belgians retiring under C.R.A's orders direct. from Trenches in 3 zone engaged & firms forming point d'appui.	
2 P.M	The bombardment commenced renewed till 2.15 under orders of Brig. Genl. PLUMER'S Force. Own batteries working directly under the French allowed to continue under orders of the French Commander.	
2.15 P.M	9.2 gun reported being called upon by aeroplane to shoot at B12 d 88 as there was enemy there. The request not complied with. An urgent appeal was made & permission given then to fire while an officer was sent to notify to French HQ informing them of action taken.	
3.15 P.M	Liaison officer returned to ask that 9.2 might fire into wood C.I.C. 2 rounds were fired. Orders were issued for an attack by the French at 7.P.M — the bombardment to commence at 6.45 P.M. Targets allotted to batteries.	
6.45 P.M	All guns opened fire & continued till 7 P.M. French attack made little progress. 2/F.B.M.R.F.A. had two farms burnt & all telephone wires & horses & mules kits destroyed.	
at 7 AM →	Heavy firing by Germans throughout the night at various hostile positions West of the canal.	
10.30 P.M	Batteries with wireless orders started to fire from 4.30 A.M at targets which the aeroplane observer indicated to them.	

(73989) W4141—463. 400,000. 9/14. H.&J.Ltd. Forms/C. 2118/10.

Army Form C. 2118.

WAR DIARY
or
INTELLIGENCE SUMMARY.
(Erase heading not required.)

28th Div Arty

Hour, Date, Place	Summary of Events and Information	Remarks and references to Appendices
VLAMERTINGHE 29th April 4 AM	From so keen that a staff officer was sent to French HQ to ask if any information was requiring from Battle Posn. He was informed that nothing was in fact the h/qrs were in TA.	
8 PM	However Major sent to French HQ by request, but by not finding out the h/qrs which the French occupied, he learnt little. An attack was intended but the hour had not been decided.	
10 PM	All batteries ordered to be prepared to open on same targets as were ordered to the morning attack yesterday. Plumer's Force CRA ordered bombardment to commence at 11.30 AM an attack to commence at 5 commence when the late he issued orders for bombardment to stand by from 11.30 AM French began. Batteries therefore redried to stand by from 11.30 AM the hour when French did.	
11.30 AM	Orders received that French would not attack. During morning aeroplanes put hun mts Tpts. N.17.12 Pts. huge reported one Prussian Gun position in which it fired about 30 rounds to effect.	
7.0 PM	French announced intention of attacking at 8 PM after a bombardment in which we were asked to participate by CRA Plumer's Force. Orders issued 7.X PM but had to be altered after receipt.	
10 PM	Final Flash line & time, Tupts & attacks to all batteries these free.	

Army Form C. 2118.

WAR DIARY
or
INTELLIGENCE SUMMARY.

(Erase heading not required.)

28th Div Art

Hour, Date, Place	Summary of Events and Information	Remarks and references to Appendices
VLAMERTINGHE 30th April	31st (Howitzer) Bty went into action during the night. hurriedly broke midst French attack for 2 hours. Canadian CRBA Div Bty Sent in intimate touch with General Joppé - with whom each he a liaison officer. A staff Officer from CRA sent to French HQ. French instructions to liaison officer does not agree with RA or Div Plummer force, no French ordered to work as French Commander desires.	
10 A.M.	The about to have was changed to Sup. Commanders, first Division, direct from Genl. of the artillery commander, & then also to hour of attack objective. It first bombardment was to commence at 10 A.M. the assault not by the French. The accent bombardment from 10.45 to 11.10 AM during which the British Batteries were to fire behind German main trench. At 11.10 assault was to be & Batteries were to continue to shoot low to maintain. Attack made with partial success. The batteries got orders direct from General JOPPE as to objective down Opin.	
1 P.M.	47 Batteries have been shooting up erratically - the division bands shifting on and on off the shell.	
2 P.M.	Belgian division reported that French infantry had received 2 hours of german attack but were held up to the end. Belgian division provided miracle from Commander of French	

Army Form C. 2118.

WAR DIARY
or
INTELLIGENCE SUMMARY.
(Erase heading not required.)

28th Div Arty

62

Hour, Date, Place	Summary of Events and Information	Remarks and references to Appendices
VLAMERTINGHE (30th Cont)	18th Division to say he right was held up & was sorry that help from Braitch would be gratefully received. He reported, no one who had fixed appeared to be no German Officers left in the trenches but only NCOs in command. This information was passed on to General MILNE.	
3.30 P.M.	PLUMERS Force about 9 incendiary shells were in front of German trenches on hill 29 about C18.a.5.12.150 to night, to make a fight for the LAHORE Division. 2 Belgian batteries turned onto this.	
3.45 P.M.	Mine received but 4 shell were falling into our own lines so that same were stopped. the 1cm was not to examine them - also he Nos 2 ammunition bgr in 108th battery which was not operation was a broken and embarrassing string. In consultation with Genl Milne orders sent to O.C.108 to draw up on this bot from mill head - which was considered to mean he O.C. Belgian group reported he considered his fire had been sufficient accurate & continue to destroy the line & he therefore ceased fire.	
4.35 P.M.	No attack appears to have been made.	
8.P.M.	Summer buoyed on various objectives. Such a firm position & Corps trench ready for an action that may later become hot fig.	

(73989) W4141—463. 400,000. 9/14. H.&J. Ltd. Forms/C. 2118/10.

WAR DIARY
or
INTELLIGENCE SUMMARY.
(Erase heading not required.)

Army Form C. 2118.

Hour, Date, Place	Summary of Events and Information	Remarks and references to Appendices
VLAMERTINGHE (30th Cont.)	1.30pm arrived to replace horse gun in 103rd Battery. FRA the Princes Mondes visited B.7.2 which it was registering with aeroplane. 3 direct hits were registered while he was in the OP. A separate report on the action will be forwarded later. 1st May 1915	28th Div Arty

Diary of the 28th Divisional Artillery during the Second
Battle of YPRES from 22nd April to the 14th May. 1915.

22nd April.   5:0 p.m. Very heavy bombardment commenced to the North on portion of line held by the French between LANGEMARCK and the YSER CANAL.

The French troops in the trenches were asphyxiated by gases thrown from the German Infantry trenches and they broke back, carrying with them the teams and wagons of the Field Artillery. This was the first experience of gas.

This withdrawal of the French exposed the left flank of the 1st Canadian Division who were obliged to throw back their left flank to meet the Germans now pouring southwards and turning to the South East.

The attack by gas still continued and, as the wind was blowing from the North West, the Canadians suffered severely but held on strongly and even counter attacked as far as the Northern edge of the wood in C.10.d. where they held on with great gallantry.

In the South East corner of this wood was placed a battery of 4.7" guns of the 2nd London Division, and the advance of the German Infantry from the North West had caused the personnal to abandon their guns after withdrawing the strikers from the breech blocks.

The later advance of the Canadians recaptured these guns but, although parties were sent out after dark to reconnoitre it was impossible to bring up teams to remove the guns over the open ground with any prospect of success.

Owing to some misunderstanding the Canadians line again fell back South of the Wood, and all chance of recovering the guns had to be given up for the present. The North Midland Battery in action at WIELTJE seeing the stragglers coming back in large numbers and on account of the heavy gun and rifle fire and the general confusion, took out the

two breech blocks from ~~th~~ one section and left the guns.
The lieutenant Colonel Commanding the Brigade with his
Adjutant and a few men who refused to leave worked two of the
guns for some time, when an order was sent out to withdraw
the entire battery and bring it into action in the neighbourhood of VLAMERTINGHE.

Eventually the G.O.C., R.A's A.D.C. personally supplied
the two missing breech blocks, the whole battery was/placed again
in action and has been firing by map since the 23rd April.

Two resting batteries, the 118th (31st Brigade) and
the 365th (3rd Brigade) were brought into action against the
wood in C.10.d, but were ordered not to fire unless
instructed to do so.

23rd.April.   At 4:10 a.m. a request was made for Artillery co-operation
in counter attack at 4:45 a.m. and 365th Battery and North
Midland Heavy Battery opened fire on allotted objectives.

A reconnaissance was made by O.C. 118th Battery of
possible gun positions on the West of the YSER CANAL North
West of YPRES.

The report was received at 10 a.m.

In the meantime the position of Batteries North of
FRESENBERG was threatened by the progess made by the enemy
to the North and West, and it was decided to make a new
~~distribution~~.distribution.

The left hand Battery near GRAVENSTAFEL was withdrawn
to WIELTJE, two sections each from the remaining batteries
(366th and 367th) were ordered to shift their position and
fire northwards.

While the 118th Battery and the 365th Battery occupied
positions West of the YSER CANAL.

Both these Batteries fired on the German trenches seen
in C.8.d. while the North Midland Heavy Battery fired on the
crossroads further north.

Soon after 1:0 p.m. orders were received to cooperate
with an attack to be made by the 13th Infantry Brigade and

Battery Commanders were ordered to get in touch with the G.O.C. who informed them that the attack would take place at 2:45 p.m.

At that hour the attack was postponed to 3:45 pm.

The batteries opened fire as arranged, but the promised attack was not made, and no further communication from the 13th Infantry Brigade appears to have been received.

All the Batteries of the Divisional Artillery were firing through the night.

24th April.

The 75th Battery, which has been lent to the 5th Division for the operations at Hill 60, was able to collect three guns, and was ordered into action West of the Canal with 2 guns, while the third went into action at WIELTJE alongside the 149th Battery, and at the same time the Officer Commanding the 8th Howitzer Brigade was ordered to report to R.A. head quarters with his staff and headquarters detachment. At 9:0 a.m. the North Midland Heavy Battery fired on two farms reported by aeroplanes to be full of Germans, and at 10:0 o'clock the fire was turned on to PILCKEM. Soon after 11:o a.m. the O.C? 8th F.A. Bde arrived and was sent to the Headquarters, Canadian Division to collect as many Canadian Batteries as possible in order to support the French counter attack.

At 12:30 p.m. information was received that the 122nd Heavy Battery was being withdrawn from its position East of FRESENBERG and placed under the orders of the 28th Divisional Artillery.

O.C.8th F.A.Bde. was ordered to find a position for this Battery North of ELVERDINGHE.

The Battery arrived during the afternoon and was placed North West of BRIERLEN.

Later in the evening a message was received from the Vth Corps that 2 Belgian Batteries would join the 28th Divisional Artillery.

When the Officer Commanding the Groupe arrived, it was found that his two batteries had only just been withdrawn out of action, and the men were exhausted, and only 100 rounds per gun were with the Battery.

Orders were given that the ammunition to make up to 200 rounds per gun should be got up during the night, and for the Batteries to be in action West of the Canal by 4:0 a.m.

The Officer Commanding the 149th Battery reported at R.A. Headquarters at 10:0 p.m. that he had retired from WIELTJE with two guns, having exhausted his ammunition and having left two guns and some wagons behind.

Teams were sent out that night to bring in the guns, one of which was damaged by shell fire and unserviceable. At 11:0 p.m. Vth. Corps telegraphed that a Battery of 60 punders would arrive, and be placed under the orders of the G.O.C.,R.A. 28th Division.

During the day the 3rd, 31st, and 146th Brigades with the 37th and 65th Howitzer Batteries were engaged on the 28th Division front in keeping down the fire of Minenwerfer, and supporting the Infantry in the trenches.

The 149th Battery which retired from WIELTJE during the evening was in action due North of the village behind a ridge facing East but much exposed from the North and North West.

The Battery was located during the afternoon by a Hostile Howitzer Battery and was subjected to a heavy shell fire.

Meanwhile the rifle fire was getting more intense and the Battery Commander was informed by the local Infantry Commander that the line they at present held could be maintained until dark but probably not later.

Captain R.S.Ellis, having exhausted his ammunition and fearing the loss of his guns, decided to withdraw them at 6:30 p.m. and called up his teams to hook in.

Under a heavy fire and with the assistance of his officers the guns were removed, the remaining gun and two ammunition wagons were so damaged as to be useless, and these were left in position for the present.

One gun of the 75th Battery in action with the 149th Battery was also brought back and came into action West of the Canal.

Further to the East in the angle formed by the original trenches of the 28th Division and the new line running East and West through FORTUIN, the two sections of the 366th and 367th Batteries supported the Infantry to the North with great success, while the remaining two sections were fully occupied in maintaining the trench line formerly covered by three Batteries.

In the centre group (31st Field Artillery Brigades) the 69th Battery silenced a short range gun which was annoying our trenches. The 103rd Battery fired with one section on the crossroads South of KEERSELAERE and with the other section on a hostile battery South East of BROODSEINDE.

The 100th Battery also fired eastwards out on German trenches as ours were suffering severely from Minenwerfer.

Practically all communications were cut off for the entire day.

The 37th (Howitzer) Battery under Major E. Harding Newman were first apprised of the German advance from POELCAPELLE by Canadian Infantry retiring through the battery very early in the morning.

The Battery Commander at once sent Captain H.O. Hutchison with a telephone to reconnoitre, and the Battery reversed and opened fire on advancing Germans under instructions from Captain Hutchison.

Three German attacks were defeated entirely by Howitzer fire and at least 500 Germans were accounted for. The lyddite shell had an excellent effect, and prevented the Germans entrenching near St. JULIEN. During these operations, which were carried out with great skill and daring by Captain Hutchison the battery was under heavy field gun shellfire from daylight until 4:0 p.m. at the rate of 250 shell per hour. One gun carriage was slightly damaged.

It was very noticeable from the Battery Observing station that the Germans were working in the open and constantly digging first and second line trenches with communications between them.

During the afternoon our Infantry suffered casualties from a Battery located 1 mile South South East of FREZENBERG.

The right Group (3rd Field Artillery Brigade) was not called upon to do more that maintain its own front, but, on being informed of the situation to the North, arranged to assist by changing the front of one Battery and firing in that direction.

25th April.
At daylight the fire of the North Midland Heavy Battery was directed on the crossroads at PILCKEM, the railway near that place and the crossroads to the East of it. Later fire was turned on to LANGEMARCK.

The 118th Battery West of the Canal was directed to send forward an observer with a telephone to reconnoitre and report on the progress of the French attack and to register the batteries West of the Canal on points likely to be useful.

Soon afterwards (6:50 a.m.) a report was received from the 146th Brigade that two sections had been placed in D.19.b. to support the attack on St. JULIEN.

A telephone message from the Vth Corps stated that the 60 punders would now be kept under Corps orders and Placed in position near the 9.2 Howitzer in wood A.30. An attack by the French northwards along the East bank of the Canal was arranged for 1:0 p.m. and instructions were issued to 118th 149th, 75th and 365th and North Midland Batteries to support it.

At 1:0 p.m. the attack was postponed to 1:15 p.m. and front line trenches and supports were shelled as arranged. No attack however was made.

7.

At 5:30 p.m. information was received from a Canadian brigade West of the Canal that the French proposed to attack northwards at 9:0 p.m. with the bayonet but without any previous Artillery bombardment.

Batteries left of the Canal were ordered to be ready to cooperate if required, and an officer was sent to French Headquarters for further instructions.

A Staff Officer was sent to all Brigades 28th Division to explain the situation and to allot areas and roads in event of movement taking place.

At 8:30 p.m. notice of the inevitable postponement of the Infantry attack was received and the hour was fixed for 2:0 a.m. the next day.

26th April.   Eventually the French advanced at 4:0 a.m. but did not press the attack home. Our batteries West of the Canal opened fire on the German Trenches to stop rifle fire. The observer of the 365th Battery, Lieutenant Bates R.H.A. reported at 7:0 a.m. that the enemy were massing in farm buildings close to their lines and the North Midland Heavy Battery opened on them.

At 8:30 a.m. a telephone message from Vth Corps indicated a reorganization of Artillery for the purpose of special operations viz. All Field Batteries of 28th and Canadian Division West of the Canal to be grouped under Lieutenant O.C. 8th F.A. Bde, while the 122nd. Heavy Battery, North Midland Heavy Battery and the 457th Canadian Howitzer Battery were to be grouped under the Lieutenant Colonel Commanding the 13th Heavy Bde. At 12:0 o'clock the Brigadier General R.A. Vth Corps reached 28th Division Headquarters and placed 18 pounder Batteries under 28th Divisional Artillery Commanders.

An attack was timed for 2:5 p.m. by the Lahore Division and the French between the wood 1,000 yards West of St. JULIEN and the YSER CANAL, and forty minutes bombardment with

with five minutes rapid fire, immediately before the assult, was arranged for and carried out by the 118th, 75th, 365th and 149th Batteries, 2 Belgian Batteries on the right of the 149th Battery cooperated. The French Commander complained that this bombardment was too early and would affect his attack adversely, but on reference to Vth Corps Headquarters, compliance with the original order was demanded.

The result of the attack was that the Lahore Division and the French centre were held up., St. JULIEN was captured by the Northumbrian Brigade, but was evacuated later in in the evening.

The French left pushed on and enfiladed the German trenches with Field Artillery capturing large quantities of prisoners.

Between 3:30 and 4:0 p.m. the same four Field Batteries shelled German trenches in front of French centre and to the South East.

At a quarter to 7, news was received of a counter attack on the French right, and fire was at once opened by 118th 365th and 75th Batteries.

The counter attack was checked.

South of St. Julien the 366th and 367th Batteries of the 146th Brigade maintained their position under heavy fire and both Battery Commanders Captain C.A.R. Scott and Major T. Carlyon as well as the personnel of their batteries maintained the best traditions of the Royal Regiment.

Captain Scott's Battery (366th) engaged German Infantry near St. JULIEN early in the day at a range of 800 yards and fired by the afternoon 1740 rounds.

Our attack was heavily shelled in enfilade from the right and no counter Batteries were available at the time, but the cooperation of the 123rd Heavy Battery, 27th Division was requested in order to silence hostile guns at PASSCHENDAELE.

Hostile aeroplanes were very busy over gun positions West of ZONNEBEKE.

The telephone lines were very difficult to maintain, being very frequently cut to pieces by shell fire. Farther to the South the 37th Howitzer Battery at an early hour shelled German trenches on the GRAVENSTAFEL ridge, and then shelled enemy's Infantry leaving them. The German Infantry took refuge in some houses whence they were turned out by a few shells.

This Battery observer informed the 100th Field Battery at 11:40 a.m. that German supports were advancing from the North, and the 100th Battery shelled them.

During the afternoon while the 100th, 103rd and 37th (Howitzer) Batteries were shelling the German trenches in preparation of the attack at 2:5 p.m. a S.O.S. call was received from No. 20 trench, whereupon the 69th, 103rd, and one gun of the 37th Battery swung round and fired in the new direction. The Infantry report that this fire stopped the German attack.

On the right flank the 18th.22nd, and 62nd Batteries poured in a rapid fire at 2:10 p.m. for 5 minutes and then 18th and 22nd Batteries turned a section each on the GRAVENSTAFEL ridge for an hour and a half.

The 65th Howitzer Battery shelled a minenwerfer and a German observing station in front of the K.O.Y.L.I. with some success.

27th April.   At 2:20 a.m. a telegram was received that owing to guns shooting by the map, their assistance was not so effective as if the fire had been observed, and in conclusion asking that in event of a continuance of the attack, fire should be directed on to the houses on the MOSSELMARKT-FORTUIN road.

The G.O.C. 27th Divisional Artillery was at once requested to place his supporting batteries in communication with the 85th Infantry Brigade and with the Officer Commanding 146th Brigade grouped with the 85th.

At 7:30 a.m. the 85th Infantry Brigade wired for more

guns as German Field Artillery were moving up very close. Orders were at once sent to the 149th Battery to move out and rejoin the 146th Brigade.

At 11:25 a.m. the orders for the attack of the Lahore Division were received, and, as fire was to be opened at 12:30 p.m. there was but little time for arrangements to be made.

The 118th, 75th and 365th Batteries were given zones and commenced firing at the time fixed.

At 2:30 p.m. the French were reported held up in the centre and suffering casualties from rifle fire.

The three Batteries were ordered to get into touch with the French Commander with a view to supporting him. At 3:15 p.m. the French Field Artillery opened fire on the German trenches and asked our batteries West of the Canal to stand by for orders to open fire. At 5 o'clock a message was received stating that the bombardment in support of the attack of the Lahore Division would commence at 5:15 p.m. On the East of the Canal the 149th Battery rejoined the 146th Brigade and came into action near the 37th Howitzer Battery, Officers and men suffering from strain and want of sleep. One section of the 65th Howitzer Battery fired on trenches North of the Railway. The 366th and 367th Batteries turned eastwards and supported an attack on trench 25. 2/Lieutenant E.W. Ffrench was wounded while in the observation station. The 37th Howitzer Battery shelled the German trenches East of St. JULIEN, and a house reported to contain maching guns. The Germans had constructed a new trench across the reentrant N.E. of St. JULIEN and this was shelled and the parapet damaged. The minenwerfer opened fire at 12:0 noon near the BROODSEINDE crossroads, and was fired on on two occasions by the 69th Battery. It was silenced at any rate temporarily. The 100th Battery fired at houses North of GRAVENSTAFEL where gun emplacements were being prepared. During the afternoon from 2 p.m. to 4 pm. the 108th and 122nd and North Midland Heavy Batteries near VLAMERTINGHE searched the wood one mile West of St. JULIEN and at the same time the 37th Howitzer Battery shelled the German trenches connecting the village with the wood, from its position East of FREZENBERG.

On the extreme right the 3rd Field Artillery Brigade and the 65th Howitzer Battery had but little fighting, and their action was mainly confined to checking minenwerfer.

The 22nd Battery was heavily shelled in the evening and a stack of ammunition in the Battery was blown up, 420 rounds of ammunition being destroyed.

No casualties occurred however among the personnel. At 5:15 p.m. a general bombardment was ordered as a prelude to an attack by the Lahore Division northwards to the West of St. JULIEN.

Little progress however appeared to have been made and the situation was unchanged.

At 10:0 p.m. arrangements were made with the Royal Flying Corps to register the 9.2" Howitzer and the Heavy Batteries at various targets to the North and Northeast of VLAMERTINGHE.

28th April. Orders were received to transfer all guns West of the Canal less those of the Lahore Division from the Command of the Vth Corps Artillery adviser to Brigadier General A.W.Gay, Commanding 28th Divisional Artillery. The Batteries involved were the 118th, 75th, 365th and four Canadian Field Batteries. The 108th, 122nd and the North Midland Heavy Batteries, one 9.2" Howitzer and the 6th Belgian Artillery Groupe. A few minutes later a copy of French Corps orders by General Cure announcing an attack across the YSER CANAL ordered to take place at 2:0 p.m. and arrangements were at once made to employ all available guns to assist, after having communicated with General Cure's Artillery Commander.

By 1:15 p.m. the hour named for the commencement of

the bombardment, the Field Batteries were ready to open fire on the German first line and support trenches East of the Canal while the Belgian Batteries layed on two alarge farms just in rear.

The 9.2" gun was directed by aeroplane on to a cross road West of BIXSCHOOTE, and the Heavy Batteries were allotted vilages, railway stations, and hostile gun positions.

Orders were then received to open fire at 2:0 p.m. instead of 1:15 p.m. and the alteration of the hour was at once telephoned out.

The aeroplane observer working with the 9.2" Howitzer having received ~~opode~~ orders direct which were not communicated to the Battery, that the French attack was held up in front of a farm and a railway bridge East of the Canal, altered the objective and turned the fire on to the latter target.

The French were at once communicated with and confirmed this action.

In the meantime the seven Field Batteries and the Belgian Groupe were working in touch with General Joppé on the French right.

At 4:30 p.m. fire was slowed down considerably to await further movements of the French advance.

Soon after midday the 149th Battery had to be withdrawn from its forward position owing to the German Infantry advance, and it came into action further back and to the West without great difficulty.

The 65th Howitzer Battery section allotted to this group fired on the farm in German hands South of the HANEBEEK. All day the guns and wagon lines were shelled and there was great difficulty in getting water as the water cart of the 146th Brigade was wrecked by a shell during the day.

13.

The greater portion of the hostile fire came from the East near PASSCHENDALE.

About 10:0 p.m. a gun of the 366th Battery which was in action 1200 yards from the enemy's Infantry was hit and disabled. Obsevation was becoming very difficult. The 146th Brigade had been requested earlier in the day to engage enemy's guns which were causing many casualties both in the Infantry as well as in our Field Batteries. Unfortunately the range was too long, and no Heavy Artillery was available to assist. In the centre group (31st Field Artillery Brigade) the 100th Battery shelled the farm South of the HANEBEEK mentioned above but found the 18 pounder H.E. not sufficiently powerful, and the 37th Howitzer Battery was put on to it using the 100th Battery observer.

For the second time the Brigade Headquarters had to be shifted owing to shell fire, and occupied a house a little further to the East on the ZONNEBEKE road.

The 37th Howitzer Battery in addition to the action described above, was very busy firing at German Infantry in view of their observing station and at 1:30 p.m. shelled German first and second line trenches with great effect. Several hits were obtained on parapets North East and North West of St. JULIEN, and debris and bodies were observed blown into the air.

Our Infantry on Hill 37, 1 mile Northeast of the Battery position were heavily shelled in enfilade by hostile guns near PASSCHENDALE.

The 3rd. Field Artillery Brigade on the right had little to do with the exception of the 65th Howitzer Battery, in action near the railway, which fired Northwards across the rear of the Brigade, in communication with the left group.

Earlier in the day at 4:30 p.m. intimation was received from 28th Division Headquarters that a French attack across the Canal at BIXCHOOTE would take place at 7:0 p.m. Orders were given to all Batteries West of the Canal to get their lines laid out on given objectives, and to be ready to open fire at 6:15 p.m.

At this hour fire was opened by all guns, and after a tremendous bombardment lasting for 45 minutes the French attack commenced.

A little progress was made, but the whole of the East bank of the YSER Canal could not be captured without further organized attack.

29th April.   3:45 a.m. A violent bombardment commenced and appeared to be of such importance that a staff Officer was sent to the French Headquarters to ascertain the situation. He was informed that no artillery assistance was required, and that it was merely an artillery duel. A French liaison Officer was also sent to French Headquarters, but, beyond ascertaining that arrangements for an attack were being made, no further information was gained.

All batteries on West of Canal were ordered to be ready to open fire at 11:30 a.m. and at this hour a notification was received that no attack would take place. The 122nd Heavy Battery registered during the morning with aeroplane observation and was able to silence one German Battery.

At 7:0 p.m. the French announced their intention to attack at 8:0 a.m. the next morning after a bombardment. Targets were therefore allotted, and hour of opening fire fixed, after a personal interview between the G.O.C. 28th Divisional Artillery and the G.O.C. French Artillery.

On the East of the Canal the 366th and 367th Batteries continued in action and were heavily shelled both in the gun positions and in the wagon lines.

Arrangements were made for the 100th Field Battery and the 37th Howitzer Battery to cooperate, by linking both with the same observer, in order that the 100th Battery might be able to take any parties of the enemy driven from their trenches by Howitzer fire.

This arrangement was made by the two Brigade Commanders concerned on their own initiative.

The 37th Battery observer reported positions of guns North and Northeast of St. JULIEN and movements of German Infantry in their trenches near the village, some mounted men and a party with packs on moving East.

30th April. A thick mist necessitated the postponement of the French attack which did not commence until 11:0 a.m. As soon as observation was possible the 31st, 108th, 122nd, and North Midland Heavy Batteries, and the 9.2" Howitzer opened on gun positions already registered. One shell from the 108th Battery blew up a house with a loud explosion, probably an ammunition store.   The 118th, 75th, and 365th Batteries supported the attack of the 18th French Division, by registering on the German front line trenches and then pouring in a rapid fire on the supports while French Infantry assulted.

Close touch was kept throughout by liaison Officers with French Headquarters as well as with the 18th French Division whose Infantry were being supported.

The attack was successful and the German front and second line trenches were captured.

It was then reported that some uncut wire existed on the Southeast side of a hill occupied by the enemy which the French had partly captured and held. Instruction were given to the Belgian Groupe to cut the wire at once. The range was 3,000 but the fire of the two Batteries was very accurate/and in less than half an hour considerable damage was done to it. The remainder of the day was devoted to firing o points of importance in rear of the German lines. On the East side of the Canal the 366th and 367th Batteries came under a heavy shell fire and had four Officers wounded, and four gun limbers disabled. In the centre group the 100th Battery registered trenches South and West of St. JULIEN to be ready for hostile Infantry bolted from them by the 37th Howitzer Battery.

1st May.

Notification received that an attack by the French on their right would commence during the morning and liaison officers were sent to the right French Division. The 112nd, 31st, 108th and North Midland Heavy Batteries and the 9.2" Howitzer were given objectives registered by each respectively and fire was opened at 11:30 a.m. Registration was also carried out by aeroplane during the morning.

All firing was stopped at 12:0 noon.

At 1:0 p.m. shooting recommenced at the same targets and a telegram was sent to the Royal Flying Corps for an aeroplane to register the 9.2" Howitzer on Hill 29. This registration commenced at 1:30 p.m. and in 15 minutes, 5 rounds had been put into the German trenches., on the hill.

From 2:15 p.m. to 2:45 p.m. all guns stopped firing except the 92" which had again been turned on to Hill 29 and the 108th Battery registered with an aeroplane. At the time fixed for the assult the French and English Infantry went forward but were driven back by gun and machine gun fire.

The Heavy Artillery stopped at 3:25 p.m. in accordance with orders and recommenced on receiving a request from the French to engage certain targets which was immediately done. Owing to the heavy firing and the fact that the 5" guns and mountings of the 31st and 108th Batteries requiring overhauling only three guns were still in action when the order to cease fire at 5:30 p.m. was given. The lyddite shell were falling abnormally short from the 4.7" Batteries, and they were ordered to fire only Percussion Shrapnel as No. 54 time fuze would not allow of sufficient range for time shrapnel.

The 31st Heavy Battery and the 9.2" Howitzer continued to engage gun targets until 7:0 p.m.

At 7:30 p.m. a 6" gun on an armoured truck arrived in charge of a Belgian Artillery Captain and arrangements were made for registration by aeroplane the following morning.

Orders were also given that night for one gun of the 31st Brigade to be moved up Northwards to endeavour to engage

17.

the German big gun West of HOULTHURST FOREST.

2nd May.
During the night the two of the three damaged 60 pdrs. were repaired and four out of eight were available to shoot. The French Artillery General reallotted the zones of fire necessitating fresh registration by aeroplanes. The registration was commenced and a series of new targets ranged in by the Heavy Artillery. All wires were cut and communication very difficult. The Officer Commanding 9th Heavy Brigade reported his arrival at 10:0 a.m. bringing 123rd Heavy Battery which was placed in action alongside the 122nd of the same Brigade. The day was dull and misty and aeroplane work was impossible. Soon after 12:0 noon the French Right Division asked for fire to be turned on to enemy's guns to the North and the 122nd Battery opened fire. Three hours later warning was received from the same quarter of an expected attack from PILCKEM, and all heavy guns were layed on targets in that neighbourhood. Immediately afterwards heavy firing was heard and news was received of an attack from St. JULIEN. Our heavy guns at once opened on PILCKEM as well as on the St. JULIEN position. Four 1½" Anti aircraft guns manned by R.M.A. arrived and were disposed of under orders of Vth Corps. No. 20 Anti aircraft section fired and hit a German aeroplane which fell near BRIERIEN. During the day there was considerable activity on the part of the enemy in the neighbourhood of St. JULIEN and all the batteries of the 146th Brigade were busy firing at targets as opportunity offered. Ranges were short and the 366th and 367th Batteries were much exposed to a heavy shell fire from two directions but they continued in action in spite of it. The 100th Battery had given again to swing its left section to the East to support the 84th Infantry Brigade, and the 69th shelled the enemy's second line trenches. The 37th Howitzer Battery shelled parties of Germans seen in the

open about a quarter to five in the evening, and shortly after asphyxiating gas was poured out from the German trenches all along the line. At first it came towards our trenches but then blew back on to their own. After a short bombardment, the enemy attacked in single line, an unusual formation, and was immediately opened on by all the Field Artillery with the result that the German attack, although reinforced, was driven back. At 6:30 p.m. a movement from East to West was observed and parties of the enemy, collected in some dugouts, were driven out and forced to scatter into the houses. At the same time a line of Germans gradually extended across the valley South of the HANEBEEK. As soon as Captain Hutchinson observed this movement he tried to telephone to his battery, to fire, but, finding the wire cut at the moment, he ran back to the battery (37th Howitzer) and turned them on to the place where he had seen the Germans collecting. Several times after this the Germans tried to advance in single line extended, but at no point did they get far from their own trenches, except at one place West of St. JULIEN where they crawled forward up a hollow. On the right little incident was reported beyond some shelling of wagon lines. Arrangements had already been made to shorten the line which was becoming untenable from enfilade fire and to withdraw the 28th Division back to the FREZENBERG RIDGE. The movement to commence on the night 2nd and 3rd and to be completed night of 3rd and 4th May. Positions for Batteries had been previously reconnoitered and plans and descriptions supplied to Brigade Commanders. The withdrawal was to be by sections, the right Brigade leading and the left Brigade (146th) covering the retirement, but later on in the evening it became evident that the tactical situation did not permit of the withdrawal of any guns of the left Brigade as the Infantry required their support. They were accordingly ordered to remain in their present positions while sections of the right and centre Brigades fell back to POTIJZE.

The movement was not accomplished without some difficulty
as the night was fine and the heavy shelling of the enemy
of the gun positions of the 22nd Battery delayed the move
considerably.

3rd. May. At 2:30 a.m. reports were received that the sections of
the 3rd and 31st Field Artillery Brigades and the 65th
Howitzer Battery had occupied their new positions. Soon
after 6:0 a.m. the 122nd and North Midland Heavy Batteries
were ordered to fire on wood West of St. JULIEN to assist
the Infantry which expected an attack. At 11:0 a.m. the
9.2" Howitzer reported out of action owing to damage of
control plunger shaft. An attack from the direction of
St. JULIEN was now threatened and a section of the 108th
Heavy Battery was ordered forward to a position West of the
Canal to fire at extreme range on enemy's trenches North/east of
this village, aeroplane assistance in observation being
requested. Orders were now issued for the completion of
the move commenced the previous evening, and instructions
for keeping roads clear were added. At 4:20 p.m. the
section 108th Battery was in position and reported 10 hits
already in enemy's trenches. A series of 40 rounds were
fired altogether and many hits recorded. As the situation
appeared critical the remainder of the heavy guns fired on
St. JULIEN and the threatened attack did not come off.
Later in the evening a further attack was reported from the
wood mentioned above and the heavy batteries were at once
directed on the most valuable points. A message was received
from French sources that this attack had failed, and forwarding a letter of appreciation from the French Commander of
the work done by the 28th Div. Arty. As the 9.2" Howitzer
was now reported fit to fire, it was ~~oreder~~ ordered to
open on PILCKEM and broke down again at the 1st round.
Infantry reported fire of 108th Battery during the evening
very effective. One Section 31st Battery ordered forward

to POTIJZE wher it dug in during the night. At midnight reports were received of completion of occupation of new line by 3rd and 31st Brigades and 65th Howitzer Battery and of the withdrawal of 146th Brigade and 37th Howitzer Battery.

4th May.   The Second half of the 3rd and 31st Brigades occupied their new positions and the whole of the 146th Brigade accompanied by the 37th Howitzer Battery were withdrawn during the evening and passed through VLAMERTINGHE to rest billets. The withdrawal was most successfully accomplished, each unit was up to time and there were no blocks in the road or congestion of traffic. This in spite of the fact that the entire road was under shell fire. Lt. Colonel H.E.T. Kelly was wounded during the withdrawal. In the Morning the French announced their intention of making a strong attack in force and arrangements were made to support it with all available guns (Heavy) However not much took place although a considerable amount of ammunition was used. During the day changes in the organization of the artillery were made, and the heavy batteries were divided up among three Divisions of the Vth Corps the 28th Division getting the 108th Heavy Battery and 1 section of the 31st Heavy Battery. Later on the Infantry were very heavily shelled and called for assistance in subduing the fire of the enemy's heavy guns. No aeroplane work was done and difficulty was experienced in coping with the mass of guns brought against the 28th Division trench line. Both the Field Artillery Brigades Commanders had great difficulty in finding any place to live as the whole country side East of YPRES was swept by heavy shell fire, even a 17" gun was used against the entrenchments at POTIJZE, causing huge craters and great loss of life. More calls for assistance kept coming from the Infantry who were being shelled from all directions. It is feared that little could be done against such a concentrated fire, but all that was possible was tried and some relief to the sorely

tried Infantry was obtained. Owing to Lieutenant Colonel
H.E.T.Kelly being wounded the 31st Brigade was commanded
by Major Ramsden and Captain Sanderman was sent out during
the night to take over command of the 100th Battery. At
daylight the heavy guns opened fire on the hostile guns
positions East and West of St. Julien. During the morning
reports kept coming through of the heavy shelling of our
Infantry trenches, but no indication could be given of the
direction from which the fire came. No assistance was
obtained from aeroplanes, so various gun positions from
which enfilade fire could be brought to bear on our trenches
were selected and these positions were engaged throughout
the day. The left section 31st Heavy Battery got into close
touch with the 83rd and 84th Infantry Brigade Commanders
as well as with the 3rd and 31st Field Artillery Brigades
Commanders, and did much useful work, which however was
seriously impaired by the orders sent by the 27th Divisional
Artillery Commander instructing the B.C. to link up with
Field Artillery Brigades, 27th Division, and to fire at
targets at their request. This situation was impossible
and reference to the Vth Corps became necessary to put
it right. At 11:30 a.m. a German attack along the railway
line was attempted, but was stopped by the fire of the 18th
and 22nd Batteries. Reconnaisances of Howitzer positions
West of YPRES were undertaken during the day, as well as
of positions for Divisional Artillery to support G.H.Q.3.
Information was given by the 5th Corps at 6:30 p.m. that
two 5" Howitzers Batteries Northumbrian Division would be
attached to the Divisional Artillery, and would arrive
shortly.

6th May.   Soon after midnight the two Battery Commanders of the
4th and 5th Durham Howitzer Batteries arrived and asked for
instructions. Orders were at once given for the Batteries
to move up to BRANDHOEK and for the Brigade Commanders

and his B.C's to report to the G.O.C.R.A' at 5:30 a.m. for further orders as to reconniassances. Areas were selected and reconniassances were carried out during the day for Howitzer positions, while the O.C's 8th and 146th Field Artillery Brigades reconnoitred to the West of YPRES and BRANDHOEK. In the meantime the 37th Howitzer Battery was ordered up again into action West of the Canal to support the left of the 28th Division and attached to the left group while the 65th Howitzer Battery was transferred altogether to the right group. The 9.2" Howitzer was temporarily repaired and fired one round without further damage to recoil gear. At 8:30 p.m. the Northumberian Howitzer Brigade and the 37th Howitzer Battery moved up into positions selected during the day, but no reports had been received as to their occupation by midnight.

7th May.

Shortly after daylight our Infantry reported that they were being annoyed by shell fire from two ridges East of FORTUIN and the 108th Battery was ordered to fire on the ridges several series at irregular intervals. The 84th Infantry Brigade who had been attacked during the night reported at 9:0 o'clock that the attack had been repulsed by fire of the 31st Brigade. Difficulty in getting messages from aeroplanes and registration suffered in consequence. The wireless operators appeared to be at fault. The wind continued to blow from the East and both the 3rd and 31st Brigades complained of the effects of gas. A good obsevation station was discovered by the 365th Battery, but wire to connect it with the battery was unobtainable. The G.O.C. 4th Division complained that certain areas could not be covered by his guns and arrangements were made to put the Belgians on to it. 2 guns of the 22nd Battery were disabled by direct hits soon after 5:0 p.m. and the 365th Battery was ordered to send up two to replace them. At 11:0 p.m. the O.C. 31st Brigade reported that a gun of the 103rd was out of action. The O.C. 118th Battery was ordered to replace it.

8th May.

Very heavy cannonade started at 7:0 a.m. East of YPRES but nothing definate could be ascertained, reports agreeing that no attack was being made but only severe bombardment of trenches along the whole front of the Vth Corps. Attacks developed later in several places which were repulsed with the exception of that on the right of the 83rd Infantry Brigade. All possible fire was turned on to the threatened point counterattacks were made, and some of the lost ground was regained. The heavy firing necessitated an enormous supply of ammunition which was promptly and fully met, the work of the wagon lines and columns being thoroughly and successfully carried out over shell swept roads and through YPRES itself under fire of 17 inch guns. Lines were broken and communication became very difficult. The Batteries made the best of a grave situation and kept firing although suffering heavy casualties. The rapid fire caused the buffer oil to spurt out through the glands and the running up springs were not equal to the work. Several guns were put out of action owing to direct hits and guns were ordered up from the resting Brigade (146th) to replace them. The 146th Brigade Ammunition Column was also ordered up to relieve the work thrown upon the other two as horses were beginning to suffer. The 75th Battery was also ordered up at 8:0 p.m. to replace the 62nd which was practically silenced. At 8:30 p.m. the G.O.C. the Division wished to have some of the heavier guns withdrawn and the two 60 pounders of the 31st Battery and the Northumbrian Howitzer Brigade were ordered to withdraw. At 12:30 a.m. Major General Bulfin sent for General Gay and informed him that owing to the situation in front all the Field Artillery should be withdrawn at once. Orders were at once telegraphed and sent by dispatch rider, and by 4:0 a.m. on the 9th nine batteries had been successfully withdrawn through YPRES and reached their allotted destination West of the Canal. This withdrawal was concluded without a hitch of any sort and the Officer Commanding 31st Field Artillery Brigade was left on the East of the town with the 69th and 100th Batteries in support of the 84th Infantry Brigade.

9th May. The enemy transferred his attacks to the 4th and 27th Divisions during the day and principally to the latter. The 28th Divisional trench line having been re-established further East than had been considered probable - the adviseability of moving more guns to the East of the Canal in order to cope more effectively with the situation became apparent. Orders were consedquently issued for the 103rd and 65th Howitzer battery to reoccupy their old positions and the O.C. 31st Heavy Battery was ordered to reconnoitre a fresh position for one section.

10th May. Hostile gun fire on the 28th Division front was much reduced during the day but the 27th Division were subjected to a heavy bombardment followed by determined Infantry attacks. As the fighting in this area was mostly amongst woods no assistance could be given by 28th Divisional Artillery, However the zone of the Belgian Batteries was extended south of the railway and north of BELLEWARDE WOOD. A position was reconnoitred for the 9.2" at closer range that it might compete the better with enemy heavy guns. I order to be in a position to retaliate suitably for the heavy bombardment to which our trenches have been subjected, arrangements were made with the R.F.C. for the registration of heavy guns and Howitzers on points of the German trenches. The front was divided into 4 zones and each battery was ordered to be put on to certain spots in each in turn. All evening reports remarked on the noticeable diminution of hostile fire on our front, but whether this is due to the removal of guns or to a desire to save ammunition for another offensive, it would be difficult to say. O.C. 31st Brigade selected his old position and moved up the section during the night.

11th May. Reports came in early of the occupation of the left trench of the 27th Division by the enemy and the consequent enfilading of our right by rifle fire. The Belgian Batteries at once opened fire on the wood in I.12.b. S.W. from which a galling fire was being brought on our trenches. Shortly afterwards an 18 pounder battery was also put on to this zone. The Infantry reported the fire very accurate and effective. By noon the Belgians Batteries began to run short of ammunition and application was made to the Vth Corps for some more. By 1:30 p.m. no Belgian ammunition remained but shortly after the 5th Division transferred 1,000 rounds and fire was reopened. During the day the registration by Heavies and Howitzers of the German trenches proceeded and by evening was completed except for the zone on the extreme right. During the process of registration several direct hits were made in the trenches and some houses were destroyed.

6 p.m. Information was received that the 1st Cavalry Division would take over 28th Division front line except that occupied by 85th Infantry Brigade and the guns East of YPRES were ordered to be placed under command of G.O.C. 1st Cavalry Division while those on the West remained under 28th Division. During the day the 9.2" Howitzer moved into new position.

12th May. The 7th Brigade R.H.A. - forming part of 1st Cavalry Division - came up and Lt-Colonel Budworth inspected the positions occupied by 31st Brigade with a view to relieving it. It was arranged that one R.H.A. section should replace one section in each of 69th and 100th Batteries during night of 12/13th and that the 103rd Battery should remain in position till night 13/14th. Registration of remaining German trenches zone failed owing to cloudy weather. Later in the day it was decided that the 3rd Cavalry Division should take over from the 85th Infantry Brigade on night 12/13th and that whole of 28th Divisional Artillery should come under command of M.G.C. Cavalry Force. During the night the relief of sections 31st Brigade by sections of "H" & "I" Batteries were carried out successfully. The relieved sections proceeding to rest area about POPERINGHE.

13th May. 5:35 a.m. A heavy bombardment of our trenches commenced and targets were allotted to the groups of Duffus and White by the Cavalry Commander with whom they were affiliated. R.A.H.Q. moved out at once to ESTAMINET near railway crossing east of VLAMERTINGHE at the order of Cavalry Force and soon established telephonic communication with all groups. 108th Battery engaged German heavy guns which had already been registered and 9.2" - not having registered anything yet from new position - fired on FREZENBERG road while 31st advanced section took on the railway line. The feu de barrage, established by the field and horse guns completely checked any attempt to advance on the part of the enemy and was reported by the 4th Division to have been extremely effective. The trenches evacuated by the cavalry were thus denied to the enemy. The 2nd. Brigade Northumbrian R.F.A. was placed at disposal of C.R.A. by Corps Artillery and was at once ordered into action East of YPRES. While the batteries were coming up positions were reconnoitred for them by Majors Scarlett and Lewin of the 3rd Brigade, and these Officers saw the batteries settled into action during the night. The R.H.A. batteries were ordered into action without delay and the relieved sections of the 31st Brigade were re-established in their original positions while the 3rd and 146th Brigades were ordered to stand by. Corps Artillery then ordered 31st Battery advanced section to move West of Canal and join remainder of Battery, so by midnight the total of guns East of YPRES was 18 pdrs. 12, 13 pdrs. 12, 15 pdrs. 12, 4.5" Howitzers 6. Orders were received that the Heavy Artillery would be taken over at 12:0 noon tomorrow by General UNIACKE, Commanding 2nd Group of Heavy Artillery Reserves.

14th May. Command of 9.2" Howitzer, 108th Heavy Battery and section 31st Heavy Battery handed over at 12:0 noon to Heavy Artillery Reserves. In the afternoon information was received of the massing of Germans on our front and left front. A feu de

barrage was at once established all along the front and
Heavy Artillery informed of situation. Essex Regiment
reported that the fire of field guns prevented any hostile
move on part of enemy and that one battalion, which could
be seen from their trenches, made no effort to advance in the
face of the shrapnel and H.E. By 5:10 p.m. observers reported
no sign of hostile movement so fire was slackened. In the
evening M.G. de Lisle sent following message to C.R.A. :-
" Please convey to the Artillery under your command my
compliments on the effective support it has afforded the
Cavalry Force during the recent operations. The rapidity of its
response and the volume of its fire has greatly assisted my
Cavalry".   Group Commanders were also thanked for their
close cooperation by Cavalry Brigade Commanders with whom they
were affiliated.

Diary of the 28th Divisional Artillery during the Second Battle of YPRES from 22nd April to the 14th May. 1915.

22nd April.   5:0 p.m. Very heavy bombardment commenced to the North on portion of line held by the French between LANGEMARCK and the YSER CANAL.

The French troops in the trenches were asphyxiated by gases thrown from the German Infantry trenches and they broke back, carrying with them the teams and wagons of the Field Artillery. This was the first experience of gas.

This withdrawal of the French exposed the left flank of the 1st Canadian Division who were obliged to throw back their left flank to meet the Germans now pouring southwards and turning to the South East.

The attack by gas still continued and, as the wind was blowing from the North West, the Canadians suffered severely but held on strongly and even counter attacked as far as the Northern edge of the wood in C.10.d. where they held on with great gallantry.

In the South East corner of this wood was placed a battery of 4.7" guns of the 2nd London Division, and the advance of the German Infantry from the North West had caused the personnal to abandon their guns after withdrawing the strikers from the breech blocks.

The later advance of the Canadians recaptured these guns but, although parties were sent out after dark to reconnoitre it was impossible to bring up teams to remove the guns over the open ground with any prospect of success.

Owing to some misunderstanding the Canadians line again fell back South of the Wood, and all chance of recovering the guns had to be given up for the present. The North Midland Battery in action at WIELTJE seeing the stragglers coming back in large numbers and on account of the heavy gun and rifle fire and the general confusion, took out the two breech blocks from th one section and left the guns. The Lieutenant Colonel Commanding the Brigade with his Adjutant and a few men who refused to leave worked two of the guns for some time, when an order was sent out to withdraw the entire battery and bring it into action in the neighbourhood of VLAMERTINGHE.

Eventually the G.O.C., R.A's A.D.C. personally supplied the two missing breech blocks, the whole battery was/placed again in action and has been firing by map since the 23rd April.

Two resting batteries, the 118th (31st Brigade) and the 365th (3rd Brigade) were brought into action against the wood in C.10.d, but were ordered not to fire unless instructed to do so.

23rd.April. At 4:10 a.m. a request was made for Artillery co-operation in counter attack at 4:45 a.m. and 365th Battery and North Midland Heavy Battery opened fire on allotted objectives.

A reconnaissance was made by O.C. 118th Battery of possible gun positions on the West of the YSER CANAL North West of YPRES.

The report was received at 10 a.m.

In the meantime the position of Batteries North of FRESENBERG was threatened by the progess made by the enemy to the North and West, and it was decided to make a new distribution.

The left hand Battery near GRAVENSTAFEL was withdrawn to WIELTJE, two sections each from the remaining batteries (366th and 367th) were ordered to shift their position and fire northwards.

While the 118th Battery and the 365th Battery occupied positions West of the YSER CANAL.

Both these Batteries fired on the German trenches seen in C.8.d. while the North Midland Heavy Battery fired on the crossroads further north.

Soon after 1:0 p.m. orders were received to cooperate with an attack to be made by the 13th Infantry Brigade and

Battery Commanders were ordered to get in touch with the
G.O.C. who informed them that the attack would take place
at 2:45 p.m.

At that hour the attack was postponed to 3:45 pm.

The batteries opened fire as arranged, but the promised
attack was not made, and no further communication from the
13th Infantry Brigade appears to have been received.

All the Batteries of the Divisional Artillery were
firing through the night.

24th April.   The 75tht Battery, which has been lent to the 5th Division
for the operations at Hill 60, was able to collect three
guns, and was ordered into action West of the Canal with 2
guns, while the third went into action at WIELTJE alongside
the 149th Battery, and at the same time the Officer Commanding
the 8th Howitzer Brigade was ordered to report to R.A. head
quarters with his staff and headquarters detachment. At
9:0 a.m. the North Midland Heavy Battery fired on two farms
reported by aeroplanes to be full of Germans, and at 10:0
o'clock the fire was turned on to PILCKEM. Soon after 11:o
a.m. the O.C? 8th F.A. Bde arrived and was sent to the
Headquarters, Canadian Division to collect as many Canadian
Batteries as possible in order to support the French counter
attack.

At 12:30 p.m. information was received that the 122nd
Heavy Battery was being withdrawn from its position East
of FRESENBERG and placed under the orders of the 28th
Divisional Artillery.

O.C.8th F.A.Bde. was ordered to find a position for this
Battery North of ELVERDINGHE.

The Battery arrived during the afternoon and was placed
North West of BRIERLEN.

Later in the evening a message was received from the
Vth Corps that 2 Belgian Batteries would join the 28th
Divisional Artillery.

When the Officer Commanding the Groupe arrived, it was found that his two batteries had only just been withdrawn out of action, and the men were exhausted, and only 100 rounds per gun were with the Battery.

Orders were given that the ammunition to make up to 200 rounds per gun should be got up during the night, and for the Batteries to be in action West of the Canal by 4:0 a.m.

The Officer Commanding the 149th Battery reported at R.A. Headquarters at 10:0 p.m. that he had retired from WIELTJE with two guns, having exhausted his ammunition and having left two guns and some wagons behind.

Teams were sent out that night to bring in the guns, one of which was damaged by shell fire and unserviceable. At 11:0 p.m. Vth. Corps telegraphed that a Battery of 60 punders would arrive, and be placed under the orders of the G.O.C., R.A. 28th Division.

During the day the 3rd, 31st, and 146th Brigades with the 37th and 65th Howitzer Batteries were engaged on the 28th Division front in keeping down the fire of Minenwerfer, and supporting the Infantry in the trenches.

The 149th Battery which retired from WIELTJE during the evening was in action due North of the village behind a ridge facing East but much exposed from the North and North West.

The Battery was located during the afternoon by a Hostile Howitzer Battery and was subjected to a heavy shell fire.

Meanwhile the rifle fire was getting more intense and the Battery Commander was informed by the local Infantry Commander that the line they at present held could be maintained until dark but probably not later.

Captain R.S.Ellis, having exhausted his ammunition and fearing the loss of his guns, decided to withdraw them at 6:30 p.m. and called up his teams to hook in.

Under a heavy fire and with the assistance of his officer the guns were removed, the remaining gun and two ammunition wagons were so damaged as to be useless, and these were left in position for the present.

One gun of the 75th Battery in action with the 149th Battery was also brought back and came into action West of the Canal.

Further to the East in the angle formed by the original trenches of the 28th Division and the new line running East and West through FORTUIN, the two sections of the 366th and 367th Batteries supported the Infantry to the North with great success, while the remaining two sections were fully occupied in maintaining the trench line formerly covered by three Batteries.

In the centre group (31st Field Artillery Brigades) the 69th Battery silenced a short range gun which was annoying our trenches. The 103rd Battery fired with one section on the crossroads South of KEERSELAERE and with the other section on a hostile battery South East of BROODSEINDE.

The 100th Battery also fired eastwards out on German trenches as ours were suffering severely from Minenwerfer.

Practically all communications were cut off for the entire day.

The 37th (Howitzer) Battery under Major E.Harding Newman were first apprised of the German advance from POELCAPELLE by Canadian Infantry retiring through the battery very early in the morning.

The Battery Commander at once sent Captain H.O.Hutchison with a telephone to reconnoitre, and the Battery reversed and opened fire on advancing Germans under instructions from Captain Hutchison.

Three German attacks were defeated entirely by Howitzer fire and at least 500 Germans were accounted for. The lyddite shell had an excellent effect, and prevented the Germans entrenching near St. JULIEN. During these operations, which were carried out with great skill and daring by Captain Hutchison the battery was under heavy field gun shellfire from daylight until 4:0 p.m. at the rate of 250 shell per hour. One gun carriage was slightly damaged.

It was very noticeable from the Battery Observing station that the Germans were working in the open and constantly digging first and second line trenches with communications between them.

During the afternoon our Infantry suffered casualties from a Battery located 1 mile South South East of FREZENBERG.

The right Group (3rd Field Artillery Brigade) was not called upon to do more that maintain its own front, but, on being informed of the situation to the North, arranged to assist by changing the front of one Battery and firing in that direction.

25th April. At daylight the fire of the North Midland Heavy Battery was directed on the crossroads at PILCKEM, the railway near that place and the crossroads to the East of it. Later fire was turned on to LANGEMARCK.

The 118th Battery West of the Canal was directed to send forward an observer with a telephone to reconnoitre and report on the progress of the French attack and to register the batteries West of the Canal on points likely to be useful.

Soon afterwards (6:50 a.m.) a report was received from the 146th Brigade that two sections had been placed in D.19.b½ to support the attack on St. JULIEN.

A telephone message from the Vth Corps stated that the 60 punders would now be kept under Corps orders and Placed in position near the 9.2 Howitzer in wood A.30. An attack by the French northwards along the East bank of the Canal was arranged for 1:0 p.m. and instructions were issued to 118th 149th, 75th and 365th and North Midland Batteries to support it.

At 1:0 p.m. the attack was postponed to 1:15 p.m. and front line trenches and supports were shelled as arranged. No attack however was made.

At 5:30 p.m. information was received from a Canadian brigade West of the Canal that the French proposed to attack northwards at 9:0 p.m. with the bayonet but without any previous Artillery bombardment.

Batteries left of the Canal were ordered to be ready to cooperate if required, and an officer was sent to French Headquarters for further instructions.

A Staff Officer was sent to all Brigades 28th Division to explain the situation and to allot areas and roads in event of movement taking place.

At 8:30 p.m. notice of the inevitable postponement of the Infantry attack was received and the hour was fixed for 2:0 a.m. the next day.

26th April.
Eventually the French advanced at 4:0 a.m. but did not press the attack home. Our batteries West of the Canal opened fire on the German Trenches to stop rifle fire. The observer of the 365th Battery, Lieutenant Bates R.H.A. reported at 7:0 a.m. that the enemy were massing in farm buildings close to their lines and the North Midland Heavy Battery opened on them.

At 8:30 a.m. a telephone message from Vth Corps indicated a reorganization of Artillery for the purpose of special operations viz. All Field Batteries of 28th and Canadian Division West of the Canal to be grouped under Lieutenant O.C. 8th F.A. Bde, while the 122nd. Heavy Battery, North Midland Heavy Battery and the 457th Canadian Howitzer Battery were to be grouped under the Lieutenant Colonel Commanding the 13th Heavy Bde. At 12:0 o'clock the Brigadier General R.A. Vth Corps reached 28th Division Headquarters and placed 18 pounder Batteries under 28th Divisional Artillery Commanders

An attack was timed for 2:5 p.m. by the Lahore Division and the French between the wood 1,000 yards West of St. JULIEN and the YSER CANAL, and forty minutes bombardment with

with five minutes rapid fire, immediately before the assult, was arranged for and carried out by the 118th, 75th, 365the and 149th Batteries, 2 Belgian Batteries on the right of the 149th Battery cooperated. The French Commander complained that this bombardment was too early and would affect his attack adversely, but on reference to Vth Corps Headquarters, compliance with the original order was demanded.

The result of the attack was that the Lahore Division and the French centre were held up., St. JULIEN was captured by the Northumbrian Brigade, but was evacuated later in in the evening.

The French left pushed on and enfiladed the German trenches with Field Artillery capturing large quantities of prisoners.

Between 3:30 and 4:0 p.m. the same four Field Batteries shelled German trenches in front of French centre and to the South East.

At a quarter to 7, news was received of a counter attack on the French right, and fire was at once opened by 118th 365th and 75th Batteries.

The counter attack was checked.

South of St. Julien the 366th and 367th Batteries of the 146th Brigade maintained their position under heavy fire and both Battery Commanders Captain G.A.R. Scott and Major T. Carlyon as well as the personnel of their batteries maintained the best traditions of the Royal Regiment.

Captain Scott's Battery (366th) engaged German Infantry near St. JULIEN early in the day at a range of 800 yards and fired by the afternoon 1740 rounds.

Our attack was heavily shelled in enfilade from the right and no counter Batteries were available at the time, but the cooperation of the 123rd Heavy Battery, 27th Division was requested in order to silence hostile guns at PASSCHENDAELE.

Hostile aeroplanes were very busy over gun positions West of ZONNEBEKE.

The telephone lines were very difficult to maintain, being very frequently cut to pieces by shell fire. Farther to the South the 37th Howitzer Battery at an early hour shelled German trenches on the GRAVENSTRAFEL ridge, and then shelled enemy's Infantry leaving them. The German Infantry took refuge in some houses whence they were turned out by a few shells.

This Battery observer informed the 100th Field Battery at 11:40 a.m. that German supports were advancing from the North, and the 100th Battery shelled them.

During the afternoon while the 100th, 103rd and 37th (Howitzer) Batteries were shelling the German trenches in preparation of the attack at 2:5 p.m. a S.O.S. call was received from No. 20 trench, whereupon the 69th, 103rd, and one gun of the 37th Battery swung round and fired in the new direction. The Infantry report that this fire stopped the German attack.

On the right flank the 18th, 22nd, and 62nd Batteries poured in a rapid fire at 2:10 p.m. for 5 minutes and then 18th and 22nd Batteries turned a section each on the GRAVENSTAFEL ridge for an hour and a half.

The 65th Howitzer Battery shelled a minenwerfer and a German observing station in front of the K.O.Y.L.I. with some success.

27th April. At 2:20 a.m. a telegram was received that owing to guns shooting by the map, their assistance was not so effective as if the fire had been observed, and in conclusion asking that in event of a continuance of the attack, fire should be directed on to the houses on the MOSSELMARKT-FORTUIN road.

The G.O.C. 27th Divisional Artillery was at once requested to place his supporting batteries in communication with the 85th Infantry Brigade and with the Officer Commanding 146th Brigade grouped with the 85th.

At 7:30 a.m. the 85th Infantry Brigade wired for more

guns as German Field Artillery were moving up very close. Orders were at once sent to the 149th Battery to move out and rejoin the 146th Brigade.

At 11:25 a.m. the orders for the attack of the Lahore Division were received, and, as fire was to be opened at 12:30 p.m. there was but little time for arrangements to be made.

The 118th, 75th and 365th Batteries were given zones and commenced firing at the time fixed.

At 2:30 p.m. the French were reported held up in the centre and suffering casualties from rifle fire.

The three Batteries were ordered to get into touch with the French Commander with a view to supporting him. At 3:15 p.m. the French Field Artillery opened fire on the German trenches and asked our batteries West of the Canal to stand by for orders to open fire. At 5 o'clock a message was received stating that the bombardment in support of the attack of the Lahore Division would commence at 5:15 p.m. On the East of the Canal the 149th Battery rejoined the 146th Brigade and came into action near the 37th Howitzer Battery, Officers and men suffering from strain and want of sleep. One section of the 65th Howitzer Battery fired on trenches North of the Railway. The 366th and 367th Batteries turned eastwards and supported an attack on trench 25. 2/Lieutenant E.W. Ffrench was wounded while in the observation station. The 37th Howitzer Battery shelled the German trenches East of St. JULIEN, and a house reported to contain machine guns. The Germans had constructed a new trench across the reentrant N.E. of St. JULIEN and this was shelled and the parapet damaged. The minenwerfer opened fire at 12:0 noon near the BROODSEINDE crossroads, and was fired on on two occasions by the 69th Battery. It was silenced at any rate temporarily. The 100th Battery fired at houses North of GRAVENSTAFEL where gun emplacements were being prepared.   During the afternoon from 2 p.m. to 4 pm. the 108th and 122nd and North Midland Heavy Batteries near VLAMERTINGHE searched the wood one mile West of St. JULIEN and at the same time the 37th Howitzer Battery shelled the German trenches connecting the village with the wood, from its position East of FREZENBERG.

On the extreme right the 3rd Field Artillery Brigade and the 65th Howitzer Battery had but little fighting, and their action was mainly confined to checking minenwerfer.

The 22nd Battery was heavily shelled in the evening and a stack of ammunition in the Battery was blown up, 420 rounds of ammunition being destroyed.

No casualties occurred however among the personnel.   At 5:15 p.m. a general bombardment was ordered as a prelude to an attack by the Lahore Division northwards to the West of St. JULIEN.

Little progress however appeared to have been made and the situation was unchanged.

At 10:0 p.m. arrangements were made with the Royal Flying Corps to register the 9.2" Howitzer and the Heavy Batteries at various targets to the North and Northeast of VLAMERTINGHE.

28th April.   Orders were received to transfer all guns West of the Canal less those of the Lahore Division from the Command of the Vth Corps Artillery adviser to Brigadier General A.W.Gay, Commanding 28th Divisional Artillery.   The Batteries involved were the 118th, 75th, 365th and four Canadian Field Batteries. The 108th, 122nd and the North Midland Heavy Batteries, one 9.2" Howitzer and the 6th Belgian Artillery Groupe.   A few minutes later a copy of French Corps orders by General Cure announcing an attack across the YSER CANAL ordered to take place at 2:0 p.m. and arrangements were at once made to employ all available guns to assist, after having communicated with General Cure's Artillery Commander.

By 1:15 p.m. the hour named for the commencement of

the bombardment, the Field Batteries were ready to open fire on the German first line and support trenches East of the Canal while the Belgian Batteries layed on two alarge farms just in rear.

The 9.2" gun was directed by aeroplane on to a cross road West of BIXSCHOOTE, and the Heavy Batteries were allotted vilages, railway stations, and hostile gun positions.

Orders were then received to open fire at 2:0 p.m. instead of 1:15 p.m. and the alteration of the hour was at once telephoned out.

The aeroplane observer working with the 9.2" Howitzer having received ~~esede~~ orders direct which were not communicated to the Battery, that the French attack was held up in front of a farm and a railway bridge East of the Canal, altered the objective and turned the fire on to the latter target.

The French were at once communicated with and confirmed this action.

In the meantime the seven Field Batteries and the Belgian Groupe were working in touch with General Joppé on the French right.

At 4:30 p.m. fire was slowed down considerably to await further movements of the French advance.

Soon after midday the 149th Battery had to be withdrawn from its forward position owing to the German Infantry advance, and it came into action further back and to the West without great difficulty.

The 65th Howitzer Battery section allotted to this group fired on the farm in German hands South of the HANEBEEK. All day the guns and wagon lines were shelled and there was great difficulty in getting water as the water cart of the 146th Brigade was wrecked by a shell during the day.

The greater portion of the hostile fire came from the East near PASSCHENDALE.

About 10:0 p.m. a gun of the 366th Battery which was in action 1200 yards from the enemy's Infantry was hit and disabled. Obsevation was becoming vary difficult. The 146th Brigade had been requested earlier in the day to engage enemy' guns which were causing many casualties both in the Infantry as well as in our Field Batteries. Unfortunately the range was too long, and no Heavy Artillery was available to assist. In the centre group (31st Field Artillery Brigade) the 100th Battery shelled the farm South of the HANEBEEK mentioned above but found the 18 pounder H.E. not sufficiently powerful, and the 37th Howitzer Battery was put on to it using the 100th Battery observer.

For the second time the Brigade Headquarters had to be shifted owing to shell fire, and occupied a house a little further to the East on the ZONNEBEKE road.

The 37th Howitzer Battery in addition to the action described above, was very busy firing at German Infantry in view of their observing station and at 1:30 p.m. shelled German first and second line trenches with great effect. Several hits were obtained on parapets North East and North West of St. JULIEN, and debris and bodies were observed blown into the air.

Our Infantry on Hill 37, 1 mile Northeast of the Battery position were heavily shelled in enfilade by hostile guns near PASSCHENDALE.

The 3rd. Field Artillery Brigade on the right had little to do with the exception of the 65th Howitzer Battery, in action near the railway, which fired Northwards across the rear of the Brigade, in communication with the left group.

Earlier in the day at 4:30 p.m. intimation was received from 28th Division Headquarters that a French attack across the Canal at BIXCHOOTE would take place at 7:0 p.m. Orders were given to all Batteries West of the Canal to get their lines laid out on given objectives, and to be ready to open fire at 6:15 p.m.

At this hour fire was opened by all guns, and after a tremendous bombardment lasting for 45 minutes the French attack commenced.

A little progress was made, but the whole of the East bank of the YSER Canal could not be captured without further organized attack.

29th April. 3:45 a.m. A violent bombardment commenced and appeared to be of such importance that a Staff Officer was sent to the French Headquarters to ascertain the situation. He was informed that no artillery assistance was required, and that it was merely an artillery duel. A French liaison Officer was also sent to French Headquarters, but, beyond ascertaining that arrangements for an attack were being made, no further information was gained.

All batteries on West of Canal were ordered to be ready to open fire at 11:30 a.m. and at this hour a notification was received that no attack would take place. The 122nd Heavy Battery registered during the morning with aeroplane observation and was able to silence one German Battery.

At 7:0 p.m. the French announced their intention to attack at 8:0 a.m. the next morning after a bombardment. Targets were therefore allotted, and hour of opening fire fixed, after a personal interview between the G.O.C. 28th Divisional Artillery and the G.O.C. French Artillery.

On the East of the Canal the 366th and 367th Batteries continued in action and were heavily shelled both in the gun positions and in the wagon lines.

Arrangements were made for the 100th Field Battery and the 37th Howitzer Battery to cooperate, by linking both with the same observer, in order that the 100th Battery might be able to take any parties of the enemy driven from their trenches by Howitzer fire.

NB. 37th H. batty. was attached to 31st F.A.Bde. to which 100th Batty belonged.

? Bailers

This arrangement was made by the two Brigade Commanders concerned on their own initiative.

The 37th Battery observer reported positions of guns North and Northeast of St. JULIEN and movements of German Infantry in their trenches near the village, some mounted men and a party with packs on moving East.

30th April. A thick mist necessitated the postponement of the French attack which did not commence until 11:0 a.m. As soon as observation was possible the 31st, 108th, 122nd, and North Midland Heavy Batteries, and the 9.2" Howitzer opened on gun positions already registered. One shell from the 108th Battery blew up a house with a loud explosion, probably an ammunition store. The 118th, 75th, and 365th Batteries supported the attack of the 18th French Division, by registering on the German front line trenches and then pouring in a rapid fire on the supports while French Infantry assulted.

Close touch was kept throughout by liaison Officers with French Headquarters as well as with the 18th French Division whose Infantry were being supported.

The attack was successful and the German front and second line trenches were captured.

It was then reported that some uncut wire existed on the Southeast side of a hill occupied by the enemy which the French had partly captured and held. Instruction were given to the Belgian Groupe to cut the wire at once. The range was 3,000 but the fire of the two Batteries was very accurate and in less than half an hour considerable damage was done to it. The remainder of the day was devoted to firing on points of importance in rear of the German lines. On the East side of the Canal the 366th and 367th Batteries came under a heavy shell fire and had four Officers wounded, and four gun limbers disabled. In the centre group the 100th Battery registered trenches South and West of St. JULIEN to be ready for hostile Infantry bolted from them by the 37th Howitzer Battery.

1st May.

Notification received that an attack by the French on their right would commence during the morning and liaison officers were sent to the right French Division. The 122nd, 31st, 108th and North Midland Heavy Batteries and the 9.2" Howitzer were given objectives registered by each respectively and fire was opened at 11:30 a.m. Registration was also carried out by aeroplane during the morning.

All firing was stopped at 12:0 noon.

At 1:0 p.m. shooting recommenced at the same targets and a telegram was sent to the Royal Flying Corps for an aeroplane to register the 9.2" Howitzer on Hill 29. This registration commenced at 1:30 p.m. and in 15 minutes, 5 rounds had been put into the German trenches., on the hill.

From 2:15 p.m. to 2:45 p.m. all guns stopped firing except the 92" which had again been turned on to Hill 29 and the 108th Battery registered with an aeroplane. At the time fixed for the assult the French and English Infantry went forward but were driven back by gun and machine gun fire.

The Heavy Artillery stopped at 3:25 p.m. in accordance with orders and recommenced on receiving a request from the French to engage certain targets which was immediately done. Owing to the heavy firing and the fact that the 5" guns and mountings of the 31st and 108th Batteries requiring overhauling only three guns were still in action when the order to cease fire at 5:30 p.m. was given. The lyddite shell were falling abnormally short from the 4.7" Batteries, and they were ordered to fire only Percussion Shrapnel as No. 54 time fuze would not allow of sufficient range for time shrapnel.

The 31st Heavy Battery and the 9.2" Howitzer continued to engage gun targets until 7:0 p.m.

At 7:30 p.m. a 6" gun on an armoured truck arrived in charge of a Belgian Artillery Captain and arrangements were made for registration by aeroplane the following morning.

Orders were also given that night for one gun of the 31st Brigade to be moved up Northwards to endeavour to engage

17.

the German big gun West of HOULTHURST FOREST.

2nd May.

During the night the two of the three damaged 60 pdrs. were repaired and four out of eight were available to shoot. The French Artillery General reallotted the zones of fire necessitating fresh registration by aeroplanes. The registration was commenced and a series of new targets ranged in by the Heavy Artillery. All wires were cut and communication very difficult. The Officer Commanding 9th Heavy Brigade reported his arrival at 10:0 a.m. bringing 123rd Heavy Battery which was placed in action alongside the 122nd of the same Brigade. The day was dull and misty and aeroplane work was impossible. Soon after 12:0 noon the French Right Division asked for fire to be turned on to enemy's guns to the North and the 122nd Battery opened fire. Three hours later warning was received from the same quarter of an expected attack from PILCKEM, and all heavy guns were layed on targets in that neighbourhood. Immediately afterwards heavy firing was heard and news was received of an attack from St. JULIEN. Our heavy guns at once opened on PILCKEM as well as on the St. JULIEN position. Four 1½" Anti aircraft guns manned by R.M.A. arrived and were disposed of under orders of Vth Corps. No. 20 Anti aircraft section fired and hit a German aeroplane which fell near BRIERLEN. During the day there was considerable activity on the part of the enemy in the neighbourhood of St. JULIEN and all the batteries of the 146th Brigade were busy firing at targets as opportunity offered. Ranges were short and the 366th and 367th Batteries were much exposed to a heavy shell fire from two directions but they continued in action in spite of it. The 10Oth Battery had given again to swing its left section to the East to support the 84th Infantry Brigade, and the 69th shelled the enemy's second line trenches. The 37th Howitzer Battery shelled parties of Germans seen in the open about a quarter to five in the evening, and shortly after asphyxiating gas was poured out from the German trenches all along the line. At first it came towards our trenches but then blew back on to their own. After a short bombardment, the enemy attacked in single line, an unusual formation, and was immediately opened on by all the Field Artillery with the result that the German attack, although reinforced, was driven back. At 6:30 p.m. a movement from East to West was observed and parties of the enemy, collected in some dugouts, were driven out and forced to scatter into the houses. At the same time a line of Germans gradually extended across the valley South of the HANEBEEK. As soon as Captain Hutchinson observed this movement he tried to telephone to his battery, to fire, but, finding the wire cut at the moment, he ran back to the battery (37th Howitzer) and turned them on to the place where he had seen the Germans collecting. Several times after this the Germans tried to advance in single line extended, but at no point did they get far from their own trenches, except at one place West of St. JULIEN where they crawled forward up a hollow. On the right little incident was reported beyond some shelling of wagon lines. Arrangements had already been made to shorten the line which was becoming untenable from enfilade fire and to withdraw the 28th Division back to the FREZENBERG RIDGE. The movement to commence on the night 2nd and 3rd and to be completed night of 3rd and 4th May. Positions for Batteries had been previously reconnoitered and plans and descriptions supplied to Brigade Commanders. The withdrawal was to be by sections, the right Brigade leading and the left Brigade (146th) covering the retirement, but later on in the evening it became evident that the tactical situation did not permit of the withdrawal of any guns of the left Brigade as the Infantry required their support. They were accordingly ordered to remain in their present positions while sections of the right and centre Brigades fell back to POTIJZE.

The movement was not accomplished without some difficulty as the night was fine and the heavy shelling of the enemy of the gun positions of the 22nd Battery delayed the move considerably.

3rd. May.   At 2:30 a.m. reports were received that the sections of the 3rd and 31st Field Artillery Brigades and the 65th Howitzer Battery had occupied their new positions. Soon after 6:0 a.m. the 122nd and North Midland Heavy Batteries were ordered to fire on wood West of St. JULIEN to assist the Infantry which expected an attack. At 11:0 a.m. the 9.2" Howitzer reported out of action owing to damage of control plunger shaft. An attack from the direction of St. JULIEN was now threatened and a section of the 108th Heavy Battery was ordered forward to a position West of the Canal to fire at extreme range on enemy's trenches North/east of this village, aeroplane assistance in observation being requested. Orders were now issued for the completion of the move commenced the previous evening, and instructions for keeping roads clear were added. At 4:20 p.m. the section 108th Battery was in position and reported 10 hits already in enemy's trenches. A series of 40 rounds were fired altogether and many hits recorded. As the situation appeared critical the remainder of the heavy guns fired on St. JULIEN and the threatened attack did not come off. Later in the evening a further attack was reported from the wood mentioned above and the heavy batteries were at once directed on the most valuable points. A message was received from French sources that this attack had failed, and forwarding a letter of appreciation from the French Commander of the work done by the 28th Div. Arty. As the 9.2" Howitzer was now reported fit to fire, it was ereder ordered to open on PILCKEM and broke down again at the 1st round. Infantry reported fire of 108th Battery during the evening very effective. One Section 31st Battery ordered forward to POTIJZE wher it dug in during the night. At midnight reports were received of completion of occupation of new line by 3rd and 31st Brigades and 65th Howitzer Battery and of the withdrawal of 146th Brigade and 37th Howitzer Battery.

4th May.

The Second half of the 3rd and 31st Brigades occupied their new positions and the whole of the 146th Brigade accompanied by the 37th Howitzer Battery were withdrawn during the evening and passed through VLAMERTINGHE to rest billets. The withdrawal was most successfully accomplished, each unit was up to time and there were no blocks in the road or congestion of traffic. This in spite of the fact that the entire road was under shell fire. Lt. Colonel H.E.T Kelly was wounded during the withdrawal. In the Morning the French announced their intention of making a strong attack in force and arrangements were made to support it with all available guns (Heavy) However not much took place although a considerable amount of ammunition was used. During the day changes in the organization of the artillery were made, and the heavy batteries were divided up among three Division of the Vth Corps the 28th Division getting the 108th Heavy Battery and 1 section of the 31st Heavy Battery. Later on the Infantry were very heavily shelled and called for assistance in subduing the fire of the enemy's heavy guns. No aeroplane work was done and difficulty was experienced in coping with the mass of guns brought against the 28th Division trench line. Both the Field Artillery Brigades Commanders had great difficulty in finding any place to live as the whole country side East of YPRES was swept by heavy shell fire, even a 17" gun was used against the entrenchments at POTIJZE, causing huge craters and great loss of life. More calls for assistance kept coming from the Infantry who were being shelled from all directions. It is feared that little could be done against such a concentrated fire, but all that was possible was tried and some relief to the sorely tried Infantry was obtained. Owing to Lieutenant Colonel H.E.T.Kelly being wounded the 31st Brigade was commanded by Major Ramsden and Captain Sanderman was sent out during the night to take over command of the 100th Battery. At daylight the heavy guns opened fire on the hostile guns positions East and West of St. Julien. During the morning reports kept coming through of the heavy shelling of our Infantry trenches, but no indication could be given of the direction from which the fire came. No assistance was obtained from aeroplanes, so various gun positions from which enfilade fire could be brought to bear on our trenches were selected and these positions were engaged throughout the day. The left section 31st Heavy Battery got into close touch with the 83rd and 84th Infantry Brigade Commanders as well as with the 3rd and 31st Field Artillery Brigades Commanders, and did much useful work, which however was seriously impaired by the orders sent by the 27th Divisional Artillery Commander instructing the B.C. to link up with Field Artillery Brigades, 27th Division, and to fire at targets at their request. This situation was impossible and reference to the Vth Corps became necessary to put it right. At 11:30 a.m. a German attack along the railway line was attempted, but was stopped by the fire of the 18th and 22nd Batteries. Reconnaisances of Howitzer positions West of YPRES were undertaken during the day, as well as of positions for Divisional Artillery to support G.H.Q.3. Information was given by the 5th Corps at 6:30 p.m. that two 5" Howitzers Batteries Northumbrian Division would be attached to the Divisional Artillery, and would arrive shortly.

6th May.   Soon after midnight the two Battery Commanders of the 4th and 5th Durham Howitzer Batteries arrived and asked for instructions. Orders were at once given for the Batteries to move up to BRANDHOEK and for the Brigade Commanders

22.

and his B.C's to report to the G.O.C.R.A' at 5:30 a.m. for further orders as to reconnaissances. Areas were selected and reconniassances were carried out during the day for Howitzer positions, while the O.C's 8th and 146th Field Artillery Brigades reconnoitred to the West of YPRES and BRANDHOEK. In the meantime the 37th Howitzer Battery was ordered up, again into action West of the Canal to support the left of the 28th Division and attached to the left group while the 65th Howitzer Battery was transferred altogether to the right group. The 9.2" Howitzer was temporarily repaired and fired one round without further damage to recoil gear. At 8:30 p.m. the Northumberian Howitzer Brigade and the 37th Howitzer Battery moved up into positions selected during the day, but no reports had been received as to their occupation by midnight.

7th May.   Shortly after daylight our Infantry reported that they were being annoyed by shell fire from two ridges East of FORTUIN and the 108th Battery was ordered to fire on the ridges several series at irregular intervals. The 84th Infantry Brigade who had been attacked during the night reported at 9:0 o'clock that the attack had been repulsed by fire of the 31st Brigade. Difficulty in getting messages from aeroplanes and registration suffered in consequence. The wireless operators appeared to be at fault. The wind continued to blow from the East and both the 3rd and 31st Brigades complained of the effects of gas. A good obsevation station was discovered by the 365th Battery, but wire to connect it with the battery was unobtainable. The G.O.C. 4th Division complained that certain areas could not be covered by his guns and arrangements were made to put the Belgians on to it. 2 guns of the 22nd Battery were disabled by direct hits soon after 5:0 p.m. and the 365th Battery was ordered to send up two to replace them. At 11:0 p.m. the O.C. 31st Brigade reported that a gun of the 103rd was out of action. The O.C. 118th Battery was ordered to replace it.

8th May.

Very heavy cannonade started at 7:0 a.m. East of YPRES but nothing definate could be ascertained, reports agreeing that no attack was being made but only severe bombardment of trenches along the whole front of the Vth Corps. Attacks developed later in several places which were repulsed with the exception of that on the right of the 83rd Infantry Brigade. All possible fire was turned on to the threatened point counterattacks were made, and some of the lost ground was regained. The heavy firing necessitated an enormous supply of ammunition which was promptly and fully met, the work of the wagon lines and columns being thoroughly and successfully carried out over shell swept roads and through YPRES itself under fire of 17 inch guns. Lines were broken and communication became very difficult. The Batteries made the best of a grave situation and kept firing although suffering heavy casualties. The rapid fire caused the buffer oil to spurt out through the glands and the running up springs were not equal to the work. Several guns were put out of action owing to direct hits and guns were ordered up from the resting Brigade (146th) to replace them. The 146th Brigade Ammunition Column was also ordered up to relieve the work thrown upon the other two as horses were beginning to suffer. The 75th Battery was also ordered up at 8:0 p.m. to replace the 62nd which was practically silenced. At 8:30 p.m. the G.O.C the Division wished to have some of the heavier guns withdrawn and the two 60 pounders of the 31st Battery and the Northumbrian Howitzer Brigade were ordered to withdraw. At 12:30 a.m. Major General Bulfin sent for General Gay and informed him that owing to the situation in front all the Field Artillery should be withdrawn at once. Orders were at once telegraphed and sent by dispatch rider, and by 4:0 a.m. on the 9th nine batteries had been successfully withdrawn through YPRES and reached their allotted destination West of the Canal. This withdrawal was concluded without a hitch of any sort and the Officer Commanding 31st Field Artillery Brigade was left on the East of the town with the 69th and 100th Batteries in support of the 84th Infantry Brigade.

9th May.   The enemy transferred his attacks to the 4th and 27th Divisions during the day and principally to the latter. The 28th Divisional trench line having been re-established further East than had been considered probable - the adviseability of moving more guns to the East of the Canal in order to cope more effectively with the situation became apparent.   Orders were consedquently issued for the 103rd and 65th Howitzer battery to reoccupy their old positions and the O.C. 31st Heavy Battery was ordered to reconnoitre a fresh position for one section.

10th May.   Hostile gun fire on the 28th Division front was much reduced during the day but the 27th Division were subjected to a heavy bombardment followed by determined Infantry attacks. As the fighting in this area was mostly amongst woods no assistance could be given by 28th Divisional Artillery, However the zone of the Belgian Batteries was extended south of the railway and north of BELLEWARDE WOOD. A position was reconnoitred for the 9.2" at closer range that it might compete the better with enemy heavy guns. In order to be in a position to retaliate suitably for the heavy bombardment to which our trenches have been subjected, arrangements were made with the R.F.C. for the registration of heavy guns and Howitzers on points of the German trenches. The front was divided into 4 zones and each battery was ordered to be put on to certain spots in each in turn. All evening reports remarked on the noticeable diminution of hostile fire on our front, but whether this is due to the removal of guns or to a desire to save ammunition for another offensive, it would be difficult to say. O.C. 31st Brigade selected his old position and moved up the section during the night.

11th May.   Reports came in early of the occupation of the left trench of the 27th Division by the enemy and the consequent enfilading of our right by rifle fire. The Belgian Batteries at once opened fire on the wood in I.12.b. S.W. from which a galling fire was being brought on our trenches. Shortly afterwards an 18 pounder battery was also put on to this zone. The Infantry reported the fire very accurate and effective. By noon the Belgians Batteries began to run short of ammunition and application was made to the Vth Corps for some more. By 1:30 p.m. no Belgian ammunition remained but shortly after the 5th Division transferred 1,000 rounds and fire was reopened. During the day the registration by Heavies and Howitzers of the German trenches proceeded and by evening was completed except for the zone on the extreme right. During the process of registration several direct hits were made in the trenches and some houses were destroyed.

6 p.m. Information was received that the 1st Cavalry Division would take over 28th Division front line except that occupied by 85th Infantry Brigade and the guns East of YPRES were ordered to be placed under command of G.O.C. 1st Cavalry Division while those on the West remained under 28th Division. During the day the 9.2" Howitzer moved into new position.

12th May. The 7th Brigade R.H.A. - forming part of 1st Cavalry Division - came up and Lt-Colonel Budworth inspected the positions occupied by 31st Brigade with a view to relieving it. It was arranged that one R.H.A. section should replace one section in each of 69th and 100th Batteries during night of 12/13th and that the 103rd Battery should remain in position till night 13/14th. Registration of remaining German trenches zone failed owing to cloudy weather. Later in the day it was decided that the 3rd Cavalry Division should take over from the 85th Infantry Brigade on night 12/13th and that whole of 28th Divisional Artillery should come under command of M.G.C. Cavalry Force. During the night the relief of sections 31st Brigade by sections of "H" & "I" Batteries were carried out successfully. The relieved sections proceeding to rest area about POPERINGHE.

13th May. 5:35 a.m. A heavy bombardment of our trenches commenced and targets were allotted to the groups of Duffus and White by the Cavalry Commander with whom they were affiliated. R.A.H.Q. moved out at once to ESTAMINET near railway crossing east of VLAMERTINGHE at the order of Cavalry Force and soon established telephonic communication with all groups. 108th Battery engaged German heavy guns which had already been registered and 9.2" - not having registered anything yet from new position - fired on FREZENBERG road while 31st advanced section took on the railway line. The feu de barrage, established by the field and horse guns completely checked any attempt to advance on the part of the enemy and was reported by the 4th Division to have been extremely effective. The trenches evacuated by the cavalry were thus denied to the enemy. The 2nd. Brigade Northumbrian R.F.A. was placed at disposal of C.R.A. by Corps Artillery and was at once ordered into action East of YPRES. While the batteries were coming up positions were reconnoitred for them by Majors Scarlett and Lewin of the 3rd Brigade, and these Officers saw the batteries settled into action during the night. The R.H.A. batteries were ordered into action without delay and the relieved sections of the 31st Brigade were re-established in their original positions while the 3rd and 146th Brigades were ordered to stand by. Corps Artillery then ordered 31st Battery advanced section to move West of Canal and join remainder of Battery, so by midnight the total of guns East of YPRES was 18 pdrs. 12, 13 pdrs. 12, 15 pdrs. 12, 4.5" Howitzers 6. Orders were received that the Heavy Artillery would be taken over at 12:0 noon tomorrow by General UNIACKE, Commanding 2nd Group of Heavy Artillery Reserves.

14th May. Command of 9.2" Howitzer, 108th Heavy Battery and section 31st Heavy Battery handed over at 12:0 noon to Heavy Artillery Reserves. In the afternoon information was received of the massing of Germans on our front and left front. A feu de

barrage was at once established all along the front and Heavy Artillery informed of situation. Essex Regiment reported that the fire of field guns prevented any hostile move on part of enemy and that one battalion, which could be seen from their trenches, made no effort to advance in the face of the shrapnel and H.E. By 5:10 p.m. observers reported no sign of hostile movement so fire was slackened. In the evening M.G. de Lisle sent following message to C.R.A. :-
" Please convey to the Artillery under your command my compliments on the effective support it has afforded the Cavalry Force during the recent operations. The rapidity of its response and the volume of its fire has greatly assisted my Cavalry".   Group Commanders were also thanked for their close cooperation by Cavalry Brigade Commanders with whom they were affiliated.

12/15481

Hd. Qu: R.A. 28th Division

Vol V 1 – 31. 5. 15

Army Form C. 2118.

WAR DIARY
or
~~INTELLIGENCE~~ SUMMARY.
(Erase heading not required.)

28th Div Arty.

Hour, Date, Place	Summary of Events and Information	Remarks and references to Appendices
VLAMERTINGHE. 1st May	Liaison officers sent to General JOFFE's Head Quarters, from RAHA, Canadian & British RFA Brigades. 118th Battery told off by Gen. JOFFE to one of his brigades & worked chiefly with them. Several targets registered by 9.2 in. howitzers including Hill 29. Arrangements made for lamps to work with Belgian Batteries.	64
Noon	At 12 noon batteries ceased fire according to instructions received from the front. But at 12.50 P.M. Genl Joffé asked for support from heavy guns against heavy batteries shooting from direction of HOUTHULST FOREST. Assistance was given by fire as registered before on farm North of farm itself.	
12.35 P.M	French asked that 9.2 how should fire on Hill 29 from 1.30 to 1.45 P.M. As the shooting had been close to French trenches an aeroplane was wired for & put the 9.2 onto target. Got 4 (?)Several 2 were direct hits. Other targets were then taken on. An effort was made to adjust the 122 "howitzers on a farm with observation done by a Belgian gunner. So many batteries were shooting as to make this impossible	
At 2.20 P.M	French asked that 9.2 how might fire on hill 29 from 2.45 to 3.10 P.M. eventually at a redoubt on the top. Shown invisible trenches	

Army Form C. 2118.

WAR DIARY
or
INTELLIGENCE SUMMARY.
(Erase heading not required.)

Instructions regarding War Diaries and Intelligence Summaries are contained in F.S. Regs., Part II. and the Staff Manual respectively. Title pages will be prepared in manuscript.

28th Div Arty.

65

Hour, Date, Place	Summary of Events and Information	Remarks and references to Appendices
2.45 P.M.	For another machine as fast [as] led to be brought to bear from position reported return.	
3.10 P.M.	All guns opened fire on allotted targets according to orders received.	
3.25 P.M.	9.2 stopped firing on 29 Hill. All guns except those ranging with aeroplane ceased firing. 7 Kerem moved on own objective North of the woods.	
4.45 P.M.	At request of French General fire was opened on U27 a 35, U26 a 35 & U25 d 47 by the 31 - 108 RB & 9.2 in front of, but was continued on the further objectives till 5.25 PM	
5.25 PM	The French aeroplane reconnaissance reported two batteries of enemy in action at U25 d 96 & U27 a 30. There were at once engaged by 9.2 How & BM # Battery respectively. It was added by the 4.7 batteries was firing as well, that batteries had to be reduced to fire piecemeal as shrapnel (two out of three rounds) throwing bursts stopping. During the day 4 60pr were laid up owing to various damages to the mounting. 10M used for.	
7.30 P.M.	An armoured train with 6" gun under command of Capt SERVAIS (Lieut BALL RN) of Belgian Navy reported. Available next afternoon have sent with them to improve fire as up with the RFA.	

WAR DIARY
or
INTELLIGENCE SUMMARY.
(Erase heading not required.)

Army Form C. 2118.

28th Div. Arty.

66

Hour, Date, Place	Summary of Events and Information	Remarks and references to Appendices
VLAMERTINGHE 2nd May	During the night some 60 pr were repaired so that out of the 7 which fired yesterday, 5 are available for use today. Orders received from French General MANGIN recalling 3mn of our British heavy artillery now given as gun SOUTH of PILCKEM–STADEN railway & EAST of PILCKEM–YPRES Roads, a list of batteries affected by another was also rendered. As this differed from the one allotted for yesterday, it was not to be sent to RFC for a flare to work in new area until night 1/2 of May. Telephone wires all around turned during night 1/2 of May. A liaison officer sent to General MANGIN's H.Q.	
8.15 P.M.	Lt Col BATEMAN reported the arrival of batteries other than 3rd Army. Ordered to inform his Brigade Hqrs its communication with H.Q. Batteries ordered to open fire on targets previously allotted in zone. To wait for aeroplane observation.	
12.15 P.M.	In response to request from Genl JOFFRE's H.Q. the fire of 60 pr heavy artillery was turned on to C.4a.88 & C.5.4.3.	
3.0 P.M.	French wanted British of splutid counter attack from PILCKEM. All heavy batteries laid in turn were now junction in West direction.	
4.15 P.M.	Heavy bombardment commenced & have received of an attack from direction of ST JULIEN. Guns at once opened fire on enemy guns	

Army Form C. 2118.

WAR DIARY
or
INTELLIGENCE SUMMARY.
(Erase heading not required.)

2nd Div Arty
67

Place	Hour, Date	Summary of Events and Information	Remarks and references to Appendices
VLAMERTINGHE	(2nd Cnl)		
	7.30 P.M.	position South of KEERSELAERE to West of C10 – also, an attack was attempted from PILCKEM, in the crown roads in that neighbourhood. 4 anticraft guns arrived from DUNKIRK now moved into position by order of V.th Corps Artillery.	
	8.30 P.M.	Attack on our right reported held up. No 20 Antiaircraft Section after having brought down German aeroplane.	
	9.30 P.M.	Report received from 146th Bde that enemy are massing in their Zone in rear of 6th Div. No 20 (recent) is to hold front. Ridge had already been warned cancelling this. More ammunition asked for & Chlumer returned to supply same.	
	12.midnight	Decided by Div. Cmdr & General CHAPMAN that 146 B Bde cannot move away til tactical situation.	
3rd April (Wed)	1.30 A.M.	Information received that batteries of 3rd & 4th B.L. Lucknow & 8th Bn. Battery	
	5.30 A.M. 6.30 A.M.	Information of new German trench south of 4th Howr Battery. Information of heavy batteries opened on West C10 to assist our infantry which have counterattacked from direction Ypres.	
	11 A.M.	9.2in How reported damage to Ypres controlling next at different direction. V.th Corps & 10th & Plumer Force informed.	

WAR DIARY
or
INTELLIGENCE SUMMARY.
(Erase heading not required.)

Army Form C. 2118.

68   28th Div Arty

Hour, Date, Place	Summary of Events and Information	Remarks and references to Appendices
VLAMERTINGHE (3rd Cont.) Noon	Information received that attack on our line from direction of ST JULIEN to the East this morning.	
12.10 P.M.	The section 906/M ordered forward to position E of military road. RIEGERSBURG CHAUSSE to fire on N. VAN HOUTHULST STREAM until out of ammunition. Kept them at its important points. When done 27 K. turned all available guns into immediate 3-in Bty turned from machine gun continues to shell horse C10. shots Southern direction.	
2.0 P.M.	61.92 round recent kill Bdr.	
4.5 P.M.	Section of the 108 Bofors Battery reported him in position just opening fire.	
4.20 P.M.	Reported Aeroplane had numbers 2 hits + at 4.45 P.M. 10 more hits registered. Attack threatened Therene entered in C13 n4. All hun guns put into ST JULIEN turned to search along HANNEBEKE STREAM to extreme limit range. Later French reported attack developing on South of trench in Squares C16 n17. French Belgian turned on when put of C15 n C16 while in heavy battery put into trench C16 n17.	
6.P.M.		
6.15 P.M.	French reported the British left was taking its own. 9.2 in. How reported ofcers had been carried out + towards to machine fire.	

Army Form C. 2118.

WAR DIARY
or
INTELLIGENCE SUMMARY
(Erase heading not required.)

28th Div Art

69

Hour, Date, Place	Summary of Events and Information	Remarks and references to Appendices
VLAMERTINGHE (3rd Cont)		
8.30 P.M.	Heavy fire on PILCKEM that was broken down again. Armament Officer sent in car to O.M.'s workshop. Report from Infantry that fire of 108th Battery was very helpful to them & had been very effective. During afternoon 31st Battery recommended position for a section about POTIJZE, which has taken over after dark. Section to reach its place by 8.30 P.M.	
4th May midnight	Col. Rundle reported his Brigade West of VLAMERTINGHE with no casualties. 37th How. Battery accompanying it.	
12.15 AM	3rd Brigade report all guns in action & Team close.	
9.0 AM 11.0 AM	Capt. E was allotted to Heavy battery in support of French. The Capt. was charged to Battalion in use as at report of French. During morning turns calls made for help from his Officer & Advanced Section 31st H.B. ordered to fire in front indicated. Arrangements were made for to verify the sections of 2nd 10.8th H. Battery on important tactical point.	
12.30 P.M.	Order received from Art Plumer's Force for Canadian forces to come again under other ypres Canadian Division.	
2.30 P.M.	Order to resist Tribular of all Battery received. The 10th Batteries & how (inspecting) to remain under CRA 28th Div. G in Am.	

WAR DIARY
or
INTELLIGENCE SUMMARY

Army Form C. 2118.

28th Div Arty

Hour, Date, Place	Summary of Events and Information	Remarks and references to Appendices
VLAMERTINGHE (4th Cont.)	With the 1st Brigade handed to 27th Div the 113th Bde RFA to the 4th Div. Orders issued accordingly. In afternoon calls were made for assistance from trenches. Div. had no wireless but nothing registered on the light was too bad. French also asked for assistance to the north. Guns were turned on but in the case of the trenches the range was too great except for Twretin near POTIJZE Field batteries worked under 94th Brigade Commanders. Horse & German 60 pdr batteries near Ennis. Report came in of German digging line in V.27 & a 60 pdr battery was turned on. Great distraction of communication was caused by the constant error in connecting batteries with B & H.Q. and in the main lines — but was almost entirely by dismounted orderly. Orders received for removal of Div H.Q. to South ground stables 4 Div towards the Chateau. 27th RFA & 123th forced to move from Imports/YPRES to day not near POTIJZE own to shell fire. Local attack which was supposed to come off during the day never appeared to materialise.	
7.0 PM		

HTF

WAR DIARY
or
INTELLIGENCE SUMMARY.
(Erase heading not required.)

Army Form C. 2118.

28th Divisional Arty.

71

Hour, Date, Place	Summary of Events and Information	Remarks and references to Appendices
1am H7 c 50. 5th May		
1.30 AM	In order to make room for the 4th Div HQ in their own area, the 28th Div HQ was moved during the morning to position S of BEAR HOTEL. Captn SANDEMAN returned to command too & Battn while Maj RAMSDEN was in temporary command of 2nd Brigade. At day light heavy battries opened fire on our position about ST JULIEN.	
11.15 AM	Report received of change HQ of 3rd Fd A Bde in order to be near 83rd Bde — new location 14 e 5.t & 1 3 c 1.9 approximately. Infantry reported heavily shelled, especially [XXX] Right centre & casualties heavy, but no indication of direction from which were coming could be given. The Germans position about C4 & 5, 10 & 11 engaged practically all day by 108th & Scott. 2nd Battery. West opened. Left Scott. 2nd Fd Battn E. & T of YPRES fired into close touch with Hostile Infantry. Brigade Commanders & worked hard all day shooting at various objectives. Batteries run in action & the other had stuck fast in a hole. The night before and not then been shifted. The Co took him not his hitched up. The 27th Div Arty which sent him reserve to link up with various artillery brigade of last division & called upon him to engage various targets. During the morning the 3rd Fd Bde stopped a German advance down the railway by gun fire.	

Army Form C. 2118.

WAR DIARY
or
INTELLIGENCE SUMMARY.
(Erase heading not required.)

28th Div Arty   72

Hour, Date, Place	Summary of Events and Information	Remarks and references to Appendices
H7c50. 5th (Cont)	During the evening a reconnaissance of howitzer positions west of YPRES particularly of positions for 5 inch Arty on G.H.Q 3 line was carried out. Two 5 inch Howitzer batteries from Northumbrian Division arrived & hold HQ 28th Divn. Arty. G.H.A. WHITE posted to 2/1st Bn. Wel. Lieut WESTKELLY wounded.	Position MHQ will in future be referred to a BRANDHOEK
6th May	Northumbrian Howitzer Brigade arrived during the night from the Cos. sent out not to reconnoitre positions East of YPRES. Colonel Rundell & Col Duffus CRA sent on reconnaissance. 9.2" How still not in action. 108th Battery assisted with aeroplanes fire reconnaissance at the front of batteries about ST JULIEN. Several targets inflicted on by aeroplane by 108 & 31 HB batteries. Infantry in/holed situation has inflicted east today as guns have the situation well in hand 4" & 5" Durham Howitzer Bde Artillery selected position to enfilade enemy lt. The force is placed under command of 3rd Bde Cinder & the batteries under 3rd Bde. 2-3½" How. Battery ordered to select a position West of Canal to shoot on the left flank under orders of 3/1st Bde.	

WAR DIARY
INTELLIGENCE SUMMARY

Army Form C. 2118.

73

28th Div Art

Hour, Date, Place	Summary of Events and Information	Remarks and references to Appendices

BRANDHOEK (6th Cont.)

Col G.H.A. WHITE joined 28th D.A. to command 2nd & 4th RFA. Arrangement made with 4th Divn by which the left of Divnl line is to be further covered by the 118th How Bde in action tr Rmt D18 b4 W of the canal belongng to 28th Divn, shooting on German trenches in the front of the 4th Divn which they can take in enfilade 9.2 in. How informed & asked, by turns, to fire a round. They need has not recurred but the Gun Groups continue to fire in front — line. Northumbrian Brigade got into action during the night.

7th May

5. AM 162nd Heavy Battery was ordered to open fire on Hills 35 & 37 in D19 + 20 as batteries behind these hills had previously caused much annoyance. Other guns were fired at their objectives during the day.

9.30 PM Rpt Cam in that an attack had been made during the night on the 84th Brigade front but failed owing to our rifle fire. The rest of the night lit had passed quietly.

Royal also reports having enjoyed several opportunities during the day, in support of the infantry. Registration was attempted with aeroplane but up to 6:30 P.M. had not succeeded.

Wind mostly from the East throughout day. 2nd & 3rd Bdy also complain of fumes from the shell bombardment made to supply retreats. Major Ross Hudson visited 12th How Bty — Cmdr. & arrangements of fire for the front stream the front against B.G. from the flanks

Army Form C. 2118.

WAR DIARY
or
INTELLIGENCE SUMMARY.
(Erase heading not required.)

28th Divl Arty.   74.

Hour, Date, Place	Summary of Events and Information	Remarks and references to Appendices
BEANDHEK (7th Cnty)		
5.30 P.M.	Observing station in Sq C24 whence good view of the country obtainable. Heart of hint for upkeep & communication greatly felt. 12th Bde report having own men with black faces & haversacks within field hospital from detachments digging in C19d. Belgian batteries at rear turned on to shell the Square. H.O.C. 4 Divn report that C17c & C23a cannot be covered by his guns. Unless arrangement made there no front can cover from C16d to C15a22. Arrangement being made to bring Belgian batteries onto its zone myined. Gris believes that 4 Div Art arrive tonight.	
6.0 P.M.	O.C. 3rd Bde reports that 22nd Battery has 2 guns disabled & unfit to fire any to direct hits. He also that 80g⁺ Battery may be sent up in relief. Orders sent to this battery to get in touch with the 3rd & ready to the half hour to have up one section & possibly the detachments & two. Pte Endie ordered up three guns manned by detachments of 86⁵th B⁵ but returned the officer.	
11. P.M.	30th B⁵ report A/am 1/103rd Battery not partim. O/C 118th ordered speed up before further damage in.	

WAR DIARY
or
INTELLIGENCE SUMMARY.

Army Form C. 2118.

75   28th Div Art

Hour, Date, Place	Summary of Events and Information	Remarks and references to Appendices

BRANDHOEK 8th- May 7.AM Huns have commanded heavy art East of YPRES, but for some hours nothing very definite could be learnt of the situation. It was known that the Germans had bombarded the whole frontage of the V th Corps.

Later an attack developed on the left of the 27th Div in rt of 84th Bde. While the attacks were delivered along the front of the Division urgent calls for ammunition were received dealt with at once. Aeroplanes went out steadily, & were reported information from same brought. The 106th & 4. PM had registered 5 Bys which 2 were apparently completely silenced.

Another what continued fiercely in churning area in which guns were collected. They were subjected to a heavy fire by

The Belgian Army tried to assist from St JULIEN N.18 to Govt west of canal on frontage of 28 Div in which was always threatened. Protection for batteries of 28 Div sub-committee to 5th Corps for approval. Field batteries fired in this Zone as wires between were broken early in the day & the 5th Divisional batteries did good work in this sector.

Army Form C. 2118.

WAR DIARY
or
INTELLIGENCE SUMMARY.

(Erase heading not required.)

76   28th Div Arty

Hour, Date, Place	Summary of Events and Information	Remarks and references to Appendices

BRANDHOEK. (8th Cont)

5.0 P.M.

No detailed report of the doings of 15th Brigade received till evening 5.0 P.M. reported that even to note at which fire had been maintained the ed. was broken in the buffers + running up springs were weakening so that shield was much reduced. Six guns at one returned up from 146 Bty to replace the worst ones & 31st Bty ordered to send guns up to 15th Bty from the battery position. The 146 Bty Ammn Column (Gun Ammn Section) returned up as the teams of battery wagons were splitting done up with continual calls made for ammn.

At same time report received from 3 RQ that 172nd Battery was Temporarily out of action. 2 Officers Wounded, killed 16 men wounded.

5.30 P.M.   The 75th Battery from hurt of canal was ordered up to relieve 62nd Battery which was ordered to be withdrawn.

X   7.2" Am fired from armourd trucks down again. No antiaircraft guns of No 20 Section were destroyed by shellfire.

9th May 7.0 AM   GOC ordered to withdraw batteries E of canal, informed by the Divisional Commander. — On the left infantry this heavy losses made it impossible to achieve much effect. The enemy was reported about WIELTJE. Orders were at once issued for the withdrawal of the 3rd Arty, 15th

WAR DIARY
INTELLIGENCE SUMMARY
(Erase heading not required.)

Army Form C. 2118.

77   28th Dn Arty.

Hour, Date, Place	Summary of Events and Information	Remarks and references to Appendices
BRANDHOEK (9th Cavt).	Huitzer Battn. The 5 in Howitzers — 60 hrs had already been ordered back, their movement made to put them out of reach, in selected positions. The 103rd Battn also was withdrawn of 3.25 A.M. to southern. The Bgs + 1m "hm" left in position but East of canal. The section 93rd Bs arty rejoined its HQ in B.27, + Centerman was heard. 3rd Bde Ack with three without difficulty, but with only 4 5mm fit for action. R.H.A. Antiaircraft will chosen to inst. of Canal that placed near BRAND HOEK to protect Cavalry Div from air observation.	
8.30 AM	From report of F.S. it would appear that the infantry did not hold ————— Merely a line as was expected, but information must travel line but yet received. During the morning a heavy bombardment broke out + spread right across the front. It was followed by an attack on the from C.2.9.b down to railway line. Our infantry reported to be falling back from VERLORENHOEK + all battns. West of canal opened on German trenches & the heavy guns engaged enemy guns to N.E., which had been reported previously. 108th + 13 attys also reported somewhere	

Army Form C. 2118.

WAR DIARY
or
INTELLIGENCE SUMMARY.
(Erase heading not required.)

78.   28th Div Arty

Hour, Date, Place	Summary of Events and Information	Remarks and references to Appendices
BRANDHOEK (9th cont) 12.30 P.M.	Position. Brig Genl Gay informed by Maj Genl BULFIN that orders have been received by him to proceed strong his home after handing over to B. Genl D. Arbuthnot. Brig Genl D. Arbuthnot arrived almost at the same time & the situation was explained to him. Firing continued all afternoon enemy output were received from 4th	
6.35 P.M.	Division that it was thought an Infm 27th Div that their front B.Os were holding the centre was a bit weak. It was decided to move another battery East of YPRES so as to cope with the situation more effectively.	
11.30 P.M.	The above line movement was not out to appear 31st Battery – 65th + 163rd. The 65th Battery (less one section) returned to its original position north of POTIJZE. The return for the 103rd was not received in time to be acted upon as the 30th RA HQ were moving into a new dug out. The order to 31st Battery was after having reconnoitred the C.O. ordered to reconnoitre a position for the section tomorrow. The night passed quietly.	

WF

Army Form C. 2118.

28th Div Arty.

WAR DIARY
or
INTELLIGENCE SUMMARY.
(Erase heading not required.)

79

Hour, Date, Place	Summary of Events and Information	Remarks and references to Appendices
BRANDHOEK 16th May	Col Duffus group of 18 pdrs put into German trenches by aeroplane observation, was invaluable for lack of wire. The 8pm fire on the front of the 28th Divn in two counterattacks reduced but a very heavy bombardment of the 27th Divn in - followed by determined attacks - took place during the day. Little assistance could be given as the Infantry line mostly amongst the woods. The zone of the Belgian batteries was, however, extended to the woods N of BELLEWAARDE Pond. Some registration was carried out by heavy battery aeroplanes.	
5.30 P.M.	A bridson was arranged for HQ 2 in Hrs. Chase to the Canal - in order to get on terms with German guns. Artifred received from Corps to retaliate for bombardment of our trenches by heavy shelling their Corps zones September 5th for Front Division was divided into 4 zones - programme arranged. It was arranged to register the 108 H ☒ 37th & 65th How on trench zone in turn. So that at any given moment any zone could be sub--jected to severe shell fire.	
10.30 P.M.	Orders were issued notifying batteries & zones and limiting the action. Some wire received from V Corps issued to Batteries in most urgent need of it, to enable them to get wire out to drawing stations. Enemy aircraft show great diminution of fire on our front.	

WAR DIARY
or
INTELLIGENCE SUMMARY.
(Erase heading not required.)

Army Form C. 2118.

80 28th Div Art.

Hour, Date, Place	Summary of Events and Information	Remarks and references to Appendices
POTYZE 11th May	Report came in early upon occupation by the Germans of the left trench of the 27th Div on the consequent enfilading of the 28th Div on that lynch pin. Fire was opened at once in support of 27th Div by 2 Belgian batteries on the hand in T.12 b.5.W. from which a galling fire was being kept on our left. The fire was reported most accurate & effective. An 18 pr was later put in the same spot & the Divn continued to Short whilst daylight lasted.	
12 noon	From then the Belgian batteries began to run short of ammn. & by 1.30 PM had none left. Divn was reported to 28th Divn & arrangements were made by V Corps for two more pieces transferred from the 5th Divn with. Reports & returns of the Bomb. of German trench preceded through out the day & have complete except for the extreme night by the enemy. Several direct hits were recorded some buildings have been destroyed. No orders had arrived during the day in reference to Potijze in most urgent need of it.	
6 PM	Orders have been received that "C" and "D" an. howitz. battery with their two Howitzers ea. apt. from 1/85 H.B. which were still to remain in the right & that from E Ypres hour x one	

WAR DIARY
INTELLIGENCE SUMMARY.
(Erase heading not required.)

Army Form C. 2118.

28th Div Arty.

Hour, Date, Place	Summary of Events and Information	Remarks and references to Appendices
POPERINGHE (11th Cont)	Under command of Gp. of Lt. Col. 4 Div. which form head of Canal defence under S.P. Div. Cmdr. that Div. may support my mvmt by the Cavy Cmdr. The front is divided into 2 sections. Right under 85 Bde Cmdr. & Left commanded by 9th Lt. Col. Bde – under 9th Cav B. Cmdr. Arrangements for communication fixed up.	81
	12th	
12 May	Communication will advanced – two batteries have been forward having station. Lt. Col. B. O. Burrows RHA noted position by 3rd Bde. RHA. With CRA with a view to taking over Batteries. It was decided that the battery recently by 6x+Cav + 7 Bde Batteries should be taken over & not received by 103 should not. Orders from for 103rd to remain in position until tomorrow night then to withdraw as a battery. The 6x + 7th to leave one section relieving tonight & the other tomorrow. CRA hosted the batteries East of YPRES from General GREENLEES & the 9th Cav Bde & General CHAPMAN 9th & 5th Cav Bde — Population by aeroplane fell on the village in clusters.	

WAR DIARY
or
INTELLIGENCE SUMMARY
(Erase heading not required.)

Army Form C. 2118.

28th Div Art

Hour, Date, Place	Summary of Events and Information	Remarks and references to Appendices

BRANDHOEK. (12 Cnt)

Orders received in afternoon that another Cav Divn would relieve the 85th Bde Infantry. That to which 9th Infantry & the 28 "Divn" would fight next was hillX. The relieving troops flown tonight. The RANGE got no mes last antenneur, where relieve of 5 or 12th Cav Divn.

Day passed quietly. No Divn in 1st Front. No heavy shelling or attack.

Artillery movements augmented by 2nd DE LISLE at least & ample force for any attack, & shall have no difficulty. Ammn has been available before for this scheme which that most have inherently adopted with success.

INN HILL 20 13th May

Relief of our section by 4 Bdo Battries in western end of 1st H Battries, R.H.A. + relieved section proceeded to refarm about POPERINGHE.

5:35AM Summer commenced heavy bombardment of your trenches. The Scouts of Dufft w. White were allotted targets by Sector Commander with whom they are affiliated. Headquarters moved to new new Cav Divn Hqs when telephones

Army Form C. 2118.

WAR DIARY
or
INTELLIGENCE SUMMARY.
(Erase heading not required.)

Army Form C. 2118.

S3   Arty Cav Force

Hour, Date, Place	Summary of Events and Information	Remarks and references to Appendices
Iron Hill (13th Cnt)	Communication had to be established afresh since all batteries had been connected with the [?] at BEARD HOEK. The cavalry were driven off the front line from South of VERLOREN HOEK Road to the WESTHOEK Track. 108th Battery were turned on to all enjected gun targets between 9.2 on to PREZENBERG to road thence to ZONNEBEKE. 31st Battery were section on to Railway line.	
2.30 P.M.	A combined attack was ordered for 2.30 P.M. + batteries were ordered to fire on forward trenches from 2 P.M. to increase elevation at 2.30 P.M. Targets were allotted to Heavy Batteries. The attack was successful on its left but failed on the right. This was enemy [?] II maintained all afternoon at a slow rate by order 9th Cavalry Corps. The trenches occupied have were found to be almost entirely obliterated by gun fire. There was no real infantry attack all day. The infantry did not come through the evacuated trenches. Orders for the counter attack were received at 3.45 P.M. At orders of Army Comdr the Section 93rd(?) Bde which had been retired were ordered back into position again + the 7th RFA Bde has retired up. In the evening the Corps Artillery advised ordered the North Umbrian (2nd)	

Army Form C. 2118.

WAR DIARY
or
INTELLIGENCE SUMMARY.
(Erase heading not required.)

64 Army Bde Cdn Arty Force

Hour, Date, Place	Summary of Events and Information	Remarks and references to Appendices

In HILL (13 cont)

FA Brigade which had fired at CRAs disposed earlier in the day, to be brought into action East of Mitchell. Positions were selected while the Batteries were coming up — by Majors LEWIN & SCARLETT. Arrangements were made for the taking over of the Left of the Canadian line as far as C29a62. VERLOREN HOEK the new line came back to 100 East of parallel to the road which runs through I5a re Menin Road. Extended to WESTHOEK Track joins old line about I12a62. 1st at guns East of Canal at midnight were 18pr 12. 13pr 12. 15pr 12.   4.5" How 6. The Corps Artillery advance relieved the withdrawal of the heavy guns to West of Canal. During the day a locomotive in area of the Combermere guns 9/08 H.B. blew some f...

4th May

Bgn 73 An. Communication was established with the 2nd Northumbrian Brigade by telephone.

3.45 P.M.

Heavy firing heard meanwhile. Gen'l Umacke took over heavy guns at noon. Information from White Group that guns were moving North of I22.b. in communication leading those to Wood in C10.b. Other same report came from Dufferin Group that guns were advancing from I6 towards. A few S. journeys were attempted along the whole front by Heavy Arty Reserve Cdn.

Army Form C. 2118.

WAR DIARY
or
INTELLIGENCE SUMMARY.
(Erase heading not required.)

Army Form C. 2118.

Arty. Cav. Force.

85

Instructions regarding War Diaries and Intelligence Summaries are contained in F.S. Regs., Part II. and the Staff Manual respectively. Title pages will be prepared in manuscript.

Hour, Date, Place	Summary of Events and Information	Remarks and references to Appendices
H.116.	Informed of the situation. Shortly after Lord Killmuir called from at orders of Cavalry Brigadier & H.Q. Regt men informed.	
5.10 P.M	General ordered no movement in the CRA & his own orders for distribution. I gave after on the front mentioned himself outside field. Opinion received by me held partly by General, which he referred to the matter tonight. Col WALKER went over from hours stream to Major STEWART advanced Command of BWBdy. Major Genl DE LISLE asked that the following heavily to the CRA should be published. Please convey to the artillery under your command my compliments on the effective support it has afforded the cavalry Force during its recent operations. The rapidity & its response to the telephone calls from here greatly assisted my cavalry. Telegram received in night that 13th Infantry Brigade would proceed as ordered above for 5 days to Ireland including tomorrow. Hrs in that time. 2nd Cavalry Division under Genl KAVANAGH relieved General DE LISLE's Cav. Force during the night. No difficulty about reliefs my Massed Pickets.	

(73989) W4141—463.   400,000.   9/14.   H.&J.Ltd.   Forms/C. 2118/10.

WAR DIARY
INTELLIGENCE SUMMARY.
(Erase heading not required.)

Army Form C. 2118.

86. Art Cav Force

Hour, Date, Place	Summary of Events and Information	Remarks and references to Appendices
7am Hill 15th May	Brigadier Smith, CRA visited Batteries. The Battery of 2nd Northumbrian Bde reported having been shelled in the morning. The 27th Divn asked for other section of 5th How. Battery to come into action S. East of Ypres — but as the battery had now no officers left — except a subaltern of subsection — the 4th How. Battery was sent to 27th Divn. The 5th Withdrew to refit.	
16th May	Quiet day. French attacked at 8.30 P.M. after bombardment of keen horse shell commenced at noon. But result not yet known. The Officer Commanding two parts of Belgian guns — the 7th Regt — attached RCHA with the 27th (Battery Commanders allotted) to the 28th Division. Arrangements made for one section of each of two batteries to relieve one section French battery in action tonight. The remaining sections to be in reserve the third battery to be the horse line ready to replace other batteries as required. Captain C.F. WARD of 75th Battery was killed by shrapnel during the day.	

Army Form C. 2118.

87. Arty 28th Div.

WAR DIARY
or
INTELLIGENCE SUMMARY.
(Erase heading not required.)

Hour, Date, Place	Summary of Events and Information	Remarks and references to Appendices
Nr H11b. 17th May	Mist during made registration difficult - however some targets were successfully engaged from dawning station. The Belgian batteries have however made to registration to new section.	
11.25 AM	2 h Hussars reported horses in I.6.d.9.8. being used by Snipers - two in our own in the neighbourhood. Heavy Artillery informed. These horses destroyed before night by 108th Battery. Observation out in by the Cavalry. 103rd Battery at the request of the Cavalry shelled a house at C.30.c.21. the fire being directed by a Cavalry officer as the house was not visible from dawning station. Several hits were made. The house was destroyed. Northumbrian Batteries successfully engaged a German dawning station.	
2.30 PM	Messages received from Staff Capt. regarding the proximity of shots by the Germans & others as to where water should be drawn from for the brigade.	8th / 17.5.15

(73989) W4141—463. 400,000. 9/14. H.&J.Ltd. Forms/C. 2118/10.

Army Form C. 2118.

WAR DIARY
or
INTELLIGENCE SUMMARY.
(Erase heading not required.)

88 28th Div Arty

Hour, Date, Place	Summary of Events and Information	Remarks and references to Appendices
Som H11b 18th May	A house which had not been destroyed yesterday, to the complete satisfaction of the Canadn was reported in the morning. The 27th Divis in was informed which to turn on the 5th How battery which shot at it before. Heavy Artillery however also informed & arrangements made for direct observation communication through to 37th How Battery. (65th Battery reported that Canadn Commander was ordered hid with the result of his obtained. Another farm was taken on by the 9.2. from registration done from 106 Battery Observing Station by means of communication through Round. 37th Battery transferred Command to Div by order of 5th Corps. The 2nd Northumbrian brigade moved new section in his battery during the night to new position between _____ Since the old one had been found out. CRA noted CRA 27th Divn - in-sufficient Batty Comder Canaln Corps this caused some Officer A line laid to 27th Div Arty reports centre at KRUISTRAAT to facilitate communication.)	

Army Form C. 2118.

WAR DIARY
or
INTELLIGENCE SUMMARY.
(Erase heading not required.)

Sg 28 Div Arty

Hour, Date, Place	Summary of Events and Information	Remarks and references to Appendices
from HQ (18th Cont)	The day has been chiefly to do much registration or to cause at the trouble signalling test asked by CRA. Orders regarding Ammunition limit received from 5th Corps. C/118 now overtook the fires as temporary taken by Capt. Halseys.	Inits
19th May	Mist day - registration was difficult. A gun with gunlayers which was known to troth undertain Witham by one STOKES has not registered, since a suitable showing station has not yet been found.	
11 AM	A test was carried out by the Cavalry Regt & The Communication with Wottunderian Butteries. A sudden call was made for fire and thereafter gun to a round Aleph fire in sequence, was fired by two batteries 2 min & 5 min, Later	
6.30 PM	The 18th Battery refused 305 in action. The battery withdrawing to billeting area with Capt YORKE - adjt 8th How Bde - in temporary Command. The 37th Battery was handed over to the division.	

WAR DIARY
or
INTELLIGENCE SUMMARY.

(Erase heading not required.)

Army Form C. 2118.

90 28th Div Arty.

Hour, Date, Place	Summary of Events and Information	Remarks and references to Appendices
Inn Hill 20th May	Day passed very quietly. 5th Durham Howitzer Battery transferred to 4th Div. by 5th Corps order No. 37 return under command of 28th Div. During the morning — at the request of 2nd Bns a Heavy gun fire was turned on 103rd Battery on some houses which were infected by snipers. There were fire for incendiary shell Tube trench. Several hits were scored & the building was set alight but, the wood being damp, it did not burn successfully. Hill 60 Battery successfully relieved the 80th in position registered during the day. No action. The Mountain Bty also registered hostile rifle & bombing batteries from which troublesome fire in New Kemm Road failed to emanate. Arrangements were made with 27 Div. to register the batteries known. Communication wire interrupted by H.E. in plus shrapnel wire. Several human working parties have shelled & driven down to day refuge from light howitzers & by the enemy was taken on by the Heavy artillery. A lot of ammunition was carried out between Northshields towards the batteries successfully engaged the points indicated	

WAR DIARY
or
INTELLIGENCE SUMMARY.
(Erase heading not required.)

Army Form C. 2118.

Hour, Date, Place	Summary of Events and Information	Remarks and references to Appendices
Zorn Hill 29th May	Orders received that 85th Bde would take over trenches from VERBRANDEN-MOLEN - YPRES Road inclusive to north of VERBRANDEN BELLEWAARDE. The 4th Division to take up its front down to former place. Arrangements made with 4 & 27 Divns that 28th D arty should extend to zone area being taken over by 4th Div. Whilst 27 Div continued to cover that south of the railway being taken over by us. Communication one by left Front visit Brigade y 4-Divn provided for & 27 Divn arranged for their left Brigade Hdqrs in touch with Hdqrs HQ at POPERINGE. Some reports received re shelling the day — The 2nd Northumbrian Bde registering down the MENIN Road, observation being taken by a 27 Divn observing officer. Reports received there were some farms shot at during the night Moved Btn 2 front MDR reinforcement cancelled meantime today. Patrols returned back to ATC tomorrow. MF	28th Div arty

WAR DIARY
or
INTELLIGENCE SUMMARY.

(Erase heading not required.)

Army Form C. 2118.

92

Hour, Date, Place	Summary of Events and Information	Remarks and references to Appendices
Farm H7c81 22nd May 8.20 P.M 10.0 P.M	During the night came heavy firing to the North of YPRES & from the direction of ST ELOI, but all was quiet on the front. The relief took place successfully, batteries continue to shoot anything all gone. Head Quarters moved back to H7c on coming from under the orders of 28th Division. Some rifle firing was carried out during the day, 1st machine from too knocked out by a Belgian Battery. Direct hit on a house was served by 15th Battery. Movement of Germans reported in T1 & T144 Heavy fire aimed at Shrapt. Relief of R.J. Regt. 27th Div taking place tonight. Firing all day from direction of ST ELOI but turning reported front in front of 28th Division. Heavy Cannonading broke out especially to the North of YPRES 's but appeared to continue as far as ST ELOI OC 8th Bde. telegrams report heavy opened fire on our left though there was heavy rifle & machine gun fire on his front. A dispatch rider after was a. hand reached him that 28th Sup Coy on front. The late R&SR Bde was cut. 27th Div report all quiet on their front. Pts 4 Div' report heavy gun fire on their left. French Hd called up reports that Fy	Postin of HQ newmoved referred to on BRAND HOEK

Army Form C. 2118.

WAR DIARY
or
INTELLIGENCE SUMMARY.
(Erase heading not required.)

93   28th Div Arty

Hour, Date, Place	Summary of Events and Information	Remarks and references to Appendices
BRANDHOEK 11 P.M.	Rifleman were attacking about POESINGHE. The Divisional Commander in that area, however, reported all quiet on his front. Firing coming from direction of STEENSTRAATE, having diminished.	
23rd Inst.	Day quiet – some heavy? reported. Belgian batteries put into a number of gunners moving up to the trenches. This seems eccentric. New dressing stations chosen for North, which are [illegible] the country South of [illegible] could be neglected. Enemy from [illegible] active in front amount? ? Shelling took place here in the morning. St Julien? [illegible] in for some attention during the day. POTIJZE area several apparent for a battery.	
10 PM	Heavy firing again from North which lasted till 10.20 PM. 4th Div reported all quiet on their front till midnight. 28th Div front. DICKEBUSCH VLAMERTINGHE shelled during the day. Telephone wires all cut in two occasions.	

Army Form C. 2118.

WAR DIARY
or
INTELLIGENCE SUMMARY.
(Erase heading not required.)

94   28th Div a/q

Hour, Date, Place	Summary of Events and Information	Remarks and references to Appendices
BERANDHOEK 24th May 3.0 AM	A violent bombardment broke out in the direction of YPRES.	
3.15 AM	Spoke to 27th Div. Arty. - Cav Corps. 74 Div Arty + located bombardment to be in front of 28th Div. Asked 27th Div to put the Royale South of Railway on to about It 2 on. hot work alone, + MENIN Road.	
3.25 AM	Suffolk group report that gas was being used by the with heavy bombardment, but that he attack had developed. The infantry were reported holding on to trench line.	
3.50 AM	Bombardment continued heavily, as orders were sent to 146th Bde + 3/1 Royal to stand by in case they were required. Inter cyclists sent round to hasten Queen's Column.	
3.55 AM	4th Division reported the fight led ahead and their front that the gas was so heavy on that front that advance was difficult in arriving their gas.	
4.5 AM	As gas appeared very heavy + gas mask 18/H02 was reported the falling back the 27th Div was asked for all possible support - 8 Nth, 85, 95 Rd was way attacked HQ Ds Pfaffenhiy 8x.	
4.25 AM	Suffolk group reported that enemy had broken through RE at the time off ernal before returning.	
5.15 AM	4th Division asked for fire astride the ST JULIEN road as an attack was reported to be developing from that direction. The message was passed onto 27th Bde. which could be opened from his own front.	
5.20 AM	Enemy reported to have broken through about the railway. 2nd Northumbrian FB Brigade ordered to concentrate without line preference.	

Army Form C. 2118.

WAR DIARY
or
INTELLIGENCE SUMMARY.

(Erase heading not required.)

28th Div Arty 95

Instructions regarding War Diaries and Intelligence Summaries are contained in F.S. Regs., Part II. and the Staff Manual respectively. Title pages will be prepared in manuscript.

Hour, Date, Place		Summary of Events and Information	Remarks and references to Appendices
BRANDHOEK (24 Cont)	5.45 AM	Wareneke R.A.F. (on right of 4th Div) report all quiet on their front.	
	6.15 AM	Cavalry astride MENIN Road reported being heavily attacked. The message was at once transmitted to 27th Div Arty.	
	6.30 AM	Northumbrian Bde. ran out of ammunition. Arrangements were at once made to procure more. Artillery time 4th Div: anti aircraft (seven rounds) were at once fired at enemy aeroplane at by 131st Ammn 1st Cnf. attack. 28th Div to find them some men.	
X	6.50 AM	The 1st 6th & 3rd Bengals reduced into their positions for GHQ O_2 on a per cent. in an emergency.	
	7.15 AM	4th Div reported that Support in St JULIEN road was no longer required.	
	7.45 AM	82nd Arty Bde. ask for all possible fire on front S. of the railway to assist a counter attack which was being launched. Batteries firing on under:—	
		3 Bn.Howr. 12 fm of 28th Div	
		9 " 75 mm Belgian	
		1 " 4.5" How 28 Div	
		2 " 13 Pr R.H.A. 28 Div all	
		4 " 13 Pr R.H.A. Can Cav. paced at 28th Div disposal at 6.20 AM	
	7.50 AM	2nd Northumbrian Bde. reported being reduced to fire of 2nd Battery of Brigade 1st Battery.	
	9.30 AM	85th — report line in tact (Capt Ruddell forced to land) aircraft immediately S. of railway, which had fallen back to I.16 (wrong)	

WAR DIARY or INTELLIGENCE SUMMARY.

Army Form C. 2118.
96. 28th Div. A.R.

Place	Hour, Date	Summary of Events and Information	Remarks and references to Appendices
BEARDSHOEK	24th (Cont) 12.30 P.M.	Batteries fired all morning in support of counter attack. Report received that enemy held WITTEPOORT FARM and ridge East to Contour 44.	
		About this time it was reported that they were moving in broad Int. & in dead ground from I.6.c. Batteries turned at once on both these & 27th Div. A.T. informed asked for assistance, also the H.A.R. Div. Cmdr saw CRA about cooperation in counter attack which 27th Div. was about to start from top ridge tm. South slope of spur running from WITTE POORT FARM to Contour 44. 28th Div. take from ridge ½ way to northern slope.	
	2.0 P.M.	27th Will 28th Div. take from this ridge tm northern slope. Observers to report progress of the attack.	108. 5?
	4.50 P.M.	Counter Attack launched. Observer 37th How. Battery (Capt Hitchins) went along with it taking a telephone. The observers & Battery left his station with a telephone to keep in touch with it. The observer of the 27th R.Div. was also to report on the progress made by the attack by the men south & attack by the 80th Bde. During the day it was decided that, owing to the number of grave attack by North-umbrian Bde. which were hit or unable to shoot through buffer trouble, & the casualties sustained by the A.M. the 146 B.S. should relieve it & early YPRES. The whole Northumbrian Bde was therefore withdrawn in the night and 2 section of 146 B.M. installed in its place. It was impossible owing to the nature of the ground to find positions for two whole batteries of the 146 B.M. and these of the 2nd Northumbrian Bde. were not suitable as they	

WAR DIARY or INTELLIGENCE SUMMARY.

Army Form C. 2118.

97 28th Div A.5

Hour, Date, Place	Summary of Events and Information	Remarks and references to Appendices
BRANDHOEK	(24 concluded) was well known to the Germans.	
	At 9:12 p.m. the Belgian Artillery had lost 3 guns in evening which were left to shoot - 3 having been rendered useless by the breech blocks jamming.	
	The R.H.A. battery had 3 guns disabled & arranged to put into action the Warwickshire R.H.A. Battery which joined the 28th Div. during the day. The Belgian Artillery was ordered to withdraw all his damaged guns to Rail head & to form a battery out of the remaining 8. Counter attack prepared for by order of Divl Cmdr contradicted information.	
25th May	Slow rate of fire maintained throughout night on the area about of the centre attack was uncertain.	
9 a.m.	B.G.R.A. 27th Div: 27 Div & H.A.R. informed of situation. Battn asked to switch on German trench which were yesterday our attack from Ibex.	
	K.M.N. YETAITE POELCAPPELLE. H.A.R. asked to enfilade to demolish BELLEWAARDE FARM & HOOGE the neighboring old trench line. All with direct observation if possible.	
?	141 Bde report having no battery in action for the remounting for position for the attack.	
	Belgian report another gun ruined from concussion - bringing up strength of remaining batteries to 7 guns.	
11 a.m.	27 Divnl Arty report half of WITTE POORT FARM in German hands. & that no British were in trench I 11 b.	
	Same time 85 Bde report that Germans were in East end of ruined buildings...	

WAR DIARY
or
INTELLIGENCE SUMMARY.
(Erase heading not required.)

98. 28th Div Arty

Army Form C. 2118.

Hour, Date, Place	Summary of Events and Information	Remarks and references to Appendices
BRANDHOEK (25" cont)	Have but considered safe to shoot a Gen Staff imagined the 62" R/A required artillery attachment. 37th Manoir reported enemy trench at I 11 b 3.4. I 11 d 9.8 + shown on return copy of hill 44. Trench also reported running from road crossing I 6 c to I 12 a 6.9. After went went to I 12 a 0.5. It may be suspected from this that the Germans are interested in the 44 contour hill with BELLEWARDE Farm as a pivot to trench the line. A.A.R. asked to destroy the Farm + 27th Div to prevent digging in southern slopes. With Dupps [?] [?] Area engaged trenches south of railway & westhoek track & west along track while the White Group assisted by 3"A" from W of Ypres fired on the West & Northern slopes of 44 contour hill, assisted by HMS Thunderer Batteries.	
5.P.M	14th Brigade reported tonight from neutrition. Divl Cmdr saw CRA to obtain situation & action which was being taken. 28th Front which - 6 morning - asked as far South as I 18 c 5 6. This point being completely outside the 28th Artillery zone & will within that of the 27th Artillery. It CRA strongly recommended Divl Cmdr to apply for the services of the Bde of 27th Bde which naturally cover this zone. CRA 27th Division was asked to send the commander of this Brigade to report for orders to the 80th Inf Bde which was responsible for this front. This was arranged.	
6 P.M	CRA Army of Corps Artillery explained the necessity for having a B.G.	

WAR DIARY
or
INTELLIGENCE SUMMARY.
(Erase heading not required.)

Army Form C. 2118.

99   28th Div Arty.

Hour, Date, Place	Summary of Events and Information	Remarks and references to Appendices
BRANDHOEK (2.5" Cnel)		
8.30 P.M.	27th - Owing this gun - Transferred Temporarily this command of to the position occupied by this Brigade to be vacated handed over to 28th Div. Orders received from 5th Corps placing under 28th CRA control of the 27th Div'l Brigade which covered area to MENIN Road. A staff officer was sent to Brdr Genl STOKES 5th batte who arranged the 1st S.A.F.A. under Major EMERY being transferred Temporarily 1st S.A. Cmdr placed himself in touch with mndr nders of 28th CRA R.F.A. During, charm'd position as it was heavily shelled during the day with 12 inch shell.	
26th hen	Some registration carried out, by all batteries.	
4 P.M	A conference about was arranged between the Heavy artillery the field Battries. An aeroplane is to spot the heavies into German trenches about BECELEWAERDE Farm & the full guns are to chastise the enemy on their halt. This worked well into the day on two occasions ... execution was accomplished.	
27th hen	During the night - 3 A.M. officers from 2nd Bde R.F.A, 6th Div, arrived for instruction regarding Battery area etc. No special intimation of their arrival was received till 7.50 when 6th Corps inmn, Third 7-30PM, was received again to by adv would arrive during the day, that twenty ... that horse planes would ... artillery later. The B.M. had then been in ... for 2 hours	

WAR DIARY

Army Form C. 2118.

28th Division

100

Hour, Date, Place	Summary of Events and Information	Remarks and references to Appendices
BRANDHOEK 27 (Cont)	The CO had at RHQ. Arrangements were made for relief of section by 31st Bty tonight. The CO, B.C. & battery leaders to meet OC 2nd Bty at 2.0 P.M.	
11 M	Cav Corps Artillery arrived with an order dated 22 inst from S.G.R. X Cav Corps ordering 7 P.B. to take intelligence on night 27/28. The men had intimation received P.S. a wire had received suggesting that on Rd. South to relieve the 2nd North'd Bty should be relieved by the 2nd Northumbrian Bty. The CO in action in RHQ position. On pointed out that 15th could not march up from RHQ positions by 15hrs had to in they must relieve the 1st & 2nd Bty further East. Divl Cmdr at same time directed RHQ bring them away at all.	
1 PM	Reply received from OC that Northumbrian would relieve 1st Bty but were not stated whether RHQ would to with drawn or not. Reply is afternoon some hours received from Canton Cps announcing that the RHQ would not be withdrawn tonight but would not taken out by 31st - but at latest. BC of the Commander of the section of 2nd Northumbrian Bde reported that a section was on its way up. It had been understood from Crps artillery that the whole Bde was coming up to relieve the RHQ in close Posn.	
4 PM		

WAR DIARY or INTELLIGENCE SUMMARY

Army Form C. 2118.

28th Div Art

Hour, Date, Place	Summary of Events and Information	Remarks and references to Appendices

BRANDHOEK 27 (cont.) — Withdrawal tonight was decided upon. Arrangements were made direct with CRA 83rd Divn that the 1st Bn Shell Lane & 2nd Fd Amb take on the O.P.'s implied. Orders received from 2nd Army that RFA batteries are to be relieved tomorrow.

9.30 P.M. —

28th May — Officer 1st Northumbrian Bde came up & arrangements were made for the relief by 3 RFA sections by 3 sections Northumbrian tonight. Registration by sections by 2nd Bde RFA carried out during the day. Some registration by 28th Divn batteries was checked. 3 sections RFA relieved by 11.0 P.M.

29th May — Registration of Northumbrian Sections carried out during the day. Some registration of other batteries. Heavies engaged hostile batteries on the ground, & shelled stables HOOGE Chateau — putting out German who were out to machine guns by cavalry. 38th Bde — relieved 28th Divn area. Relief of RFA completed.

30th May — 38th Bde Officers visited 146 "A" "B" & "C" Battery positions. CRA also took CRA 6th Divn round present him the front. Arrangement made for relief & front section gun by 38th Bde and sections relieved during the evening. Do had been fruitless except for attack by French in evening.

Army Form C. 2118.

WAR DIARY
or
INTELLIGENCE SUMMARY.

(Erase heading not required.)

28th D.J.C.K

102

Hour, Date, Place	Summary of Events and Information	Remarks and references to Appendices
30th (contd)	Relief of 1st portion 146th Bde carried out & nearly full.	
31st May	G.O.C.R.A. 6th Division came over during the day. Rearranged quietly & relief of remaining Section 146th Bde & joint Section 3rd Bde carried out without difficulty. Command of artillery transferred to Brig Genl HUMPHREYS at midnight & HQ returned to WATOU	

1.6.15.

McQueen
Maj RFA
Comdg 28

121/5871

28th Division

H.Q.rs R.A. 28th Division

Vol VI. 1. — 30.6.15.

Army Form C. 2118.

28th Div Art

WAR DIARY
or
INTELLIGENCE SUMMARY.
(Erase heading not required.)

103

Hour, Date, Place	Summary of Events and Information	Remarks and references to Appendices
WATOU 1st June	Remaining sections of 3rd Brigade were relieved	
2nd June	The 3rd, 31st and 146th Brigades were all in rest area. Divisional Ammunition Column but four wagons left for supply of 8th Brigade Batteries, also in rest area.	
3rd June	At 12 noon Battery and Brigade Parades were held in honour of H.M. The King's Birthday	
4th June	C.O.C. 28th Division visited the 3rd, 31st, 146th Brigades and Divisional Ammunition Column and made a short address to each, thanking them for the work they had done.	
5th June	G.O.C. R.A. inspected 146th Brigade	
5th – 14th June	Divl Artillery remained in rest.	

Army Form C. 2118.

WAR DIARY
or
INTELLIGENCE SUMMARY.
(Erase heading not required.)

28th Div A.5.

Hour, Date, Place	Summary of Events and Information	Remarks and references to Appendices
WATOU 15th June	CRA visited CRA of 14th & 5th Divisions to arrange about the relief of the 14th Divl Artillery which has a period under the 5th Divn. Another unit the 4th of the Third under its own control. B.C's visited the Cmdr of Bdes to be relieved. W.E	
16th June	CRA visited CRA of 5th & 14th Divn. Battery Commanders of the day reconnoitring the battery positions & making arrangements for taking over. W.E	
17th June	4.40 AM orders received for relief 9th Section 5/4th Divl Bty Ammn tonight. 31st Bde to relieve the 46th - the 31st to relieve the 48th & the 146th to 47th. One battery "A/1" from 6th: to remain in action under 28th Divl Arty. CRA advised the two new Commanders of Bdes in 28th Div area of these arrangements. 31st Bde Cmdr to assume Cmd of own Group Bty of B/1 at the same hour. While they two B. Commanders report to CPA at 35 Divn as instructed for orders. Relief has completed by 19 o'clock without light. Relief successfully carried out during the night. W.E	
WEST OUTRE 18 June Noon	The CRA assumed command of the artillery in 28th Divl Area - consisting of the 8 sections 31st Bde artillery the remaining batteries section of 48th Bde & A battery 9/4th Bde have attached to 28th Divl Artillery. Damp but in execution. Owing to night the relief was completed without difficulty.	

Army Form C. 2118.

WAR DIARY
or
INTELLIGENCE SUMMARY.
(Erase heading not required.)

28th Div Arty

Place	Hour, Date	Summary of Events and Information	Remarks and references to Appendices
WESTOUTRE	19th June	At daylight A/49 Howitzer Battery became lost after 28th Div Arty in place of B.A. now with 5th Div Div. During the day the 25th Howitzer battery arrived to join Divnl Arty, then settled a bank by Divnl Comdr. The Commander - Captain Gilpin, however, reported having been made to fire off all his ammunition by the 5th D. inn before leaving. Efforts to get more bombs taken in hand by Army. Registration completed by all batteries. 83rd In parks B - milium Regt - SB in the trenches rifle 3rd BAA Comm under CRA 28th Dvn on completion of relief. M.F.	Nominal roll of officers attached.
	20th June 6.30 AM	Information received of completion of relief. + 3rd BAA rejoined the 28th Division. CRA visited 3rd BAA. Registration continued during the day. M.F.	
	21st June	Registration continued. Arrangements made with No1 Squadron RFC for registration. Aeroplane of front behind German lines which an invisible from observing station. asked by 5th Divn to have drawn on the hotel at daun for hostile flash, in case of aerial for attack on HOOGE which 3rd Divn delivered the evening. M.F.	

Army Form C. 2118.

WAR DIARY
or
~~INTELLIGENCE SUMMARY.~~
(Erase heading not required.)

28th Div Arty

Hour, Date, Place	Summary of Events and Information	Remarks and references to Appendices
WESTOUTRE 22nd June	Registration continued. Nothing to report. Naval Kite Balloon found the 28th Div RA Commanders recommended position for ascending from. CRA visited Kemmel wire.	WiF.
23rd June	An anti-aircraft gun attached to join Div Arty. 3rd & 3rd BY have to settle communication to suit fresh m/c disposition & emergent move of Inf & By HQrs.	WiF.
24th June	Nothing to report	
25th June	Divl Commander inspected gun positions of 100th A/Bg. Batteries of the 3rd Brigade.	
26th June	Daylight fire work trial carried out at BERTHEN. CRA attended with representatives from each of the batteries. Div Arm open a report centre in SCHERPENBERG.	WiF.
27th June	83rd Trench Mortar Battery joined Divisional artillery. It is commanded by Capt Marsh. Elek & is equipped with 4 four howitzers. Two hun and rounds have been issued from the school with the howitzers. CRA with Col BRUCE visited the 83rd Bty trenches to look for places when round significantly with KEMMEL could be established. Three places were selected.	WiF.

A/49th Battery R.F.A. (Howitzer)

Rank	Name	Battery	Date of Joining	Class of Commission	Remarks.
Major	Bridges A.H.	A/49	19.6.15.	Regular	Commanding Battery
Lieut.	Campbell-Johnston P.B.C.	"	"	Temporary	
2/Lt.	Hughes P.E.	"	"	Temporary	
2/Lt.	Groom S.A.E.	"	"	Temporary	
2/Lt.	Penny C.H.L.	A.C.	"	Temporary	

28th Division

Hd Qtr RA 28th Division

Vol VII

1-31-7-15

101/496

a²
a 96

Army Form C. 2118.

WAR DIARY
or
INTELLIGENCE SUMMARY.
(Erase heading not required.)

28th Div Arty

108

Hour, Date, Place	Summary of Events and Information	Remarks and references to Appendices
WESTOUTRE 1st July	Some registration with aeroplane by R/Reg carried out. B de C order hum ammunition position for Scottish division hui WF. Dickebusch shelled.	
2nd July	Nothing to report. 11.30 PM Violent outburst of fire for 5 minutes from N of YPRES. Enemy guns more active in the Salient. YPRES shelled. Second balloon from No 4 K A B. section. WF	
3rd July	Nothing to report. WF Some registration. WF	
4th July	A combined shoot with 12th Heavy battery by 3rd LB4 carried out with ammunition used during the week. Six feet of ground in unknown but few observed & accurate. Enemy artillery more active. YPRES shelled with 17th. Trench by 3rd B- fired in enfilade the 18th howr. of No 17. Reconnaissance for 9th A.L. carried out on position of hostile trench. YPRES still active. WF	
5th July	Reconnaissance 6 HQ3 carried out. Hostile guns active. YPRES shelled in afternoon. Some damage made near DICKEBUSCH vicinity. WF	

WAR DIARY
or
INTELLIGENCE SUMMARY.
(Erase heading not required.)

Army Form C. 2118.

109 28th Div Arty

Hour, Date, Place	Summary of Events and Information	Remarks and references to Appendices
WESTOUTRE 6th July	Active gunnery Recce continues. Preparation of HA lines continued - also digging in of wires. Dec Mondy booking into Kruispre & 9.S.	
7th July	Strong wind - no balloon observation possible.	
8th "	Nothing to report. Wind still destroying to balloon observed.	
9th "	Some trench mortar shooting, which we rather whole, successful. The positions seem to have been fairly accurately located.	
10th "	An enfilade shoot was abandoned owing to the high winds. Battria was asked to experiment in a shoot at the obstacles seen in case they interfered with a timed shoot after 3rd Sum But these have not been registered. Back positions will be hard to reach myself.	
11th "	During the night 6th/7th battery was shelled - enemy employed enemy enemy trench mortars, with good effect - while its premier movements by B & S gun to Bde & Div Rounder. This fire puts by the men in the trenches. Their fire, at one, stops enemy trench mortar when it attempts to trouble us at night, the excellent result obtained encourage us in our Gradually. From present observation we can telegraph to the intact taken in the firing of the battery by the Infantry in the trenches.	

Army Form C. 2118.

WAR DIARY
INTELLIGENCE SUMMARY.
(Erase heading not required.)

No. 110. 28th Div Art

Hour, Date, Place	Summary of Events and Information	Remarks and references to Appendices
WESTOUTRE (cont)	Divisional Commander writes that "I have heard of the prompt & substantial support given by the guns of the 31st Bty to the Infantry in some of the guns are enemy. I am very glad to read the message from 85 & B & commdr. Nothing else to report. WWF	
12th July	Nothing to report.	
13th July	Heavy firing heard at 7.30 p.m. in evening. Balloon ascended, and reported heavy shelling on both sides in direction of BOESINGHE. Sixth Corps reported that Germans had shelled their front line trenches with heavy gas shell, and that they had retaliated. No infantry attack. German working party reported digging trench from O.19.c.94 – O.19.c.98 men wearing brown trousers & white shirts. Possibly civilian labour is being employed.	

Army Form C. 2118.

WAR DIARY
or
INTELLIGENCE SUMMARY.
(Erase heading not required.)

28th Div Arty.

Hour, Date, Place	Summary of Events and Information	Remarks and references to Appendices
WESTOUTRE July 14th.	The CRA and Lieut. Colonels Curely, 31st, 146th Brigades and O.C. Afqq reconnoitred positions occupied by the 1st and 2nd Northumbrian Brigade. The 27th Brigade 5th Division relieve 146th Bde & 28th Brigade " " 31st Bde These Brigades in turn relieve 1st & 2nd Northumbrian Brigade. 65th Howitzer Battery (one section) & these Afqq. All reliefs to take place on nights of 16/17 and 17/18th. At 8.45 pm the Germans exploded a mine in front of 4th 43 Trench. 62nd & 365th Batteries opened fire on a twelve opposite, and the enemy were unable to gain any advantage.	

Army Form C. 2118.

WAR DIARY
or
INTELLIGENCE SUMMARY.
(Erase heading not required.)

28th Divl Arty

Hour, Date, Place	Summary of Events and Information	Remarks and references to Appendices
WESTOUTRE 15th July	Battery commanders sent on during the morning to reconnoitre the positions they were to take over from the Northumbrian (50th) Division. At 1.30 p.m. Officer of 62nd Battery reported 3 Battalions of Germans moving North along road running through P2a P2a.	
16th July	1st sections of 31st & 146th Brigades were relieved by sections of 28th & 27th Brigades and in turn relieved sections 2nd & 1st Northumbrian Brigades. Relief reported complete at 11.10 p.m.	
17th July	Registration carried out in the morning. O.C.'s 31st & 146th handed over command at 12 noon, assuming command in new area at 6.0 p.m. At this hour the 10th Heavy Brigade came under the orders of C.R.A. 28th Division. Relief has been completed successfully at 1.40 a.m. 18th July.	

Army Form C. 2118.

WAR DIARY
or
INTELLIGENCE SUMMARY.

(Erase heading not required.)

113   28th Divl Arty.

Hour, Date, Place	Summary of Events and Information	Remarks and references to Appendices
WESTOUTRE 18th July	C.R.A. visited the Batteries of 10th Heavy Brigade during morning.	
19th July	18th B. Battery shot with aeroplane observation. Balloon co-operated + sent in this observation. Correct Co-ordinates obtained in 7 rounds. Div Cmdr visited 10th Heavy Bty.	628. W/E
20th July	3rd B. again registered Targets with aeroplane observation. Observer dropped wireless machine at 9th plan received rounds later. Incl Maj DE BERRY who to relieve Col RUNDLE CRA joined.	W/E
21st July	Heavy registration with balloon aeroplane was successful, carried out. Some that in advice of firing fire was carried out from KEMMEL in the presence of CRA General PILCHER - 17 Divn. 3rd B. worked with aeroplane + registered some target by fire shortful morning. Two officers for battn of B. which is to relieve 3rd B. arrived + are attached to 3rd B.	
22nd July 17		
23rd July LOCRE CHATEAU	Aeroplane - shot with 87+9 - reduced to 1 - W Coy, has not succeeded from on account of the wind which prevents balloon from being up. RA HQ moved to LOCRE CHATEAU	

WAR DIARY
INTELLIGENCE SUMMARY

Army Form C. 2118.

114   28th Div Arty

Hour, Date, Place	Summary of Events and Information	Remarks and references to Appendices
LOCRE CHATEAU 24th July	Heavy Battery registered on balloon templates on different targets. Seen starting. Flying and balloon registered two front seen starting. At 9.30 PM a shot at MESSINES - organised by II Corps Artillery - by 1st 6th Siege, 2, 4.7 Batteries & Canadian Heavy Batteries, Experiment rather was carried out. 62nd Bty attery	
25th July	A shoot with a heavy battery on two balloons was attempted during the afternoon but did not work satisfactorily. The heavy was also invited out by the Balloon at the full of the river head the battery. Shoot post-poned till tomorrow. 62nd Battery moved into Canadian area where German trenches can be enfiladed.	
26th July	Balloon Heavy Battery shoot not executed. The area to be found by CRA Moved Right to Canadian 33 T. Joint lik scene in 8 rounds. Still himself thus by himself. Great activity of enemy aeroplanes over whole divisional area. Inft.	
27th July	Looking patrol fired at but there was not so much activity on that has been noticed. Lot of German diggers. Lt. J H Strink commanded 33 Trench than the battery whereas it can mortar	
28th July	62nd Battery went into action in its new position. Which is strongly held by 3rd Bay Cands for tactical purposes. Exp is the 62nd under 145th Bde Cmdr.	15th Heavy Bty shoot under control of III Corps HAR. Memorial Roll of Officers attached.

Army Form C. 2118.

WAR DIARY
~~INTELLIGENCE SUMMARY~~
(Erase heading not required.)

28th Division Arty. /15

Instructions regarding War Diaries and Intelligence Summaries are contained in F.S. Regs., Part II. and the Staff Manual respectively. Title pages will be prepared in manuscript.

Hour, Date, Place	Summary of Events and Information	Remarks and references to Appendices
LOCRE CHATEAU (28 Cont)		
29 July	Owing to B" B" having taken over from the 63rd & 4th Trenches H.S. etc. To which an annex by the 365 Battery, that battery in place under Tactical control of O.C. 31st B.A. when Artillerie cover the C.+ B.M. front. MtE	
	A combined shoot was carried out by the 2nd Siege Battery — After Howitzer, the 3rd Canadian Artillery on the HOSPICE – WITSCHAETE. The results are not known, but the North end, which is used for observing home was distinctly hit. MtE	
30 July		
3.30 AM	Heavy firing heard to North.	
3.35 AM	3rd Bde Army up. They reported that firing appeared much further North.	
4.45 AM	Firing continued. So 10th H. Bde was rung up and reported to shoot on probable gun emplts.	
5.0 AM	Balloon asked for hours & to put hostiles on to any batteries seen firing. Balloon reported to wish to see enemy gun flashes, but it would seem 5th attack to between ZILLEBEKE POND and HOPE.	
5.15 AM	R.F.C. asked for an aeroplane to look for Hostile B⁵ reported on about 5th.	
5.20 AM	The French H.A.R. informed M.F.E. G.M. Lyt Section No 2 Mountain Battery under 2Lt H.A.S. WORTLEY joined Divnl Artillery.	
3 PM	Heavy firing to S.S.W.II.	

Army Form C. 2118.

WAR DIARY
or
INTELLIGENCE SUMMARY.
(Erase heading not required.)

116.   28th Divn Arty

Hour, Date, Place	Summary of Events and Information	Remarks and references to Appendices
COCRE CHATEAU. 31st July	Heavy firing during the night but have not prevented storming of Kemmel from being accounted communication to enemy trenches. During after examination of some trenches hints was carried out by Balloon observation. W.F.	

AG Bear
Brig 28th Divnl Artillery for
July, turnovver
1st August 1915.

Witspoen.
ing power
for AZ. Pa
28 Div

Brigade Major R.A.

    28th Division.

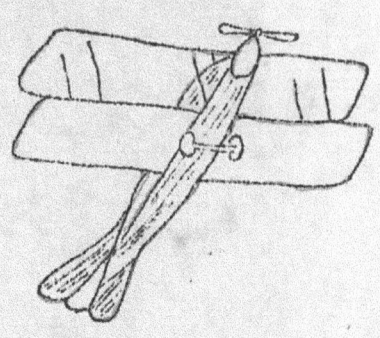

    Rough sketch of German aeroplane seen yesterday at 5.45 a.m. This is the ALBATROS scout and this is the first time it has been seen by this section.

Peculiarities :- Planes short and of same length, very slight stagger and dihedral, closed in fusillage, albatros tail.

    Machine is much smaller than the ordinary Albatros biplane. Out of range when seen.

                                      sd/ J.B. Leefe Capt.RGA

7.7.1915.   Commanding 10th Anti-air-craft.

Officer Commanding,

                For information.

                                          Ferguson. Major.

7.7.1915.   Brigade Major R.A. 28th Division.

Items of Interest.   15th July 1915.

Yesterday morning at 6.30 a.m. a German aeroplane circled over the 3rd Brigade dummy battery and dropped a light. This was shortly followed by a heavy bombardment of salvos from a Howitzer Battery.
The Officer Commanding 1st York and Lancaster Regiment forwards the following extracts from reports sent in by Company Officer.

O.C. 'B' Company reports in J.1. As a result of firing by our Artillery on N.W. corner of Petit Bois, enemy's trench Mortars were quiet during the night. The first few rounds on Petit Bois about 9.15 p.m. July 14th, must have been very close to the Mortar which has fired on J.1 during the last few days. In H.3 the flash of a trench
     Mortar which was firing in front of the G. trench after the explosion of the mine, appeared to come from a point about 50 yards N.E. of road running diagonally through right hand corner of H.24.c. (sheet 28) and just in rear of German trenches.

O.C. 'D' Company in J.2. reports – Immediately following the explosion of the mine to my right the enemy began throwing trench Mortars in to the area of the explosion. From my position in J.3 Right I was able to locate one of these guns in right edge of Petit Bois (100^x half right from J.3 Right) I therefore opened fire from J.3 Right on this area and was about to signal to the Artillery to do so too, but they had apparently already been given this target which they shelled accurately and completely silenced the Mortar.
There has been no mention of any trench Mortars having fired on our trenches since last night.

                                                      P.R.Burkhardt
                                                                       Captain.
15.7.1915.   for Brigade Major W.A. 28th Division.

A.a.G.H.Q./280/2 (C)   2nd Corps Q.C. 619/7   28th Divn. 2209/7.
R.A. 28th Divn. 1952.

- - - - - - - - - - - -

2nd Army.

It has been found that Dibromoxylene has little effect except on the eyes, and that "goggles" form an adequate protection. A selected type of "goggle" has been ordered through Ordnance Services on a scale of one per man of Formations at the front.

Experiments are being carried out to find a solution capable of neutralising this substance in shell holes and trenches for use as a spray. Promising results are being obtained and progress will be reported to you later.

        sd/- C.F.Macready Lt.General.
11th July 1915.   A.G. British Army in the Field.

Officer Commanding,

     Forwarded for your information, in continuation of this Office circular memo No. as above, dated 7th instant.

        C.R.Burkhardt Captain
17th July 1915. for Brigade Major, R.A. 28th Division.

SUBJECT :- Target Reports and Progress Reports.

B/62

Attention is drawn to Divisional Artillery Routine Order No. 322 dated 25th June 1915.

Target Reports - must not be mixed up with Progress Reports. The Target Report is a tabulated register of all targets fired at during the day, including registration, which should be stated. e.g. "registered on ---- -----" vide sample of Target Report issued.

The Progress Report is a diary of the days events, in which should be included -

    (a) More or less important or interesting targets which have or have not been fired at, such which justify a description, and, if fired at, the effect obtained.

    (b) Movement of the enemy.

    (c) Work done or being done by the enemy.

    (d) Information about anything seen, such as -
        1. A suspected observing station.
        2. A suspected machine gun emplacement.
        3. The building of a redoubt.
        4. Flashes or lights seen.
        5. New trenches being made or existing ones improved.
        6. In fact anything new or altered in the hostile area.

The day for the purpose of these reports is from 3.0 p.m. to 3.0 p.m. and if kept written up during the day and not left until the last moment, should be despatched a very few minutes after 3.0 p.m.

Brigade Commanders will cause suitable arrangements to be made for the collection and despatch of these reports. Mounted orderlies should be sent to suitable points near Observation Posts to which dismounted orderlies from Observation Posts can take the reports at a given time.

                                                                                       To.

To save time these reports may be sent direct to Divisional Artillery Headquarters, but this is a matter for Brigade Commanders to settle, - they should in any case receive a copy.

The object of the Progress Report is to enable a Report in the daily "doings" and "observations" of the Artillery, to be made out for the information of the G.O.C. the Division and Infantry generally.

The only satisfactory Progress Reports received so far have been those of the 62nd and 365th Batteries.

-o-o-o-o-o-o-o-o-o-o-o-o-o-o-

Officer Commanding,

31st Brigade R.a.

-o-o-o-o-o-o-o-o-o-o-o-

For your information, and necessary action.

M Fergusson. Major.

20.7.1915. Brigade Major R.A. 28th Division.

-o-o-o-o-o-o- I T E M S   O F   I N T E R E S T -o-o-o-o-o-o-

21st July 1915.

(1) Work was seen going on in O.31.a.3.5. from T.18.a.2.7.
It is thought that working party at SPANBROUCK MOLEN is
making communication trench to their first line.
L.4 trench reported men seen entering farm O.31.a.4.0.
Party seen working between L.4. and ruins N.36a.7.4.
5 four horsed wagons were seen moving to MESSINES and
returning.   Working parties also seen at O.25.a.9.9. and
O.25.d.2.5.

(2) A suspected trench mortar position is at N.18.d.10.8.
This should be watched and more information sent in
regarding it.

(3) Item No. 5 of yesterday should read S.E. corner of N.20.c.
In same place yesterday at 5.30 p.m. men were seen coming
up in two's and three's and afterwards appeared carrying
planks about.   Two Officers turned up in a dogcart.

(4) At P.2.d.2.3. at 5.0 p.m. yesterday a company of Infantry
halted on the road and was addressed by a mounted Officer
who came from the house in P.8.b.
N.C.O's were seen urging on the stragglers.   It is
suggested that this house is a Battalion Headquarters.
At 2.0 p.m. a company was seen drilling near the same
place.
In the same place there are a lot of white crosses
scattered over the ground.   They have not the appearance
of graves.   It is wondered what they are for.

(5) Flashes were seen last night at -
N.W. corner of PETIT BOIS.
L. of brickstack about O.13.c.8. (or 9.) 1 probably behind
a hedge or a reverse slope L. of VIERSTRAAT) WYTSCHAETE
Road O.15. centre.

M.Ferguson Major
BmRA.

ITEMS OF INTEREST
{o}{o}{o}{o}{o}{o}{o}

22nd July 1915.

B/91

1.   Work still continues at SPANBROEK MOLEN where the Germans appear to work right out in the open in spite of being continually fired on by our guns.

2.   Working party seen at O.25.a.9.8. in redoubt. Enemy seen carrying timber at N.30.d.3.9., N.30.c.4.5., and N.30.c.7.5.
The principle work seems to be carried on in the front trench close to our advanced work in N.30.c.3.3.

3.   Lights have been seen at night some distance behind WYTSCHAETE - MESSINES Road. Lamp signalling appears to be   carried on about O.26.c.5.5.

4.   A fatigue party was shelled as it moved along road O.36.a.10.5 to O.36.a.8.7. and dispersed.

5.   At 10.0 p.m. last night a large fire was visible in the direction of MESSINES or beyond.

C.R.Burkhardt Capt
for Major.

Brigade Major R.A. 28th Division.

ITEMS OF INTEREST
-o-o-o-o-o-o-o-

26th July 1915.

1.   Two German aeroplanes were brought down by us last night. One fell at MAPLE COPSE I.23 24. The other was shot down by one of our airmen and fell at I.34.d.5.6.

2.   Machine gun in Black Redoubt was very active last night and was taken on by 62nd Battery at 10.0 p.m. at request of infantry. Fire apparently effective as the gun remained silent for the rest of the night.

3.   A working party of the 5th Lancers at N.26.d. in full view of the Germans drew fire near some of the observing stations from guns whose flash was seen on bearing of 86° true from KEMMEL Tower.

4.   Working parties seen and fired on at O.25.a.8.8., N.30.c.3.3., O.32.a.6.3., and U.2.a.5.10, O.31.d.2.8. South West corner of Bois de WYTSCHAETE.

5.   366th Battery fired on two occasions yesterday afternoon to stop the bombing of N.15 trench.

6.   At 8.40 p.m. O.3 trench was shelled by short range gun from the East, which was probably trying to find the trench mortar Battery. The 75th Battery retaliated on German trench opposite.

7.   The 116th Battery is registering with balloon observation this afternoon. Results not yet known. The shoot with double observation which was attempted yesterday was not a success - the balloon had to come down.

8.   At 7.0 p.m. last night an unusual amount of smoke was seen behind the German first line trenches in front of the BOIS de WYTSCHAETE about N.24.d.4.8.

9.   A/49th Battery reports a German Battalion seen at 1.5 p.m. moving East or South East on a road which is thought to be the WYTSCHAETE - WARBEEK Road.

10.   A Whizbang is suspected of living in or behind the BOIS de WYTSCHAETE - a flash was seen from H.4. trench. Can we get any more definite information about this.

11.   The shoot of the Heavy Battery on the brickstack is reported to have completely obliterated the observing station there.

12.   A number of men in Two's and three's seen on the road at O.15.b.5.6.
        2 or 3 men were seen to enter house in clump of trees in O.13.d.5.5.

13.   The square barn at O.24.d.1.1. has had the sacking removed from the window since   yesterday. It is probably slept in at night.

14.   What appears to be a loophole for a machine gun has been noted in salient trench at O.24.c.7.1. Should like more information about this.

15.   Registration and retaliation carried out as usual.

16.   The balloon was shot at both in the morning and afternoon, but none of the shell appeared very close to it.

V.R.Burkhardt Capt
                    Major R.A.
Brigade Major R.... 28th Division.

ITEMS OF INTEREST
-o-o-o-o-o-o-o-

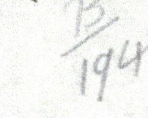

29th July 1915.

(1)   At 3.30 p.m. this afternoon the 21st Siege Battery, in cooperation with the 3rd Divisional Artillery, attempted to destroy the HOSPICE.   The building itself was not actually hit direct.
     The Germans replied with 5.9" shrapnel and 8.2" H.E. on KEMMEL.

(2)   Retaliation was carried out on following :-
On Mortar N.36.d.7.3. which was bombing D.1., opposite trench 15 which was being bombed on several occasions, and at N.18.b.2.5. at request of Infantry who were being shelled.

(3)   Working parties have been seen and fired on at -
N.30.c.2.8. near SPANBROEK MOLEN.
O.32.c.1.7.
N.30.d.9.6.

(4)   149th Battery observer located a sniper on the top of SPANBROEK MOLEN.

(5)   B/79 Battery of 17th Division commenced registration today.
     62nd Battery started registering in its new position.

(6)   Three batteries report having seen the new markings on German aeroplanes.

(7)   18th Battery report having seen 2 guns and 1 wagon moving N.W. from P.1.

8.   Flashes seen about O.25.c.9.5. - thought to be 8.2" shooting in direction of PLOEGSTEERT at 8.10 - 8.25 p.m.
last night.

(9)   A British Field Battery, in the direction of YPRES, is reported to have been very busy firing gun fire at 10.0 p.m. last night.   A farm was also observed burning in the direction of DICKEBUSCH.

10.   One observer reports having seen a woman walking about at O.25.d.3.3. which is curious, as the inhabitants were believed to have been removed from the vicinity of the German line.

(11)   Ten or twelve salvos (each of three rounds) were fired from direction of BOIS QUARANTE last night and fell near K.L. farm.

          sd/   V.H. FERGUSSON   Major R.A.
          Brigade Major R.A. 28th Division.

| 2nd Army | 2nd Corps. | 28th Divn | 28th R.A. |
| I.G.862 (21/5) | G.608 | G.324 | 2122 |

B/191

2nd Corps.

      As very little information is available regarding gas shells employed by the enemy, it is particularly desirable that all possible details should be collected to throw light upon the subject, especially as regards the nature of the fuzes and calibre of the guns.

25th July 1915.
                sd/ B. WALCOT Captain G.S.
                for M.G.G.S. 2nd Army

Officer Commanding,

      For information and necessary action.

                                      Major.

29.7.1915.   Brigade Major R.A. 28th Division.

ITEMS OF INTEREST
-o-o-o-o-o-o-o-

B/231

30th July 1915.

1. A dark coloured doorway is reported to have been erected to fill up a breech made in the wall of the farm at N.18.d.10.2.

2. Trench Mortar in front line trench at N.W. corner of PETIT BOIS was engaged at 4.45 p.m. and silenced.
 Another Mortar at N.30.c.2.8. opposite F.2. was silenced.
 What appears to be an emplacement for a trench mortar has been constructed at N.24.d.5.10.

3. A test call was replied to by 118th Battery in 6 seconds from the time the message was received at O.P.

4. Working parties seen and fired on at -
 N.30.a.6.1. (behind SPANBROEK MOLEN)
 N.30.c.1.9. at request of Infantry who assisted observation
 O.25.a.10.8.
 O.19.c.10.5.
 On road O.32.b.3.2.

5. Movement was seen by 18th Battery observer in the most southerly house in WYTSCHAETE.

6. A/49th Battery reports that at 8.15 p.m. last night a light was seen shining at irregular intervals, varying from 3 to 16 seconds on a bearing of 148° magnetic from KEMMEL TOWER. The light continued throughout the night and was still showing at 11.30 a.m. this morning.

7. Retaliation was carried out several times during the 24 hours on the German trenches opposite N.15 by the 366th Battery at the request of the Infantry.
 The time was taken on three occasions as being 20, 30, and 40 seconds from receipt of order to gun being fired.

8. An observer reports that he thinks he detected the flashes of field guns near the east end of BOIS L'ENFER (O.25d) This point should be watched.

9. The 10th Anti Aircraft section fired six series at hostile aeroplanes during the day.

sd/ V.M. FERGUSSON Major R.A.
Brigade Major R.A. 28th Division.

28th Divisional Artillery

Routine Orders

No. 213.

31st July 1915.

400. **Court Martial.** A Field General Court Martial composed as under will assemble at the Headquarters, 146th Brigade Ammunition Column, at 10.0 a.m. on Monday 2nd August 1915 for the trial of the undermentioned N.C.O. and men and such other accused persons as may be brought before it.
PRESIDENT :- Major G.S. Hoare 28th D.A.C.
MEMBERS :- A Captain 31st Brigade R.F.A.
A Subaltern 146th Brigade R.F.A.

No. 39104 Cpl. P. McGovern 366th Battery R.F.A.
No. 91159 Dr. J. Kilmartin)
No. 61301 Dr. P. Ford   ) 146th Brigade A.C.

The accused to be warned and all witnesses directed to attend.

401 **Blankets.** Reference G.R.O. 930. Officers Commanding will arrange to return to D.A.D.O.S. before 12.0 noon on 2nd proximo, 75% of all winter blankets. A report as to the handing over of these blankets to be rendered to this office not later than 2p.m. on the same day.

402. **Orders.** The attention of all concerned is directed to the following orders.
Claims for Damages. G.R.O. 1036
Monthly Army List G.R.O. 1041
War Loan G.R.O. 1045

C.R. Burkhardt Captain.
Staff Captain R.A. 28th Division.

ITEMS OF INTEREST
-o-o-o-o-o-o-o-

31st July 1915.

1. A/49th Observer reports that at 11.0 a.m. this morning he saw two triangular flags - having the top post white and the lower red - erected in the German lines about 50 yards behind the front line trenches and a hundred yards South of SPANBROEK MOLEN.
   They were displayed for about 15 minutes.
   The points of the poles - which were 25 to 50 yards apart - were inclined inwards. This signal is supposed to indicate that the space between the two flags has been captured by the Germans, and it may have been displayed to inform our Infantry that the enemy had succeeded in occupying a trench or two in the salient.

2. Some German heavy shell - probably 8.29 inch - fell in the Grounds of KEMMEL Chateau on the 29th instant. The bearing of two of the rounds was taken and read 101° and 106° magnetic respectively from the Chateau. The fuze Dopp Zo/92 was set at 25.6
   3.2

3. A/49 reports a Howitzer Battery, probably a 4.2 inch, fired yesterday on F.2 and F.4 trenches. The O.C. saw the flash which appeared to come from the west edge of L'ENFER WOOD. If this is correct the battery has been pushed very close up.

4. Working parties were seen and fired on at following places :-
   N.30.c.2.8. behind SPANBROEK MOLEN plank carriers, O.25.a.9.8. which is suspected of being a battery position, Red Chateau.

5. Retaliation has been carried out on
N.30.c.3.7.   opposite L.2
N.30.a.4.6.   "   F.5
O.36.a.   2   15   on several occasions for rifle
                                 grenade fire.
N.30.c.5.4.   "   L.1 for crumping
N.30.d.4.3.   "   L.1 for rifle grenade fire
N.24.c.8.4.   "   G.4 Infantry being shelled.

6. 9.50 a.m. A/49th Observer reports hostile aeroplane with new design in red was seen at WULVERGHEM.

7. The magnetic bearing of the guns which put about 45 shrapnel into LINDENHOEK Cross Roads at 1.45 p.m. yesterday and set alight to a building there is 105° from KEMMEL TOWER.

8. Observers report having watched the heavy firing last night apparently about YPRES, and endeavoured to get bearing to flashes, but were unable accurately to do so, on account of the mist.
   The signal for the attack was a shower of rockets all along the front, and the guns opened at once.
   A red flare was seen to go up more than once, upon which the enemy's fire was redoubled, and the bursts appeared to be in the
                       in intensity
   direction of the flares.

9. In a Brigade test today the 365th Battery responded in 15 seconds. This was the record during the test.

                              sd/ V.M. FERGUSSON Major.
                              Brigade Major R.A. 28th Division.

28th Div.   2nd Corps.
G. 353.   G. 934.

B/274

28th Division.

Following message received from 6th Corps timed 11-35 p.m. 30th, is forwarded for your information:-

"G. 644. 30. Result of enquiry into use of liquid fire by Germans this morning at HOOGE briefly as follows AAA Position held by enemy very quiet no reply to bombing A A A Loopholes observed eighteen inches square concealed AAA Sudden appearance of mines apparently without explosion AAA Then five jets of fire appeared west of crater and fifteen jets east of it AAA Flames ten feet high lasted two minutes smoke twenty feet high on a front of one hundred to one hundred and fifty yards AAA Germans advanced in irregular groups without masks or respirators getting over parapet almost simultaneously with fire AAA Heavy bombardment of supports AAA Jets of flame thirty to forty yards long AAA Moral effect and element of surprise very great but actual damage slight no one seriously burned AAA Germans preceded attack by firing two shells some distance in rear of trenches and two hundred and fifty yards apart AAA these shells did not explode but burst into flames which burned for about ten minutes AAA Chief danger apparently surprise and panic".

2nd Corps.   SD/ ALICK RUSSEL, Lieut-Colonel,
31.7.1915.   for B.G.G.S.,

2.

83rd Infantry Brigade.
84th Infantry Brigade.
85th Infantry Brigade.
C.R.A., 28th Division.

         The result of the above emphasizes the importance of (i) strong support trenches about 80 to 100 yards in rear of front fire trenches, (2) strong continuous obstacles, wire entanglements etc., at least 30 to 40 yards in front of fire trenches (3) front fire trenches held comparatively lightly while support trenches are held strongly (4) all extra ammunition bombs etc., kept in support trenches ready to be instantly sent up to the fire trenches when required.

         It is important that all ranks should thoroughly understand this new method of war and realise that its success depends on surprise more than on any destructive effect.

         Therefore the men must be taught to keep cool and to fire straight.

31st July, 1915.   R.H.HARE, Lieut-Colonel,
                           General Staff, 28th Division.

10th Heavy Brigade R.G.A.
-o-o-o-o-o-o-o-

Rank	Name	Battery	Date of Joining	Class of Commission	Date of promotion to present rank	REMARKS.
Lt.Col.	Marshall	T.E.	H.Q.	9.4.15	Regular	31.5.13	Cmdg. Brigade
Capt.	Charles	E.E.	"	25.7.14	"		Adjutant
Lieut.	Crawford Clarke	R.W.B.	"	9.4.15	Spec. Res.	23.7.14	Ord. Officer
			27.5.15		6.3.14	
Major	Macalpine Leny, D.S.O.	W.H.	115th	26.9.14	Regular	30.10.14	Cmdg. Battery
Capt.	Hogg	O.F.G.	"	6.6.15	"	30.10.14	
Lieut.	Hartree	A.	"	15.1.15	"	19.12.14	
Lieut.	Milligan	E.D.	"	26.9.14	"	23.12.14	
Lieut.	Bolsover	G.	"	14.2.15	Spec. Res.	12.8.12	
2/Lt.	Addenbrooke Prout	R.	"	9.2.15	Temporary	5.10.14	
Major	Sweyne, D.S.O.	O.R.	116th	6.9.14	Regular	30.10.14	Cmdg. Battery
Capt.	Becker	L.A.B.	"	5.3.15	"	30.10.14	
Lieut.	Floyd	B.E.	"	9.9.14	"	23.7.13	
Lieut.	Banks	C.D.A.S.	"	31.3.12	"	23.7.13	
Lieut.	Wildey	A.W.G.	"	13.9.11	2	23.12.13	
2/Lt.	Borrowdaile	G.H.A.	"	10.12.14		22.7.13	
2/Lt.	Hill	W.	"	2.7.15	Temporary	30.1.15	
Major	Rolland	C.E.	12th	28.1.15	Regular	7.9.14	Cmdg. Battery
Capt.	Briggs Davison	J.	"	5.11.14	"	21.12.13	
2/Lt.	Russell	A.	"	10.10.14	Temporary	7.10.14	
2/Lt.	Dick	H.P.	"	12.10.14	"	9.10.14	
2/Lt.	Sale	S.E.	"	7.2.15	"	16.1.15	
2/Lt.	Watkins	W.L.	"	12.2.15	Regular	10.2.15	
2/Lt.	Patch	R.A.	"	11.7.15	Temporary	24.2.15	

121/6598

38th Division

HdQd RA. 28th Division

Vol VIII

From 1 - 31. 8. 15

WAR DIARY or INTELLIGENCE SUMMARY.

Army Form C. 2118.

28th Div Arty.

Hour, Date, Place	Summary of Events and Information	Remarks and references to Appendices
LOCRE CHATEAU. 1st August	Owing to the mist it was impossible for observers to get readings to hostile guns which fired on YPRES during the night. A test of communications was held in 3rd B⁴⁵. M/y(How) Battery was registered during the morning by Reman hear Kelley with aeroplane observation. A new position was selected. WµF	
2nd August	5 in Naval Gun put a round into BAILLEUL at 9 am. The demolition of German aerial was interrupted by the RA wireless mast. 2 B⁴⁵ Communications that were carried out by the 146 B⁴⁵. WµF	
3rd August	It was decided owing to the unsettled nature of the front amongst Infy B⁴⁵ that the 62nd Battery should be withdrawn from its enfilade position — its place being taken by a battery (149) of 146 B⁴⁵ — should rejoin the 3rd B⁴⁵.	
4th August	CRA, OC 3 146 B⁴⁵, OC (49) B⁴⁵, visited 62nd Battery position. News received from RA Army that 2 Horse Batteries in 10 Division front to army. WµF	
5th August	CRA visited trenches to inspect the work done by No 2 Wire Battery in the way of improving positions. 149 Battery Commander relief 9/62 Battery in its enfilade position on night 5/6. WµF	
6th August	Nothing to report.	
7th August	B/89 Howitzer Battery joined the Divisional Artillery was affiliated with the 3rd B⁴⁵ in whose area it will work. WµF	Nominal Roll of Officers attached

Army Form C. 2118.

WAR DIARY
or
INTELLIGENCE SUMMARY.
(Erase heading not required.)

118   28th Division

Hour, Date, Place	Summary of Events and Information	Remarks and references to Appendices
LOCRE CHATEAU 8th August	Officers & specialists 123rd I.B. attached to 28th Div Arty for 8 days instruction. HQ & B Btys to 3rd B.A. A & D Btys to 3rd. D Bty to 146th. C Bty Battery also to 108/145. A/73 How Battery joined Div Arty & affiliated with 3rd R.B.A. MiE	Nominal roll of officers attached
9th August	To create a diversion during an attack which was delivered on another part of the initial front, the 28th Div Arty bombarded SPAN-BROEK MOLEN. Bombardment in two phases. 3. 5-3.10 A.M. Field batteries 18 prs. & 5 in. Bty firing on the firm trenches behind, aimed at the MOLEN. 3.20 to 3.40 A.M. on fig 2 How. 4.5" & 4.7" Hos. Divisional Artillery manned. The batteries were arranged to explode the trenches & bombardment. Little activity was aroused. fire, support from our machine guns. Day has been too windy to judge of results. MiE	
10 August	Aeroplane reported SPANBROEK MOLEN completely destroyed. Corps Commander expressed dissatisfaction with communication between batteries Kemmel & C Trenches. MiE	
11th August	Divisional Commander inspected 146th Bde positions & a test call from trenches to east during the inspection by a staff officer. One battery reported in 30 seconds, the other five in 40. Divnl Cmdr quite satisfied. MiE	

Army Form C. 2118.

WAR DIARY
or
INTELLIGENCE SUMMARY.
(Erase heading not required.)

119   28th Div Arty.

Hour, Date, Place	Summary of Events and Information	Remarks and references to Appendices

LOCRE CHATEAU

12th August — Mountain Artillery Section continued preparing emplacement, bringing the total up to 57.
A blind trench mortar shell was measured today. It is 41 inches long 9.2 in diameter. Capt Commander inspected trenches.

13th August — Divisional commander inspected 146th Bty. A staff officer in the trenches sent call for fire during the inspection. One battery responded in 30 something or other in 40 seconds.
SPANBROEKMOLEN was seen clearly & considerable damage noted. MESSINES Tower again made an object in station. Heavies ordered to deal with it.

14th August — Emplacements in C trenches completed by Mountain Artillery Section. Total on 94, 185 & 5th Bdy front is now 9.
Nothing to report.

15th August — A test was carried out by the Divn of R.A. communication from batteries had batteries. Divnl Cmdr directed first that terminal on various points of Capt Commanders front. Some delay caused on front of Bryant as the Bdres were given before the hour decided upon, in batteries knew this infantry had not cleared the trenches then challenged the order of the target & would not fire.

MWF

Army Form C. 2118.

WAR DIARY
or
INTELLIGENCE SUMMARY.
(Erase heading not required.)

28th Div'nl Artillery

120

Hour, Date, Place	Summary of Events and Information	Remarks and references to Appendices

LOCRE CHATEAU

16th August — The 3rd L.B. engaged a new German redoubt opposite trench No. 4. B/64 Battery made direct hits. It is considered that the redoubt which is being driven from the redoubt is very close to our trenches. A mine is being driven from our trenches. In the afternoon some experiments were carried out by a form of the 149th B.S. on small Concrete protection but up to the R.E. The T.N.T. Guncotton very good detonation.

17th August — Two aerial fired at German redoubt opposite trench No. 4 to the trenches but did great damage done. It is impossible to tell any material damage with 4.5" How. & the trenches are too close for any thing heavier to be employed. If mm 4.5 in. Amunt were available we have damage might be effected.

18th August — Lord Kitchener, the French Pres. have him to visit 28th Div'nl area. In his representation 9/D and Artillery heads for his inspection. Lord Kitchens after lunch visit the SCHERPENBERG where the C in C Commander saluted the troops for the firm to be turned out to. This has been and at the first troop each 4 battalion had fired six round Volley for 5 seconds in 2 mins 1st Battn. in 1.2 min. etc.

19th August — CRA went round listen to shells inspected 33rd T.H. Battery.

Army Form C. 2118.

WAR DIARY
or
INTELLIGENCE SUMMARY.
(Erase heading not required.)

28th Divnl Arty

121

Hour, Date, Place	Summary of Events and Information	Remarks and references to Appendices
LOCRE CHATEAU 20th August	Consolidated position for a battery which the 7th Divn wish to place in 28th Divnl Area to replace to front of their Divn.	
21st August	Barium tine tests carried out with the 3rd Bde with satisfactory results. W.F.	
22nd August	CRA 17th Divl Arty visited position allotted on the 20th. Arranged with CRE that in providing timber etc for dug out & material for horse line etc — The OC CoRE attached to affiliated Bdes should deal direct with FA Bde Cmdr. In this way it is hoped [illegible] may be saved. W.F.	
23rd August	One howitzer in 368 Bty — one in 47 Bty how, no damage done. They say some Bty O.Ps were hit. 366th Battery scored several direct hits on a H.Q. Cmdg post.	
24th August	Greater activity amongst enemy heavy guns, hence aeroplane strut.	
25th August	Left Section of No 2 how battery completed 12 aeroplanes met in front of the Division.	
26th Aug	Greater activity of enemy aeroplanes.	
9.30–10.30 P.M.	Sound of Zeppeline on POPERINGHE received.	
27th Aug	Selection of Gun position in rear wood line for close defence completed.	

Army Form C. 2118.

WAR DIARY
or
INTELLIGENCE SUMMARY.
(Erase heading not required.)

122   28th Div Arty

Hour, Date, Place	Summary of Events and Information	Remarks and references to Appendices

LOCRE CHATEAU 28th August Major T.S. Cafu resumed command of the 18th Battery - vice Major Eo. LEWIN - now Brevtr 12 Div Art. mF

28th August Nothing to record. mF

30th " Nothing to record mF

31st " Heavy Enemy Offensive to turn 8 in Hrs on PECKHAM but infantry able to hear short Tomorrow instead. mF

Items of Interest for 24 hours ending 3.0 p.m. 1st August 1915.
----

1.   75th and 366th Batteries carried out registration on some unseen localities by means of balloon observation. Two balloons were tried first but the method was found very slow.

2.   Working parties were seen and fired on at -
O.19.c.2.4.
N.36.b.7.9.
O.32.b.3.6.   Series effective. Some men carried away on stretchers Others on mens backs.
N.30.c.4.7.   Boards being carried in SPANBROEK MOLEN.
O.13.c.3.6.
N.30.c.2.7.

3.   Fire in retaliation.
Opposite G.2.   Made things much quieter
N.30.c.2.8. opposite F.2.

4.   Flashes seen at -
9.56 p.m. on bearing 83° magnetic from 18th Battery O.P.
8.0 p.m.   "   "   86° true from N.26.c.2.8. Time between flash and report 20"

5.   A fire is reported at U.11.b. Observer suggests it was a barn or hayrick.

6.   Test calls.
18th Battery responded in 40"
69th   "   "   " 30" to call from F.5.

7.   Brown cottage O.13.c.3.3. orignally thought to be an observation station again shows signs of occupation.

8.   From 6.15 p.m. to 7.0 p.m. parties of men left LOMM TREE FARM O.32.b.14 and disappeared over the top of the crest. 50 or more men and a couple of cyclists must have left during this period.

9.   149th Battery distinctly saw a rifle fired from the top of SPANBROEK MOLEN at 7.5 p.m. This has been reported before as a certain snipers post.

10.   367th Battery carried out successfully visual signalling tests between trenches and observing stations last night and between Battery and O.P. this morning.
   69th Battery had successful signalling test between Battery and O.P.

11.   Near PLOEGHAM FARM between 7.0 and 8.0 p.m. red and white very's lights were let off. One white one was also observed which burst into several/stars.
                                white
12.   At 10.0 a.m. this morning an enemy aeroplane registered an Heavy Howitzer battery on one section of A/49, but scored no success.

13.   365th Battery again report having seen a hostile aeroplane with the new markings.

sd/ V.M. FERGUSSON Major.
Brigade Major R.A. 28th Division.

Items of Interest for 24 hours ending 3.0 p.m. 2nd August 1915.

1. The 15" naval gun that fired at CASSEL and DUNKIRK, dropped a shell into the Asylum at BAILLEUL at 9.0 a.m. The wireless operator at R.A.H.Q. immediately afterwards intercepted the observations being sent by an aeroplane - which was invisible owing to the clouds - to the battery, which reads as follows :- "One shot not observed. Appears to be well aimed. Not possible to come any closer. Am flying away"

2. A hostile aeroplane was brought down by one of our aviators this morning, and fell into the German lines. It was seen to fall by different observing officers, but the place could not be located with sufficient accuracy to engage it on the ground.

3. Working parties were seen and fired on at the following points
   O.32.b.7.2.
   N.30.c.3.7. Working party near SPANBROEK MOLEN.
   N.24.d.3.9. Behind 1st line trench. 5 men digging.
   Farm N.18.d.10.2. Infantry reported fire as excellent.
   O.14.c.9.6. 60 men. Series reported effective.
   O.32.c.0.6.

4. Fire in retaliation was carried out -
   opposite L.4. to stop rifle grenades.
   O.32.a.7.2. Trench 15 to stop bombing on several occasions.
   N.30.c.5.2. Trench opposite L.2. which was being crumped.
   N.30.c.5.2. opposite L.1. to stop rifle grenades.
   N.W. corner of PUMP BOIS for shelling of Infantry
   Opposite J.1. and J.2. to stop rifle grenades.

5. Test calls. 366th Battery responded in 30, 25, and 16 seconds to three Battery test calls and in 17 seconds to an appeal from No. 14 trench.

6. Flashes seen - 5 rounds
   10.15 p.m/Bearing 81.40 magnetic from N.26.c.2.7.
   7.35 p.m. 2 rounds. Bearing 123.0 magnetic from KEMMEL TOWER.

7. A German was seen to walk slowly across a field and enter a dugout at O.25.a.7.5 at 4.5 p.m. Shortly afterwards crumps began to fall on our trenches.

8. Farm house on Hill 64 - O.19.d.4.7. was on fire yesterday evening.

9. Between German front line trench and the right of L.1. there is reported to be a black and white flag supported on 2 poles.

10. Reference item 3 of 31st ultimo, O.C. 365th Battery reports that last January a small calibre howitzer Battery was known to be in this position. As far as Captain Yorke remembers, the square address was O.31.b.2.7.

11. More work is reported by the 69th Battery to have been done on the enemy's front trenches, opposite F.5 and G.1. Three small works can be observed from his observing station, which are not noticeable from the trenches.
    These works are about 20 yards apart and the centre one is at point N.30.a.4.5. and is probably a machine gun emplacement like the others.

2.

12. In return for some direct hits on the Black Redoubt N.30.a.4.4 by the 60 pounders, the enemy shelled F.4,5, and 6 heavily from 6.30 p.m. till dark.

13. A German Heavy Battery was registered on one of the Howitzer positions this morning, and bombarded it for some time.
When our Heavy Battery opened fire later on, the 4.5-inch Howitzer got the credit of doing the shooting and was crumped again.

14. The following description of the work proceeding in the enclosure of LONE TREE FARM -- whose correct square address is O 32 c O 6 -- is given by the 75th Battery.
"At 6.0 p.m. on 1st instant planks and beams were being taken into the enclosure from the communication trench which runs West from the MESSINES - WYTSCHAETE road and along the road from SPANBROEK MOLIN. The men disappear underground at the edge of the enclosure on both sides. A few heavy shell would be most beneficial. Heavy guns please note."

15. Five lights in the formation as shown in diagram were seen from KEMMEL TOWER and bearings were taken. They could not be seen by the naked eye. At 10.15 p.m. they were still shining.

sd/- V.H.FERGUSSON Major

Brigade Major, Royal Arty., 28th Divn.

B/314

Items of Interest for 24 hours ending 3.0 p.m. 3rd August 1915.
------

1.   Following wire was received yesterday from G.O.C. 85th Infantry Brigade.
         D.4 trench was troubled this afternoon by grenades and asked 62nd Battery for enfilade fire.
         Fusiliers report excellent effect entirely freed us from rifle grenades.
         Shell appeared to fall in enemy's support trenches left of D.4.

2.   Working parties were seen and fired upon at the following places :-
         South West corner PETIT BOIS - work stopped.
         Near SPANBROEK MOLEN.

3.   Shooting in retaliation is recorded as under :-
         N.W. corner of PETIT BOIS to stop shelling of trenches
         Shelling stopped.
         N.36.d.5.9. on front line trench - effective
         N.30.c.7.1 to stop shelling of trenches
         N.25.c.2.1.   "   "   "   "   "

4.   Flashes seen -
         11.5 p.m.   82° Magnetic from N.26.b.4.8.
         11.15 p.m.   70°   "   "   "   (3 flashes)
         11.20 p.m.   63°   "   "   "
         11.25 p.m.   70°   "   "   "   (3 flashes)
         11.40 p.m.   70°   "   "   "
         12.5 a.m.   78°   "   "   "
         12.20 a.m.   73°   "   "   "

5.   Brigade test was carried out this morning in the 31st Brigade the fire of the Batteries being concentrated successively on 4 different points.
         The 75th Battery were called up by the Infantry to fire on communication trench N.36.b.4.2. which entailed a switch of 10° and replied in 1 minute 20 seconds.

6.   18th Battery saw two trucks being handled on minature railway on a bearing of 91° magnetic from N.26.b.3.8.
         More information is required about the light railway.

7.   The trenches between Red Chateau O.13.c.4.6. and fork road O.13.c.3.8. have been strengthened since the heavy guns fired on them.

                                           sd/ V.M. FERGUSSON   Major.
                                           Brigade Major R.A. 28th Division.

Items of Interest for 24 hours ending 6.0 a.m. 5th August 1915.

1. Working parties seen and fired on at following points. -
    In communication trench in rear of SPANBROEK MOLEN.
    N.36.d.2.5. opposite trench 15, by request. Good series.
    N.30.c.3.7. near SPANBROEK MOLEN. Work stopped.
    N.3.b.7.2. Parties on road scattered

2. Series in retaliation fired on -
    N.24.a.6.9. Fire trench by request.

3. Battery zones having been slightly changed to accord with new Infantry fronts some registration was carried out.

4. Infantry report that some heavy object was being dragged about near SPANBROEK MOLEN. Observers should try and spot this and report on it.

5. The 69th Battery report that a mine was exploded in G.1 trench during the night. Nothing was seen or heard and no communication was received from the Infantry on the subject.

6. A lot of visual signalling tests were carried out both by day and night, all worked successfully except in the case of G.3 trench from which the expected light could not be seen. It is suggested that the Infantry may have lost the correct setting.

7. Flashes seen -

    5.0 p.m. 96° magnetic from KEMMEL Tower. Possibly an antiaircraft gun, as one was firing at the time. 4 flashes.
    8.30 p.m. 103° magnetic from KEMMEL Tower. 2 flashes.

8. The light was bad all day and very little movement was seen in the German lines.

    sd/ V.H. FERGUSSON Major

    Brigade Major R.A. 28th Division

B/384

Items of Interest for 24 hours ending 6.0 a.m. 6th August 1915.

1. At 4.30 p.m. the German trenches were decked with flags opposite the PETIT BOIS and suitably decorated notices were displayed referring to the fall of WARSAW.
   At 10.30 a.m. a white flag was waved about in front of the PETIT BOIS probably part of the rejoicing.
   A board decorated with German flags was also displayed from fire trench S.E. of SPANBROEK MOLEN.

2. A good deal of work has been done in the last two or three days behind the N.E. corner of PETIT BOIS at N.24.b.10.8. The ground which used to show green between the trees now shows freshly turned earth.

3. A heap of faggots has made its appearance at the Southern edge of DIAMOND WOOD. It is suggested that it was to conceal an observing station or possibly a gun for flanking defence. More information about this is required.

4. German observation balloon was up yesterday on a bearing of 68° magnetic from N.26.b.4.8.

5. Working parties fired on at -
   SPANBROEK MOLEN. Party did not resume work.
   N.36.d.3.3. In communication trench.
   N.30.c.6.6. SPANBROEK MOLEN.
   N.36.d.4.5. Opposite D.1.

6. Fire in retaliation was opened on -
   N.36 repeatedly to stop grenading of 14 trench. Observation was done by Infantry Officer in the trench. Commander of trench reported at 9.30 p.m. that the last series had been effective, as he had heard a whistle blown in the German trench which is the call for stretcher bearers. No more grenading.
   N.36.b.0.5. Opposite D.4., by request.
   O.31.b.2.0. BOIS L'ENFER, by request.
   N.30.c.5.0. Fire trench. To stop rifle grenades.

7. The 75th Battery reports a curious phenomenon. The clock on WULVERGHEM Church tower which has persisted for the last three weeks in making out the time to be 6.3. has now changed its mind and indicates 6.15 as being more probably correct. The clock is innocent of works.

8. In the reserve trench opposite D.4. an earth coloured box 4ft x 4ft x 2ft has made its appearance. There is a mirror on it which sometimes flashes in our direction. It would appear to be some sort of signalling device.

9. 69th Battery reports that there is a wall built trestle at
C.25.a.9.10 and to the south of this place there are a good many
yards of yellow canvas screens. Can more be found out about this.
Is it the light railway again?

10. At 6.30 p.m. a frame was erected opposite G.1. trench where
a saphead is suspected. Two trench flags were fastened to the
frame which it was thought might be connected with mining.
    The position was registered and one of the flags was carried
away during registration.

11. Between 8.30 p.m. and 9.3 p.m. 8 flashes of a gun were seen
on bearing of 105 magnetic from KEMMEL Tower.
    3 other flashes were seen on a bearing 113° from same place
and during same time.

                                sd/ V.M. FERGUSSON Major.

                            Brigade Major R.A. 28th Division.

28th Divisional Artillery
-o-o-o-o-o-o-o-o-o-o-

Items of Interest for 24 hours ending 6.0 a.m. 7th August 1915.

1. Working parties seen and fired on at -
    In front of F.2. at saphead, by request.
    O.32.b.2.6. Large party cutting crops. Work stopped.
    N.30.a.4.7. Putting up barbed wire.
    O.31.d.10.5. At LONE TREE farm.
    SPANBROEK CABARET.

2. Retaliation on -
    N.36.a.5.9. To stop fire on support trenches in rear of L.1 and 15.
    N.18.d.2.3. On fire trench.

3. Flashes seen -
    8.40 p.m. 81° magnetic from N.21.d.10.0. 1 flash appeared to be in the open near RED CHATEAU.
    6.30 p.m. Smoke ring of howitzer seen on bearing 79° magnetic from N.26.b.3.6. 3 rings were seen
    8.5. p.m. 110° from EIFFEL TOWER 3 flashes
    2.0 a.m. 82°   "   "   "   1 flash.

4. Enemy observation balloon was up on bearing of 67° magnetic from N.26.b.4.8. during afternoon.

5. 69th Battery suggest that the heavy object which the Infantry heard being moved about at SPANBROEK MOLEN may be one of the large beams of the Mill which were thrown about by the 60 pounder.

6. The screens near the trestle bridge mentioned in Item No. 9 of yesterday have been removed and earth works have been disclosed behind.
    The sandbags, reports the 69th Battery have been laid in a peculiar fashion. They appear to form letters, but, owing to the angle from which they are viewed, these cannot be read.

7. A new communication trench runs N. and S. into work 67. O.26.c.1.1.

8. 100th Battery reports that a lot of work has been put in on front trench at N.30.c.2.7. - transforming it into a redoubt - like black redoubt. The presence of a gun there is suspected.

9. Trench in front of house N.18.b.9.0. is reported by the 18th Battery to have been strengthened. What appears to be a machine gun emplacement is visible at S.W. end of trench.
    The wire in front of this position is very heavy.
    A new trench has been dug since the last clear day on North Western slopes of hill 57 - O.9.c.0.0.

10. The corn which was being cut O.32.b.2.6. is being placed in front of what appears to be strong wire entanglement at that place.

11. WULVERGHEM time is now 6.20 by the North face of the clock and 6.10 by the southern face.

12. A/49th Battery reports having seen men entering and leaving a dugout at O.25.a.7.5. also that a train was seen on the YPRES - COURTRAI railway moving in the direction of COMINES at 3.30 p.m. yesterday afternoon and another at 7.35 p.m.

sd/ V.M. FERGUSSON Major.

Brigade Major R.A. 28th Division.

B/452

28th Divisional Artillery
-o-o-o-o-o-o-o-o-o-o-o-o-

Items of Interest for 24 hours ending 6.0 a.m. 9th August 1915.

1. The bombardment of SPANBROEK MOLEN was carried out at 3.0am this morning, but with what results is not yet known, as a ground mist has prevented observation.

2. There was a heavy artillery fight last night between 7.0pm and 8.0pm in the vicinity of BOESINGHE and HETJAS.

3. Fire in retaliation opened on -
   N.36.a.7.6. fire trench to stop hand grenading.
   N.36.a.5.9. for 2 shell in support trench L.4.
   Opposite D.3. and 4 to stop grenading of those trenches
   Opposite H.2. fire trench for shelling of H.E. support trench.

4. Working parties seen and fired on at -
   N.36.a.7.9. 6 out of 40 men were knocked out.
   O.31.a.0.4. party dispersed.

5. 62nd Battery reports that behind German second line opposite K.1 and K.2 trenches, a third line is being built.
   The parapet along W. edge of PETIT BOIS has been heightened.
   In hedge N.18.d.4.2. a brushwood screen has been erected partially filling the gap. Near this are emplacements or dugouts which it is suggested are for machine guns.

6. Flashes seen from N.14.c.9.9. at 3.0 am on magnetic bearings of 89°, 87°, 85°, 84°. 3.20 am bearings 112°, 94°, and 105° from KEMMEL TOWER.

7. The 15 rounds which fell about H.2. trench between 2.15 and 2.45 pm appeared to come from just south of the line KEMMEL - WYTSCHAETE.

8. 25th Trench Howitzer Battery reports firing 2 heavy bombs yesterday evening from M.15 at the ground just beyond the mine crater which the enemy are suspected of sapping.

9. A Field Artillery Brigade of the 37th Division and a 4.5' Howitzer Battery are attached to 28th Divisional Artillery for 8 days instruction.

sd/ V.M. FERGUSSON Major.
Brigade Major R.A. 28th Division.

28th Divisional Artillery.

Items of Interest for 24 hours ending 6.0 a.m. 10th August 1915.

1. The light remained too bad yesterday to enable observers to estimate the damage done on SPANBROEK MOLEN, but the 84th Brigade report that a heavy shell fell on the Black Redoubt and caused much foul language from the Germans who left their trenches near that place. In other parts of the position visible from the observing station sand bags were seen to have been thrown about. An observer was asked to go out from the R.F.C. to report and he wired to say that SPANBROEK MOLEN appeared to be completely destroyed.

2. Working parties seen and fired on at -
    SPANBROEK MOLEN - some of the party were hit.

3. Fire in retaliation was opened on -
    N.30.c.1.10.
    N.36.a.8.8. by request. Trench howitzer temporarily silenced.

4. Flashes were seen at -
    10.30 pm on bearing 88½ and 76½ magnetic from N.26.b.2.7. Guns thought to be field guns.
    3.45 am 99½, 98 and 97½ magnetic from same place and guns thought to be heavy.
    11.0 p.m. on bearing 96 magnetic from N.33.d.1.5.
    Between 3.0 am and 3.40 am on 9th on bearing 121°, 107°, 102½°, 98½° and 94½° magnetic from N.26.c.1.9.
    3.16 am 9th on bearing 116.30' from N.26.c.2.7.
    4.10 am on bearing 92° and 93° from N.26.c.2.7.

5. The enemy has brought up a heavy trench howitzer with which much damage was done to D.4.
    It is supposed that there is more than one of these heavy howitzers, as three or four bombs were fired in a minute.
    The howitzer was located at N.36.a.9.5. and fire opened by two 18-pr batteries on the front and one on the flank and by 4.5' howitzer Battery.
    It is reported that our fire shifted it several times.
    A/49th Battery eventually located it again at N.36.d.6.1. and after firing a few rounds of lyddite the bombing ceased.
    The Infantry reported that a red rocket was sent up when the Trench Howitzer ceased firing.

6. 25th Trench Howitzer Battery reports having fired 18 light bombs from L.15 against enemy trenches in N.36.d. in retaliation. The bombs are described as being 30 ins long by 4" in diameter and the range was estimated at 500 to 600 yards.
    O.C. Battery says the field Artillery got quickly on to it and seemed to get the line well.

7. 33rd Trench Howitzer Battery reports the preparation of new emplacements and dugouts in a different area.
    He fired two rounds at N.24.d.8.3. where he takes the trench in enfilade.

                          sd/ V.M. FERGUSSON Major.

                Brigade Major R.A. 28th Division.

13.8.1915.

Brigade Test

	Target	Time taken
69th Battery	SPANBROEK MOLEN	15 seconds
100th Battery	HALDELSTEAD Farm	40 "
	Point 74	20 "
	" "	42 "
103rd Battery	SPANBROEK MOLEN	30 "
B/89th Battery	SPANBROEK MOLEN	5 minutes to 1st round
		7 minutes to 2nd round

Very slow, but messages had to be sent from new Brigade observation station to Headquarter billet to the Battery, as no wire available to lay out line direct

28th Divisional Artillery

Items of Interest for 24 hours ending 6.0 a.m. 14th August 1915.
-o-o-o-o-o-o-o-o-o-o-o-o-o-o-o-o-o-o-o-o-o-o-o-o-o-o-o-o-o-o-o-o-

1. Working parties seen and fired on at -
    N.30.a.6.4. opposite L.3.
    N.30.c.8.4. in support trench
    SPANBROEK MOLEN work stopped for day. Fire appeared
                    very effective.

2. About 11.0 a.m. a party was seen occupied with some work on the top of MESSINES TOWER. As this is suspected of being an observing station, the 75th Battery opened fire. The work stopped for the time.
    The 3rd Group H.A.R. have been asked to put some 9.2 inch into it.

3. KEMMEL was shelled with 8.inch yesterday evening and the 3rd Group H.A.R. were asked to "crump" MESSINES.

4. The 366th Battery report new trenches behind the German first line opposite our No. 15 trench.

5. The farm at T.6.a.3.3. was shelled steadily for an hour yesterday with 5.9" shell.

6. 118th Battery fired, by request, on a snipers post constructed in a willow tree between the front line trenches at N.24.c.5.4

7. At 4.30 p.m. 84th Brigade reported that some loopholes had been constructed in German trench opposite No. 14. They asked to have them destroyed.
    A/49th Battery fired on them and it is reported to have done a certain amount of damage to the parapet in that place, but did not get any of the loopholes.

8. Both Trench Howitzer Batteries report a quiet day in the trenches. Neither Battery fired. The H.Q. of the 33rd Trench Howitzer Battery has moved to SLIGL FARM.

9. O.C. Mountain Artillery has now completed 9 emplacements in the 84th and 85th Brigade trenches.

                            sd/ V.M. FERGUSSON Major.
                    Brigade Major R.A. 28th Division.

Hd Qrs.
No 2220
14-8-15
28th Divl Artillery

28th Div B/
G. 406 543

C.R.A.
    With reference to G. 406 dated 9th August, the signals for appearance of aeroplanes and for "Carrying on" will be as laid down in Divisional Standing Order No. 22 (b).

14th August 1915
                R H Hare   Lieut Colonel
                General Staff 28' Division

O.C.
  31st Bde R.F.A.
    For Information.

15 · VIII – 15
                Sd/V M Fergusson Major
                B.M.R.A.

28th Divisional Artillery
-o-o-o-o-o-o-o-o-o-o-o-o-

Items of Interest for 24 hours ending 6.0 a.m. 15th August 1915.
-o-o-o-o-o-o-o-o-o-o-o-o-o-o-o-o-o-o-o-o-o-o-o-o-o-o-o-o-o-

1. Working parties seen and fired on at -
    N.30.c.8.4. support trench
    N.36.b.7.9. near a house
    Front of Petit Bois
    N.30.c.5.5. SPANBROEK MOLEN

2. Fire in retaliation, or by request, opened on -
    U.1.a.2.6. to stop crumping
    N.24.d.4.6. front trench, by request
    S.W. corner Petit Bois to stop shelling of H.5.

3. Flashes seen at -
    8.35 pm on bearing 105° magnetic from KEMMEL TOWER
    8 - 8.15 pm on bearing 94° magnetic from N.26.b.1.9.
    8 - 8.15 pm   "   "   103°   "   "   "

4. Much has been done in German trench opposite L.1.R.

5. 149th Battery suggest that the box like apparatus opposite D.4., which was thought to be a signalling apparatus, is in reality a periscope The same battery reports that a square black shield has appeared on top of a mound just in front of the German fire trench opposite D.2.
More information is required about this.

6. During the 13th an 18-pr shell marked March 1915 was fired by the Germans and dropped behind E.1. trench. The trench Commander says there is no doubt about the direction it came from.

7. 18th Battery reports a small camp in O.12.c. in a small copse An officer and an orderly stayed there some time. Some Battery up to the North might be able to reach this.

8. 69th Battery report a very heavy shelling of its old position near DICKEBUSCH, between 10.30 a.m. and noon, by 6" or 8". One gun was hit, but the detachments had been withdrawn and no casualties were caused.

9. Infantry report seeing a telescope at the HOSPICE yesterday morning.

sd, V.H. FERGUSSON Major.
Brigade Major R.A. 28th Division.

28th Divisional Artillery Practice. Carried out Sunday 15th August 1915.

-o-o-o-o-o-o-o-o-o-o-o-o-o-o-o-o-o-o-o-

TARGET	ORDER RECEIVED	BATTERY	FIRED	T.I.L	REMARKS.
PLOEGH.	31st Bde 3.26 pm	103rd	3.27	1 min.	The reason for this long delay is that the Bde. was informed that the shoot would not commence till 3.30 and they were aware that the infantry had not vacated the trenches. The B.C's therefore questioned the correctness of the order.
		100th	3.29	3 min.	
		69th	3.32	6 min.	
		118th	3.34	8 min.	
		B/89th	doubtful		
	146th Bde 3.25½ pm	A/49th	3.37	11½min.	The operator would not until after a long delay accept the word PLOEGH.
PLATT BOIS	3rd Bde 3.40 pm	62nd	3.40 1/3	20sec.	3rd Brigade Target on the usual zone of this brigade.
		22nd	3.41	1 min.	
		18th	3.41	1 min.	
		365th	3.41½	1½ min.	
		A/73rd	3.42½	2½ min.	
	31st Bde. 3.44 pm	100th	3.45	1 min.	31st Brigade Target of this brigade's usual zone.
		103rd	3.45	1 min.	
		B/89th	3.52	8 min.	
SPANBROEK MOLEN	31st Bde 3.54 pm	100th	3.55	1 min.	A very good switch as this Bty. had been ordered previously not to shoot on 83rd Bde. front.
		103rd	3.55½	1½ min.	
		118th	3.56	2 min.	
		69th	3.57	3 min.	
		367th	3.58	4 min.	
		B/89th	3.58	4 min.	
	146th Bde 3.52 pm	149th	3.54	2 min.	This entailed a switch of 9°
		366th	3.55	3 min.	
		A/49th	3.57	5 min.	

28th Divisional Artillery

Items of Interest for 24 hours ending 6.0 a.m. 16th August 1915.

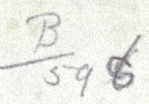

1. Working parties seen and fired on at -
    O.31.d.8.7.   party dispersed
    N.36.b.7.9.   "   "
    N.30.c.8.4.   "   "
    N.36.b.   party carrying planks
    O.31.d.9.9.   party scattered
    Near Petit Bois   work stopped

2. Fire in retaliation or by request opened on -
    U.1.a.2.7. opposite C.2 & C.3. to stop shelling of
              those trenches
    O.32.b.3.6. to stop shelling of D.4. on three occasions
              The battery got off the first round in
              answer to the call for help in 24, 31, and
              28 seconds.
    N.18.d.2.5. by request
    N.24.d.7.8.

3. Flashes seen -
    10.40 pm on bearing of 75°)
    11.10 pm   "   "   75°)
    11.5 pm   "   "   70°) from N.26.b.4.6.
    11.50 pm   "   "   72°)
    10.10 pm   "   "   91½°   " N.26.b.2.7.

4. 75th Battery report that C.2. and C.3. trenches were rather
   heavily shelled at 2.30 pm yesterday afternoon. Hitherto
   these trenches have hardly been shelled at all. It is suggested
   that the Germans have discovered some position from which these
   trenches can now be observed.

5. At 3.0 pm and at intervals throughout the afternoon a helio was
   seen working from a house, which is probably the large farm
   in U.6.b. Owing to the direction in which the instrument was
   facing the messages could not be read.

6. 367th Battery scored 2 direct hits while registering an
   emplacement in German fire trench at N.36.a.6.4.

7. 22nd Battery reports that a machine gun was engaged at 9.30 am
   and silenced.

8. The 365th Battery reports that two openings appeared in the
   parapet of the German fire trench on the edge of PETIT BOIS
   about N.24.a.8.6. while our guns were firing fairly heavily.
   Later - when the firing had ceased - these appeared to be
   closed by shutters or doors covered with some sack coloured
   material exactly the same as the neighbouring trench. This
   should be watched and further information sent in about these
   openings.

9. Work is still proceeding about N.24.b.3.2. where shovels full
   of earth can be seen thrown up.

10. A trench mortar put some bombs into K.1. and J.3.L. at 4.30 pm.
    This mortar has been inactive for some time.

11. Some very heavy shell were put into DICKLBUSCH about midday.

P. T. O.

12. O.C. 31st Brigade reports, I visited the trenches opposite German earthworks in N.36.a.5.5. yesterday evening. A good view can be obtained from the front trench 14a and a still better one from the support trench No. 14. The earthwork is in the form of an appendix as shewn in the trench map. At the end is a small redoubt which appears strongly made and loopholed. Probably it is a position for a machine gun. On the right of this redoubt is a large embrasure of sandbags and sacks, then still further to the right 3 smaller embrasures close together about 2 yards apart. The whole of the earth works round these embrasures, and still further to the right are covered with large sacks full of earth scattered about at various angles. These sacks must be very heavy, and the opinion of the GOC 84th Brigade is that they have come out of a mine. I also am of opinion that mining is in progress there. As regards the loopholes, they could be used for guns but I do not think the 3 smaller ones are intended for that purpose. There is no attempt at concealment. I am turning on the B/89th Howitzer Battery to shell these trenches with H.E. shell. The front trenches are being cleared and a forward Observing Officer is in the support trench.

13. The camp in O 12 c mentioned in para 7 of yesterday's items of interest is reported to contain many horses. About 100 were seen to be apparently leaving stables about 4.45 p.m. yesterday.

14. The Trench Howitzers have nothing of interest to report.

15. The Mountain Artillery Section spent the day overhauling the guns.
The preparation of positions in the 83rd Brigade area will now be proceeded with.

sd/- V.M.FERGUSSON Major
Brigade Major, R.Arty., 28th Division.

28th Divisional Artillery

Items of Interest for 24 hours ending 6.0 a.m. 17th August 1915.

1. Working parties seen and fired on at -
   75th Battery 0.31.d.8.7. party dispersed.
   103rd Battery N.30.c.1.9. right rear of SPANBROEK MOLEN work stopped.

2. Fire in retaliation, or by request, opened on
   62nd Battery N.24.d.5.7. by request - a test call - 60 seconds to first gun.
   A/49th Battery N.36.d.6.0. to stop shrapnel falling in C4
   367th Battery N.36.a.7.5. on fire trench to stop crumping of F. trenches
   "   "   N.30.c.5.0. on fire trench to stop crumping of F. trenches
   "   "   N.30.c.4.5. on fire trench to stop crumping of F. trenches.

3. Flashes seen -
   Three times on bearing 90° magnetic from N.26.b.3.8. Gun probably 6", was firing N., smoke seen after each round. More information can be got, as a good view can be obtained on clear day. Range probably 10,000 yards.
   10.0 p.m. on bearing 37° magnetic from T.18.c.2.5.
   9.35 p.m. "   " 103°   "   " KEMMEL Tower.

4. The 18th Battery Commander carried out a test from the trenches yesterday morning. His battery responded to three calls in 1'45", 39 seconds, and 33 seconds respectively. This battery shoots directly over the road, on which there is considerable traffic, and delay is often caused by people passing in front of the guns at the moment they are required to fire.

5. During an Infantry test of the 22nd Battery communications, rounds were fired in 8, 3, 2, and 20 seconds after receipt of order in the Battery. The target was the same in each instance.

6. The 146th Brigade have now got buried lines connecting Battle Headquarters and three batteries.
   The buried line to R.A.H.Q. is already in use.

7. On two occasions B/89th Battery fired on the loopholed redoubt opposite trench No. 14, mentioned in para 12 of yesterdays Items of Interest.
   Light direct hits were scored on the second occasion.
   The O.C. 31st Brigade has been to the trenches to inspect the damage done and reports the following :-
   I visited trench 14 this morning with my adjutant and inspected German earthworks in N.36.a.5.5. The works had been hit in several places and sacks and sandbags had been displaced. Some of the damage appeared to have been repaired during the night, as fresh earth and sandbags had been placed in position. The large loophole A with iron plate had not been displaced though shell fell on either side of it. The sandbag embrasure B was not hit though the redoubt at the end of appendix appeared to have been struck in two places. The accompanying sketch shows roughly the earthworks from 14 support trench.
   These earthworks are strongly built and would require at least 50 H.E. to really knock them about.

P. T. O.

The Germans retaliated early this morning with rifle grenades inflicting several casualties amongst our Infantry.

8. The 100th Battery had a successful lamp signalling test from G.2. trench yesterday evening.

9. A telephonist in G.2. trench, wishing to inform the 69th Battery that the telephone wire was working properly rang up that Battery at 7.45 p.m. and said "Test G.2. line correct". The Battery operator heard the Anglo words Test G.2. and did not wait for any more. A gun was fired at once, and the mistake only discovered when .... was rung up for the time at which the call was sent.

10. Some light shell and a few 4" were fired at P.H.4 and 5 about 6.15 p.m. probably in retaliation for some shell which were put into PLUHAN.

11. 25th Trench Howitzer battery was not employed yesterday. The 33rd fired 11 rounds into German fire trench opposite J.3. left to silence rifle grenades.

12. The section of the Mountain Artillery is reconnoitring 83rd Brigade area for positions.

Brigade Major ... 28th Division.

[sketch with labels:]
Iron loophole
Large Sandbag loophole
A
B
New earth
Black Redoubt
New Earth
Redoubt
GERMAN TRENCH

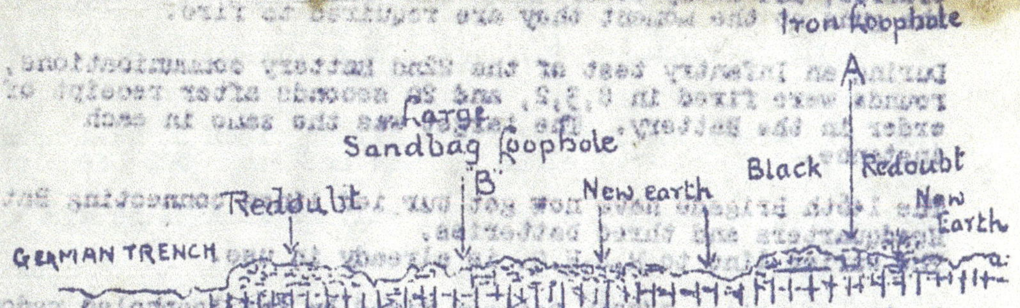

28th Divisional Artillery
-o-o-o-o-o-o-o-o-o-o-o-

Items of Interest for 24 hours ending 6.0 a.m. 18th August 1915.
-o-o-o-o-o-o-o-o-o-o-o-o-o-o-o-o-o-o-o-o-o-o-o-o-o-o-o-o-

1. Working parties seen and fired on at -
   367th Bty. N.36.a.9.7. Behind front line trench. Party scattered
   118th Bty. N.24.c.2.9. Work stopped
   149th Bty. N.36.b.7.9. Two men were hit and rest disappeared
   A/49th Bty. O.32.c.7.5. men in communication trench
   A/49th Bty. N.36.a.10.5. work ceased.

2. Fire in retaliation, or by request, opened on -
   367th Bty. N.36.a.7.7. G.4. Fire trench to stop shelling of trenches 14 and 15.
   367th Bty. N.36.a.9.4. Fire trench to stop shelling of trenches 14 S.
   367th Bty. N.36.a.7.9. Fire trench to stop shelling of trenches L.1. right.
   103rd Bty. SPANBROEK MOLEN to stop shelling of F.4.
   62nd Bty. N.24.b. opposite H.3. and H.4.
   365th Bty. opposite J.3.Right to stop shelling of that trench.
   366th Bty. N.35.d.5.6. to stop shelling of D. trenches.

3. Flashes seen -
   On bearing of 98° magnetic from N.26.b.1.8. Field gun. no time given
   8.45 pm on bearing of 91.30° magnetic from N.26.c.3.9. 15 rounds
   9.5. - 9.30 pm on bearing of 87 and 93° magnetic from N.26.c.3.9.
   5.30 pm bearing of shell scoop 108° magnetic from N.27.c.4.7 light shell
   9.10 pm bearing 92° magnetic from INSULL Tower. Many flashes.

4. At 4.30 pm the enemy exploded a mine in front of G.1. trench which sent up a large cloud of dust and smoke but did little material damage.
   The Infantry report that one bay only of front line was knocked about.
   Very little disturbance was caused though the enemy threw some hand grenades after the explosion.

5. A number of Infantry seen by 18th Battery moving in small parties of about a company in O.13.a. yesterday afternoon.

6. Some movement was seen by 149th Battery during the afternoon in the red tiled house with two chimneys at O.19.d.9.8. It is suggested this building may be used as an observing station.

7. 8.30 pm there was considerable rifle fire on the 17th Divn front, where both the guns and trenches seemed rather restless. Firing died down after about ½ hour.

8. 69th Battery reports having seen a British aeroplane - Bristol Scout descend about ST ELOI about 12.30 pm. The machine was wobbling much in flight and it is supposed it must have been hit.

9. As the result of the fire of the 146th Brigade yesterday

P. T. O.

evening, the Commander of D.4. trench reports that an explosion took place about 300 yards behind the front line trench opposite Bay 14 in L.4.

10. Mountain Artillery section reconnoitred H. and J. One place for gun found in H.3. and none in J. trenches.

11. 25th Trench Howitzer Battery reports - At the request of the Cheshires who had been much harassed, and had suffered casualties from rifle grenades in 15 trench, the Battery fired three series at the enemy trenches opposite. One series in the morning, one in the middle of the day, and one in the evening. 46 rounds were fired in all, of which about 10 exploded directly in the enemy's trenches or dugouts, sending up a deal of timber and pieces of sandbags. In the morning the enemy replied first with rifle grenades, then with shrapnel, and finally with heavy H.E. shell. At midday they replied first with shrapnel and then with a number of H.E. shell - 3 of the latter being fired in quick succession immediately after the first of each of our bombs. In the evening they replied with a few shrapnel and a number of H.E. shell, their shrapnel found the line of the emplacements but was bursting high. Their heavy guns searched all round the emplacement but seemed to have vague ideas as to its whereabouts. There were no casualties.

sd / V.M. FERGUSSON Major,
Brigade Major R.A. 28th Division.

OC
69th Battery R.F.A

[Stamp: HEADQUARTERS 31ST BRIGADE R.F.A. Date 18/8/15 No. B/609]

The Attached cancels all previous issues

18/8/15

L B Holloway Lieut R.F.A
Adjutant 31st Bde R.F.A

2nd Corps
G. 389.

REGISTRATION BY SQUARES.

1.C = 1st Canadian.   1.N. = 1st Northumbrian.

Brigades Divl. Arty.			Batteries Army Artillery			Brigades Divl. Artillery.			Batteries Army Artillery.		
O. 13	3					U. 2.	2.C	118	115	114	
						3	2.C	118	115	114	
14	3		12	116		4	118		115	114	
15			12	116		5	118		115	114	14
16			12	116							
17			12	116		6			114	14	
18			12	116		9	1.C	118	115	114	
19	31	3	116			10	1.C	118	115	114	
20	31	3	12	115	116	11	118		115	114	14
21			116	12		12			114	115	14
22			116	12		16	3.C	118	65	114	14
23			116			17	118	65	114	14	
24						18			114	14	
25	31	3	115	116	114	23	64	65	114	14	
26	31	146	115	116	114	24	65		14		
27			116	115	114	29	64	65	14		
28			116			30	65	64	14		
29			116			V. 7.			114		
30						8			14		
31	146	31	115	114		13			14		
32	146	31	115	114		14			14		
33						19			14		
34			114	115	116	20			14	9	
35			114	116		21			14	9	
36			114			25			14	9	
						26			14	9	
						27			14	9	

28th Divisional Artillery
-o-o-o-o-o-o-o-o-o-o-o-o-

Items of Interest for 24 hours ending 6.0 a.m. 19th August 1915.
-o-o-o-o-o-o-o-o-o-o-o-o-o-o-o-o-o-o-o-o-o-o-o-o-o-o-o-o-o-o-o-

1. Working parties seen and fired on at -
   100th Bty. O.25.a.9.8. One round hit the roof of the house into which the party went.
   149th Bty. N.36.b.7.9
   366th Bty. O.32.c.4.7. Working in communication trench. 3 direct hits on trench
   75th Bty. O.31.d.8.7. Several men seen to fall. Stretcher bearers came later and took them away.

2. Fire in retaliation, or by request, opened on -
   365th Bty. S.W. corner of PETIT BOIS to stop shelling of H. trenches. Shelling ceased
   4/73rd Bty. N.24.c.8.4. by request. Machine gun emplacement reported by Infantry in H.2
   75th Bty. N.36.d.2.8. One direct hit on machine gun emplacement.

3. Flashes seen -
   9.25 pm on bearing 99°45' magnetic from N.26.c.2.8.
   10.15 pm on bearing 91°30' magnetic from N.26.c.2.8.
   Bearing of 5.9" shell scoop 120° magnetic from N.9.d.2.5 fuze set at 23.4

4. In Divisional Test carried out before Lord Kitchener and the French Minister of War yesterday morning two targets were selected and one round of battery fire was fired by two Batteries of 3rd Brigade at each.
   The times between the order leaving R.A.H.Q. and series of both Batteries concluding, worked out at 2 minutes for the first and 2½ minutes for the second target.

5. 365th Battery report that the strengthening of the defences on western edge of PETIT BOIS continues.
   The Infantry report that it took the Germans two nights to repair the damage done by our guns on Sunday at the S.W. corner of the wood.

6. At 6.30 pm sounds of heavy firing were heard from the left. Observers reported that the fire seemed to come from N. of Hill 60. They were unable to state who started the firing but that our guns seemed to be doing most of the shooting.

7. 69th Battery reports that much digging seems to have been done just in rear of front trenches at SPANBROEK MOLEN.

8. Another position for an emplacement has been selected by the Mountain Artillery section in the K. trenches

9. Neither Trench Howitzer Battery fired during the 24 hours.

        sd/ V.M. FERGUSSON Major,
     Brigade Major R.A. 28th Division.

28th Divisional Artillery

Items of Interest for 24 hours ending 6.0 a.m. 20th August 1915.

1. Working parties seen and fired on at -
    367th Bty. O.32.c.7.5. party dispersed.
    A/73rd Bty. N.24.d.2.3. MAIDDLSTEDE
    18th Bty. N.24.d.8.8. behind White tree in Wytschaete wood

2. Fire in retaliation, or by request, opened on -
    Opposite H.2. by request.

3. 2 direct hits made on Red Chateau during registration by B/89th Battery.

4. A test call was sent to the 69th Battery from the trenches while the wire was under repairs.
    The message was picked up by a linesman and passed on to the Battery.
    Fire was opened 2 minutes 24 seconds from time message started and 10 seconds after receipt in the Battery.
    The 100th Battery fired a round in 30 seconds from the time the message was sent from G.2. trench.

5. 100th Battery reports that a lot more work has been done on the communication trench running out of the front German trench at N.24.c.7.1.

6. Many fresh sandbags have been added to the front line trenches in front of the BLACK REDOUBT and also at N.30.c.3.6.

7. A/49th Battery made a direct hit on machine gun emplacement at N.36.d.1.10.

8. 366th Battery reports seeing the Germans working in couples examining and repairing wire at O.26.a.5.5., O.26.d.7.2., and O.32.d.2.5.

9. 18th Battery report what is thought to be a machine gun emplacement at N.18.d.8.0.

10. Neither Trench Howitzer Battery fired yesterday, which was a quiet day on the front.
    The 33rd Trench Howitzer Battery was inspected yesterday in the trenches by the C.R.A.

11. Section Mountain Artillery has selected some sites for emplacements in the 83rd Brigade area.

12. About 10.0 am yesterday about 30 heavy shell were dropped about TIA FARM.

sd/ V.M. FERGUSSON Major

Brigade Major R.A. 28th Division.

B
680

B/63

-o-o-o-o- ITEMS OF INTEREST. -o-o-o-o-

1. Continual work is being carried out on Trench O 19 c 9.6 also near SPANBROEK MOLEN N 30 c 1.9 where, in addition to great digging activity, men have been seen dragging up something heavy. Observers have been asked to watch this place, and report on work which is in progress.

   Work also proceeding at following points:- N 30 a 6.3, O 25 a, West end of WYTSCHAETE Wood, and N 24 d 5.10.

2. Single forward gun position reported O 19 c 0.5 or O 20 c 4.4

3. A Trench Mortar has been located at N 18 d 9½, where some dug-outs are visible.

4. Central window of HOSPICE is being used as an Observing Station. Another O.S. appears to have been established in sandy bank on edge of DIAMOND Wood about N 18 d 10.5. A third place for Observation Station has been spotted in brick stack from which view is probably obtained by periscope.

5. On a bearing of 76½ true from S.W. corner of N 20 c, movement can be seen from 365 Bty. O.P. up to a building with a wood behind it. There is continual traffic on the road and the house is evidently occupied.

6. Dug-outs in open ground between DIAMOND Wood and BOIS DE WYTSCHAETE are being much strengthened.

20/VII/15

W.Fergusson, Major
BM RA 28th Dn

28th Divisional Artillery

Items of Interest for 24 hours ending 6.0 a.m. 22nd August 1915.

1. Working parties seen and fired on at --
   - 149th Bty. N.36.b.1.5. work ceased
   - 149th Bty. N.36.c.7.9.   "   "
   - 366th Bty. N.36.a.2.2.   "   "
   - A/49th Bty. O.32.c.7.5. party scattered. See item 6.
   - 69th Bty. O.25.a.10.9. appeared effective

2. Fire in retaliation, or by request, opened on -
   - 75th Bty. N.36.d.8.1. fire trench to stop shelling of C.4. Battery fired shell for shell
   - 62nd Bty. N.24.c.9.5. to stop shelling of G.4.

3. Flashes seen -
   7.55 pm on bearing 98° magnetic from KEMMEL Tower 3 flashes.

4. 149th Battery reports that there is a dugout, which looks as if it might be a machine gun emplacement, South of the road and 30 or 40 yards East of the ruins at N.36.a.10.5. This is the first time it has been seen.

5. German flag was displayed in front line trench opposite D.4.

6. About a platoon of Germans were seen by A/49th Battery to enter a house at O.32.c.7.5. yesterday afternoon. They returned bearing planks and took a short cut across the open instead of using the communication trench. They finally entered communication trench when fired on and proceeded probably to house O.31.d.10.9.

7. 69th Battery reports 2 rounds were fired apparently on G.2. trench from a hedge between O.25.a.3.8. and N.30.b.6.5. As it is supposed that G.2. is mined the O.C. 69th Battery concluded a gun had been brought up to assist when the mine was exploded and that it was registering. The Battalion Commander was informed. As a matter of fact the German mine was successfully exploded by our own people at 8.29 p.m. last night.

8. The house at O.19.d.5.6., BOX HOUSE, has been reported before as an observing station. O.C. A/73rd Battery reports a hole in the wall whence bricks seem to have been removed. Movement and the glint of a telescope or field glass was also observed.

9. 365th Battery observer reports the explosion of a mine last night between 6.0 and 7.0 pm in the direction of HOLLANDS-CHLSHUUR Farm. The explosion was followed by gun fire from German lines, which was quickly responded to by our guns.

10. Neither Trench Howitzer Battery was employed yesterday and each reports a quiet day on the front.

11. The O.C. Mountain Gun Section reports he has prepared positions in H.3. and 26.   L 6

sd/ V.M. FERGUSSON Major.
Brigade Major R.A. 28th Division.

28th Divisional Artillery

Items of Interest for 24 hours ending 6.0 a.m. 23rd August 1915.

1. Working parties seen and fired on by -
   - 18th Bty. at N.24.d.8.8. dugout hit and work stopped
   - 62nd Bty. .. N.24.d.10.5. two hits on German trench
   - 365th Bty .. O.13.c.1.4. a quantity of timber thrown up. (see item 6)
   - 149th Bty .. N.30.d. 30 men cutting grass. Party scattered.
   - 149th Bty .. N.36.a.9.5. Work stopped
   - 366th Bty .. O.32.c.4.5. effective (see item 8)

2. Fire in retaliation, or by request, opened by
   - A/73rd Bty on N.18.b.5.6. M.G. emplacement, by request.
   - 75th Bty .. N.36.b.5.2. to stop shelling of C.4.
   - 69th Bty. .. O.25.b.5.8. to stop short range gun
   - 100th Bty .. It was supposed that G.2. was being whiz-
   - on N.24.c.6.1 banged, but it turned out afterwards that an officer in G.2. was throwing hand grenades.
   - 118th Bty .: Hospice to stop shelling of TEA Farm
   - 118th Bty .. O.19.d.1.5. To stop shelling of PONKERSHOF Farm.

3. German aeroplanes more active than they have been lately.

4. 18th Battery saw a German aeroplane (Aviatak) cross from LINDENHOEK over the German lines to a point on a bearing of 99.30° magnetic from N.26.b.8.2½. When over this place the machine fired 2 white lights and then descended to about 200 feet, dropped a message and ascended again. It then moved in an Easterly direction and finally spiralled down on a bearing of 101° magnetic from same spot.

5. Several Batteries report seeing a red spherical balloon pass over LA CLYTTE at about 5.30 p.m. moving in a south easterly direction. It was at a great height and it was impossible to tell if there was a car attached. It was first seen near a German aeroplane.

6. 365th Battery reports that a lot of work has been done at O.13.c.1.4. on the edge of DIAMOND Wood. It is suggested that a flanking work is being constructed behind the edge of the wood. It is described as presenting the appearance of a large open ended dugout opposite the open end of which the bank is shaped like an embrasure. The dugout is half concealed by a heap of faggots or dead brushwood. A gun might possibly be concealed in the dugout ready to be run out into the embrasure in case of attack.

7. 149th Battery reports that a sandbag parapet has now been built in front of the square black shield in front line trench opposite E.3. which was previously reported.

8. 366th Battery reports that the communication trench at that place and leading to MESSINES is continually being used by the enemy, parties of whom were fired at by the Battery yesterday. After one series stretcher bearers were seen running out of the farm at O.32.c.4.5. which is reported to be much used by the enemy.

28th Divisional Artillery

Items of Interest for 24 hours ending 6.0 a.m. 22nd August 1915.

1. Working parties seen and fired on by :-
   10th Bty .. at N.24.d.0.5.   dugout hit and work stopped
   63rd Bty .. N.24.d.10.5.   two hits on German trench
   365th Bty .. O.13.c.1.4.   a quantity of timber thrown up.
                                (see item 6)
   104th Bty .. N.30.d.   20 men cutting grass. Party
                                scattered.
   169th Bty .. N.36.c.4.5.   Work stopped
   96th Bty .. O.32.c.4.5.   effective (see item 8)

2. Fire in retaliation, or by request, opened by
   A/73rd Bty on N.16.b.5.6. N.G. emplacement, by request.
   75th Bty .. N.36.a.5.2. to stop shelling of C.4.
   69th Bty .. O.15.a.5.3. to stop short range fire
   100th Bty .. It was supposed that G.Z. was being whizz-
                on N.24.d.8.1bergod but it turned out afterwards that
                an officer in G.Z. was throwing hand grenades.
   128th Bty .. Hooplic. to stop shelling of Bn. Hrs
   119th Bty .. O.19.d.1.5. To stop shelling of HOLLEBEKE
                Fam.

3. German aeroplanes were active more than they have seen lately.

4. 18th Battery saw a German aeroplane (Aviatik) arose from
   LINDENHOEK over the German lines to a point on a bearing of
   93.30° magnetic from N.25.c.0.2. When over this place the
   machine fired 2 white lights was then descended to about 500
   feet, dropped a message and ascended again. It then moved in
   an Easterly direction and finally spiralled down on a bearing
   of 101° magnetic from same spot.

5. Several Batteries report seeing a red spherical balloon pass
   over LA CLYTTE at about 5.30 p.m. moving in a south easterly
   direction. It was at a great height and it was impossible to
   tell if there was a car attached. It was first seen near a
   German aeroplane.

6. 365th Battery reports that a lot of work has been done at
   O.13.c.1.4. on the edge of INVERN Wood. It is suggested that
   a flanking work is being constructed behind the edge of the
   wood. It is described as resembling the appearance of a large
   open ended object, the slope the open end of which the bank is
   shaped like an archway. The front is half concealed by a
   hedge of trees and is well constructed. It might possibly be
   concealed. An organ ready to be run out into the embrasure
   in case of fire, &c.

7. 169th Battery reports that a machine Parapet has now been built
   in front of the double black circle in front line trench
   opposite J.9. Which was previously reported.

8. 96th Battery reports that the communication trench at that
   place and Cortez Farm Sap TRENCH is continually being used by the
   enemy parties of whom were fired at by the Battery yesterday.
   After one German autocratic because were seen running out of the
   farm at N.13.d.3.3. which is reported to be much used by the
   enemy.

9. The balloon attracted a lot of attention during the day. German observation balloons were up nearly all day yesterday and prevented our batteries from taking full advantage of working parties which exposed themselves.

10. 25th Trench Howitzer Battery did not fire.
    33rd Trench Howitzer Battery reports an uneventful morning but in the afternoon our field guns drew retaliation fire from the enemy which did material damage to two dugouts and to parapets but without causing casualties. No. 5 gun was placed in H.2. on "V.C. Road" opposite suspected machine gun emplacements. Two successful rounds were fired at this target. The second round sent up a mass of flying splinters and left an appreciable mark on the target. Rifle grenades were fired from J.2. which drew a reply. Three rounds were fired from J.2. emplacement. No more rifle grenades were fired from either side.

11. Another platform has been completed by the Mountain Artillery Section in 83rd Brigade area.

                      sd/ V.M. FERGUSSON Major.
            Brigade Major R.A. 28th Division.

28th Divisional Artillery
-o-o-o-o-o-o-o-o-o-o-o-o-

Items of Interest for 24 hours ending 6.0 a.m. 24th August 1915.
-o-o-o-o-o-o-o-o-o-o-o-o-o-o-o-o-o-o-o-o-o-o-o-o-o-o-

1. Working parties seen and fired on by -
   - 62nd Bty on N.24.b.1.4. in open. party dispersed
   - 366th Bty .. O.25.d.4.6. repairing telephone wires. dispersed.
   - 366th Bty .. N.36.d.1.8. repairing M.G. emplacement, on two occasions (see item 4)
   - 69th Bty .. N.30.a.5.6. effective.

2. Fire in retaliation, or by request, opened by -
   - A/73rd Bty on N.24.d.5.3. M.G. emplacement, by request of H.2. one direct hit.
   - 366th Bty .. N.36.d.1.8. M.G. emplacement, by request. (see item 4)
   - 118th Bty .. O.19.d.5.4. BOX HOUSE to stop shelling of LINDENHOEK
   - 118th Bty .. N.24.c.8.6. German front trench
   - 367th Bty .. N.36.a.7.7. to stop bomb throwing. Temporarily successful
   - 367th Bty .. N.36.a.9.4. To stop bomb throwing. Stopped it for a time.
   - B/89th Bty .. PECKHAM To stop bombing of G.2. Two direct hits on farmhouse.
   - B/89th Bty .. N.30.a.5.5. Opposite F.5. to stop bombing. Infantry reported mortar to be 130° magnetic from notice board G.1.
   - 100th Bty .. PECKHAM To stop bombing G.1.
   - 69th Bty .. BLACK REDOUBT N.30.a.3.3. to stop a whizbang.

3. 25th Trench Howitzer Battery did not fire.
   The 33rd Trench Howitzer Battery fired 4 rounds, by request, at a working party in PETIT BOIS with good effect. In the afternoon 2 rounds were fired to silence an enemy mortar.

4. Yesterday afternoon the 366th Battery took on the machine gun emplacement at N.36.d.1.8. by request of the Infantry. The 5th round was a direct hit and after that 2 rounds in 3 were direct hits. Twenty four rounds in all were fired and the emplacement was completely destroyed.
   On two occasions during the evening the Battery opened fire on working parties at that spot, which were endeavouring to repair the emplacement.

5. 69th Battery reports much digging has been done at N.30.a.5.6. just North of where a communication trench joins front line trench near PECKHAM. Other Batteries have observed this activity also.

6. Mountain Artillery Section has labelled his emplacements.

7. 31st Brigade reports - The 100th Battery was called up at 2.7 am to retaliate as MINENWERFER fired two rounds into G.2. trench and the Battery had just fired a round when the Infantry reported that another round from the MINENWERFER had burst. The 100th Battery fired three rounds in reply to this. About 3.17 am the Infantry reported 2 rifle grenades had dropped in their trench. In reply to this the Battery fired two rounds. At about 3.25 am the B.M. 84th Infantry B.ge asked for Howitzer fire and the B/89th Battery fired two rounds, after which everything was quite quiet for the remainder of the night.

            sd/ V.M. FERGUSSON Major.
         Brigade Major R.A. 28th Division.

28th Divisional Artillery
-o-o-o-o-o-o-o-o-o-o-o-

Items of Interest for 24 hours ending 6.0 a.m. 25th August 1915.
-o-o-o-o-o-o-o-o-o-o-o-o-o-o-o-o-o-o-o-o-o-o-

1. Working parties seen and fired on by -
    365th Bty. on edge of PETIT BOIS
    149th Bty at N.36.b.7.9. men returning from the trenches
    366th Bty. O.32.b.3.6. on six occasions. party stopped each time
    366th Bty " N.36.d.4.7. party stopped work.

2. Fire in retaliation, or by request, opened by -
    62nd Bty   on N.24.d.4.6. on front trench to stop shelling. shelling ceased
    365th Bty .. S.W. of PETIT BOIS to stop shelling. Shelling ceased.
    100th Bty .. N.24.c.7.1. to stop whizbang on G.2. (see item 4)
    100th Bty .. House N.24.d.8.2. to stop whizbang on G.2.
    100th Bty .. HALDENSTELL N.24.c.7.6. to stop whizbang on G.3.
    118th Bty .. N.24.c.8.2. Black Redoubt
    367th Bty .. N.36.a.7.7. fire trench to stop whizbang
    366th Bty .. N.36.d.1.8. M.G. emplacement by request.
    A/49th Bty .. Ruins N.36.d.6.2. to stop shelling of D. trench.

3. Flashes seen -
    7.41 pm on bearing 102° magnetic from KEMMEL Tower probably trench mortar
    8.15 - 8.45 pm on bearing 101° magnetic from KEMMEL Tower. Heavy Howitzer.

4. O.C. 100th Battery has studied the whizbang which was worrying G.2 yesterday and has come to the conclusion that the propelling force is compressed air. The time between the report of the gun and the burst of the shell is less than a second which proves the gun to be very close to the trench line, but no flash of any sort is to be seen even at night. Another argument favouring the contention is that the damage done to the parapet is not so great as it would be were the velocity as high as that of an ordinary gun.
    The damage is entirely caused by the explosion of the shell.

5. 367th Battery reports that at 7.30 pm a short range Battery opened fire on the L. trenches. Flashes were seen on bearing of 100° magnetic from N.26.c.2.9. The time between the flash and the report of the gun was 2 seconds.

6. Enemy heavy guns were busy yesterday.
    (a) Between 12.30 and 1.0 pm several heavy shell fell about F.4 support trenches, and at 4.45 pm a salvo from the same battery fell in rear of F.2. An officer in that trench took the time and states 16 seconds elapsed between the report of the Howitzer and the arrival of the shell.
    (b) 4.35 pm a number of rounds of 8 inch from the direction of HOLLEBEKE fell in N.23.c. The same square is reported to have received a contribution of 30   5.9 inch at 5.0 pm from WYTSCHAETE.
    (c) A 77 mm Battery in O.26. direction put some 12 rounds about the F. trenches in the morning and about 6 rounds about G.4., H.1., and H.2. in the afternoon.

7. 25th Trench Howitzer Battery did not fire.
   33rd Trench Howitzer Battery reports having taken two guns into G.1. at request of 84th Brigade, but the bombing had stopped when he got there and he was asked not to shoot. At dusk however three rounds were fired by request.

8. Mountain Artillery Section has built two more platforms in the K and L trenches.

9. B/89th Battery fired 1 series on Black Redoubt at 12.30 pm yesterday in retaliation for rifle and machine gun fire from that place, which very much annoyed the Infantry.
   Six very effective rounds are reported. The enemy retaliated with 5.9" and whizbangs but did no damage.

                                    sd/ V.H. FERGUSSON Major.
                            Brigade Major R.A. 28th Division.

Officer Commanding,
    ~~3~~
    146 Brigade R.F.A.

1.   The 1½" Trench Howitzer of the 25th Trench Howitzer Battery will be attached to the 33rd Trench Howitzer Battery.

        Similarly one 3.7" Trench Howitzer of the 33rd Trench Howitzer Battery will be attached to the 25th Trench Howitzer Battery under the following arrangements :-

2.   One officer and suitable detachment from each Trench Howitzer Battery will be transferred to the other, for attachment as early as possible, under arrangements to be made by the O.C's 3rd and 146th Brigades.

3.   The O.C's 25th and 33rd Trench Howitzer Batteries will arrange for mutual instruction to be given to all ranks, in order that both natures of howitzer may be employed by each Battery.

4.   The O.C's 3rd and 146th Brigades will report -
    (a) When these arrangements have been carried out
    (b) When training in both weapons is completed.

5.   When report (b) has been rendered, authority will be given for detachments to rejoin their own batteries. The transferred weapon will however remain.

6.   Report (b) will be accompanied by a certificate from Trench Howitzer Battery Commanders that all ranks of their Batteries are efficiently trained, and capable of using the 1½" and 3.7" Howitzer as the case may be.

7.   Please acknowledge.

                                        M Fergusson.
                                            Major.

26th August 1915.   Brigade Major R.A. 28th Division.

G.O.C.
    85th Infantry Brigade

                    For information.

                                        M Fergusson
                                            Major.
26th August 1915.   for C.R.A. 28th Division.

28th Divisional Artillery

Items of Interest for 24 hours ending 6.0 a.m. 26th August 1915.

1. Working parties seen and fired on by -
    - 69th Bty at N.30.c.5.4. work stopped
    - 366th Bty .. N.36.a.7.4. .. ..

2. Fire in retaliation, or by request, opened by
    - 100th Bty on Peckham front trench, N.24.c.7.1. and MAEDELSTEADE to stop whizbang on G.1.
    - 103rd Bty .. SPANBROEK MOLEN and Black Redoubt to stop whizbang.
    - 118th Bty .. SPANBROEK MOLEN and PECKHAM to stop whizbang
    - 367th Bty .. N.36.a.9.1. by request to stop trench mortar. Fire reported effective.
    - 366th Bty .. Machine gun emplacement off D.2. by request.
    - 365th Bty .. at 9.0 pm N.W. Corner of PETIT BOIS. To stop trench mortar from bombing J.3.R.

3. Flashes seen -
    - 9.15 pm on bearing 98° magnetic from N.26.b.8.2½ (20 flashes)
    - 8.10 pm .. .. 103° .. .. KEMMEL Tower
    - 8.35 pm .. .. 112° .. .. (3 flashes)

4. A German flag was observed to have been planted on a willow in front of their fire trench opposite 14, no doubt with the idea of celebrating their naval victory in the Gulf of Riga. After dark an officer went out and brought the flag in to our trenches.

5. Work continues to be done at SPANBROEK MOLEN and at N.36.b.7.9 where the support trenches appear to have been greatly strengthened.

6. 25th Trench Howitzer Battery did not fire.
   33rd Trench Howitzer Battery reports that an enemy mine was exploded to the right of J.32 at 8.0 pm. No damage was done. An outbreak of hostile hand grenading followed the explosion.

7. The Mountain Artillery Section has now completed 12 emplacements on the Divisional front.

sd/ V.M. FERGUSSON Major
Brigade Major R.A. 28th Division.

28th Divisional Artillery

Items of Interest for 24 hours ending 6.0 a.m. 27th August 1915.

1. Working parties seen and fired on by -
    - 366th Bty at N.36.d.1.8. opposite D.1. by request. Work stopped on two occasions.
    - 62nd Bty .. N.24.c.9.5. Opposite G.4. Party dispersed.
    - 69th Bty .. N.30.c.1.9. SPANBROEK MOLEN. Fire very effective.
    - 118th Bty .. N.30.a.4.5. Work stopped.

2. Fire in retaliation, or by request, opened by -
    - A/49th Bty on U.1.a.0.9. Redoubt opposite C.4. Infantry reported fire effective.
    - 22nd Bty .. N.18.d.2.5. Opposite K.1. by request
    - 62nd Bty .. N.24.c.9.8. Opposite G.4. to stop whizbang.
    - 100th Bty .. N.24.c.8.6. MAEDELSTEDE to stop shelling of G.2. Shelling stopped
    - 100th Bty .. N.30.a.5.8. PECKHAM to stop shelling of G.1 and 2. Shelling stopped
    - B/89th Bty .. N.24.c.8.5. MAEDELSTEDE to stop whizbang

3. Flashes seen -
    8.10 pm on bearing 102° magnetic from KEMMEL Tower.

4. 149th Battery reports that in retaliation for fire of Canadian Batteries the enemy shelled PLOEGSTEERT village and Hill 63 with light howitzers and field guns and NEUVE EGLISE with heavy shell from 5 to 5.25 pm.

5. A/49th Battery report the appearance of a red and white flag supported on two poles on the German parapet in front of the ruins in N.36.a.9.5. About 200 yards to the South was a white flag on a single pole.

6. 18th Battery reports that a new line of trenches appears to have been made running from Hill 69 (O.13.c.1.6.) in front of the brick stacks to N.E. corner of the BOIS de WYTSCHAETE.

7. 365th Battery reports that the newly turned earth behind German fire trench in PETIT BOIS has now extended to the extreme N.W. corner of the wood. The infantry report that the heaps of earth in centre of front of wood have disappeared.

8. 69th Battery reports having spotted 2 peculiar black holes in the hedge at O.19.c.4.1. which it is suspected is a whizbang position. The possibility of a covered approach from the sunken road strengthens this idea. A whizbang has undoubtedly fired from that direction and the place should be marked down.

9. At N.30.a.5.4. where communication trench joins front line trench a great deal of work has been done.

10. The German flag mentioned in item 4 of yesterday has been flying from trench 14.

11. The light was bad for observation yesterday.

12. Between 9.30 and 10.30 pm the sound of aeroplane or Zeppelin engines was heard by most batteries, but nothing was visible.

13. Neither Trench Howitzer Battery fired.

        sd/ V.M. FERGUSSON Major.
Brigade Major R.A. 28th Division.

69

6/5

5th Divisional Artillery.
-o-o-o-o-o-o-o-o-

Items of interest for 24 hours ending 6.0 a.m. 27th August 1915.
-o-o-o-o-o-o-o-o-o-o-o-o-o-o-o-o-o-o-o-o-o-o-o-o-o-o-o-o-

1. Morning patrol seen and fired on by :-
    60th Bty at N.30.d.1.5. D.L. by request. Guns stopped on two occasions.
    52nd Bty .. N.24.a.8.5. Opposite G.4. Party dispersed.
    69th Bty .. N.30.c.1.5. SPANBROEK MOLEN. Fire very effective.
    11Oth Bty .. N.30.c.4.5. Work stopped.

2. Fire on WYTSCHAETE, or by request, opened by :-
    N/294 Bty on U.1.a.0.9. Ribbons opposite G.8. Intended reported fire effective.
    52nd Bty .. N.18.d.6.5. Opposite D.1. by request.
    61st Bty .. N.24.b.8.5. Opposite C.4. to stop enemy shelling.
    11Oth Bty .. N.24.a.8.5. Instructions to stop shelling of G.24 shelling reported.
    1OOth Bty .. N.30.a.5.9. TREGEL, to stop shelling of G.1 and 2, shelling stopped.
    2/290th Bty.. N.24.a.0.5. Salbachurts to stop shelling.

3. Phones used.-
    6.10 p.m on bearing 102° magnetic from Middel Tower.

4. 14th Battery reports that in retaliation for fire of Germans Registered has been medium TRONES-ST village and HILL 75 the light howitzers and rifle guns and HEAVY again with heavy small arms 7.30 p.30pm.

5. 149th Battery report the appearance of a red and white flag, apparent on the pole of the German parapet in front of the ruins in N.30.a.7.5. About 200 yards to the south was a white flag on a single pole.

6. 14th Battery reports that a new line of Trenches appears to have been made running from HILL 60 (U.15.c.1.5.) in front of the Trench shewn in T.L. corner of the Hole de Witschaete.

7. 14th Battery reports that the newly turned earth noting German fire trench in SMALL BOIS has now extended to the extreme N.W. corner of the wood. The Infantry report that the heaps of earth in centre of front of wood have disappeared.

8. 6th Battery reports having spotted 7 hostile black lines in the hedge about 12 n.m. which it is supposed is a wildgame position. The howitzer fired a ranging approach from the monkey road along the hole 160...... wildgame was successfully fired from that direction and the place shall be marked down.

9. At 6.20 p.m. smoke observed arising from JOHN FROST HILL. Appears a short deal of work had been done.

10. The German flag mentioned in item 4 of yesterday has been flying from Trench 141.

11. The light was bad for observation yesterday.

12. Between 9.30 and 10.30 pm the sound of aeroplane or zeppelin engines was heard by most batteries, but nothing was visible.

13. Trench Mortar Howitzer battery fired.

                                   Sgd. T.S. HAMRDEN, Major.
                                Brigade Major R.A., 5th Division.

28th Divisional Artillery
-o-o-o-o-o-o-o-o-o-o-o-o-

Items of Interest for 24 hours ending 6.0 a.m. 28th August 1915.
-o-o-o-o-o-o-o-o-o-o-o-o-o-o-o-o-o-o-o-o-o-o-o-o-o-o-o-

1. Working parties seen and fired on by -
   62nd Bty   at N.24.b.8.0. Bois de WYTSCHAETE on four
                                occasions. Work was stopped
   62nd Bty   .. Opposite H.2. by request. Enemy reported
                                to be sapping.
   22nd Bty   .. N.24.b.5.3. Party dispersed
   A/49th Bty .. O.32.c.6.1. Work stopped for the day.

2. Fire in retaliation, or by request, opened by -
   18th Bty   on N.18.b.2.5. front line trench - by request
   118th Bty .. O.19.d.8.9. to stop shelling of T.3.a.3.8.
   367th Bty .. N.36.a.9.9. to stop shelling supports behind
                                trench 14.

3. 146th Brigade reports. At about 9.15 am yesterday about 20
   rounds of 4.2" .... were fired round T.3.a.5.5. Four burst in
   the air the rest on graze. Some came in pairs and some in salvos.
   At 11.0 am salvos of four were again fired. The right section's
   range being 300 yards longer than the left section's. The first
   two salvos were short of the farm T.3.a.3.8. The next one
   Bracketted it. The next was a 100 yards bracket, all short of
   the farm.
   Fuzes were of 4.2" Howitzer. Bearing of troughs 95° magnetic
   from T.3.a.3.8. (South end of farm) A German aeroplane was
   flying up and down above the LINDENHOEK - NEUVE EGLISE Road at
   the time.

4. O.C. 365th Battery went to examine new German trenches West
   of PETIT BOIS. From J.3. right a half completed trench could
   be seen, and was narrow, shallow and unoccupied.

5. 69th Battery reports heavy firing in direction of YPRES at
   6.0 pm and that a distant smell of gas was discernable at that
   hour in square M.24.d.

6. 103rd Battery reports that about 10 shell fell in squares
   N.16.c.and d. yesterday of which 50% were blind. The bearing
   of the shell scoops was 113° magnetic from N.16.c.9.1. Fuze,
   brass, marked Dopp Z 9/92 Sb, was graduated up to 28, the
   decimals being in twos.

7. At 10.15 pm the 367th Battery manned the guns on account of a
   sudden burst of rifle fire at trench 14. Their assistance
   however was not required.

8. 149th Battery reports having seen an aeroplane yesterday
   morning bearing the new markings.
   PLOEGSTEERT Wood and NEUVE EGLISE were shelled in the
   afternoon.

9. 33rd Trench Howitzer Battery fired five rounds at machine gun
   emplacement opposite H.3.

10. A bearing to an enemy object from the trenches is of little
    value unless the spot in the trench from which the bearing is
    taken is indicated. To do this bearings should also be taken
    to some prominent objects, such as KEMMEL Tower, SCHERPENBERG
    Mill or churches at NEUVE EGLISE, BAILLEUL &c.

                            sd/ V.M. FERGUSSON Major.
                            Brigade Major R.A. 28th Division.

28th Divisional Artillery

Items of Interest for 24 hours ending 6.0 a.m. 29th August 1915.

1. Working parties seen and fired on by -
    - 365th Bty   at W. edge of PETIT BOIS, by request.
    - 118th Bty   .. N.30.d.10.2. effective
    - 366th Bty   .. N.36.d.5.3.) in reply to calls from D.
    - 366th Bty   .. N.36.d.1.8.) trenches. Work continually recommenced.
    - 75th Bty   .. O.32.c.6.0. party dispersed see item 6

2. Fire in retaliation, or by request, opened by
    - 18th Bty   on N.18.b.2.5. to stop shelling of L.4. shelling stopped
    - 22nd Bty   .. N.24.a.7.9. Communication trench
    - 62nd Bty   .. N.24.c. Front trench to stop whizbang on the N. trenches. Fire ceased

3. A column of ... transport was reported by the 85th Brigade trenches to be moving towards MESSINES on the MESSINES - WYTSCHAETE Road. A/49th Battery turned on to this and caused the wagons first to trot and then to gallop. It could not be seen whether any casualties were caused.

4. 18th Battery carefully registered the S.W. corner of PETIT BOIS. The same battery claims to have carried away the sack which covered the observation post, under the N. corner of the brickstack in O.19.d.7.10, in 2 rounds.

5. 365th Battery thinks fresh work has been done at O.13.c.1.3. and also at N.24.b.1.2. S.W. corner of PETIT BOIS. In this place it looks as if a communication trench were being dug forward to the fire trench. Work is also being carried on on the west edge of the wood.
The A/73rd Battery fired a series with lyddite on the trenches in the centre and near the wood.

6. A working party at Lone Tree Farm put in appearance yesterday for the first time since the 75th Battery caused them some casualties there on the 19th.

7. The enemy shelled Hill 63 in U.13.a.S.W. and searched behind it with field guns and light howitzer.

                          sd/ V.M. FERGUSSON Major.
                    Brigade Major R.A. 28th Division.

No.283 - 29th August, 1915.

2ND ARMY CORPS SUMMARY OF INFORMATION.
THIS SUMMARY IS ISSUED FOR THE GENERAL INFORMATION OF ALL RANKS OF THE CORPS, BUT THE CONTENTS OF IT ARE NOT INTENDED FOR GENERAL CIRCULATION AND WILL, ON NO ACCOUNT, BE COMMUNICATED TO THE PRESS OR TO ANY INDIVIDUAL OUTSIDE HIS MAJESTY'S SERVICE.

RUSSIA.
The Russians have evacuated OLITA, which has been occupied by the Germans. This fortress is about 30 miles south east of KOVNO and 45 miles N.E. of GRODNO.

South and north of BREST LITOVSK the German advance continues, but they are being held up on the SWENTA section, and their efforts to reach the DWINA about JACOBSTADT where the river is fordable have so far been unsuccessful. The military experts at PETROGRAD seem to think the Germans are rearranging their forces somewhat and are strengthening their armies in the north.

It is claimed that the German cavalry have driven a wedge in the Russian line towards the PRIPET marshes (south east of BREST LITOVSK).

MISCELLANEOUS.
The Secretary of State for the Colonies has received the sum £100 2s 3d collected by Dagadu, Chief of Kpandu, in TOGOLAND, towards the successful prosecution of the war. This Chief, in 1886, had applied to be taken under British protection, and had been given a British flag but his territory came within German influence when TOGOLAND boundary was delimited. Eighteen months ago, on account of British sympathies, he was exiled to DUALA, and the flag was discovered and taken from him. When DUALA was occupied by the Allies, Chief Dagadu was released and returned to Kpandu in January.

In forwarding his contribution, which was entirely spontaneous and came as a surprise to the political officer in TOGOLAND, the Chief wrote as follows :- "I the Head Chief Dagadu of Kpandu, have given here £50, fifty pounds, and my Village-youngmen have also assisted me with cash £51 10s., fifty-one pounds and ten shillings (to total £101 10s). One hundred and one pounds and ten shillings, being a fund given to help the English Government towards the Imperial war between England, France, Russia, and Germany, Austria-Hungary, and Turkey. It was my willing to give more than what I have done above, but on account of the Germans, and owing to their bad treatment giving, most of my Village youngmen have removed from this land and entered into another Colony for their daily bread; and also my land is very poor to say. May God the Almighty bless the Great Britain to master the victory. I congratulate the local and Imperial Government, and the District Political Officer, Mr.R.S.Rattray, who is treating us here very well and gentle; may he live long. And Mr.J.T.Furley (the Senior Political Officer of Lome), who is a best and good gentleman, carrying his duty very pleasant in order, by my eyewitness, may he live long. May God bless the English Government and prolong their power to be second to none.

God Save the King!
Yours obediently
HEAD CHIEF DAGADU OF KPANDU. XXX mk."

The sketch-map overleaf shows times and routes of Cookers of 5th Bav. Regt. from details supplied by a deserter from that regiment.

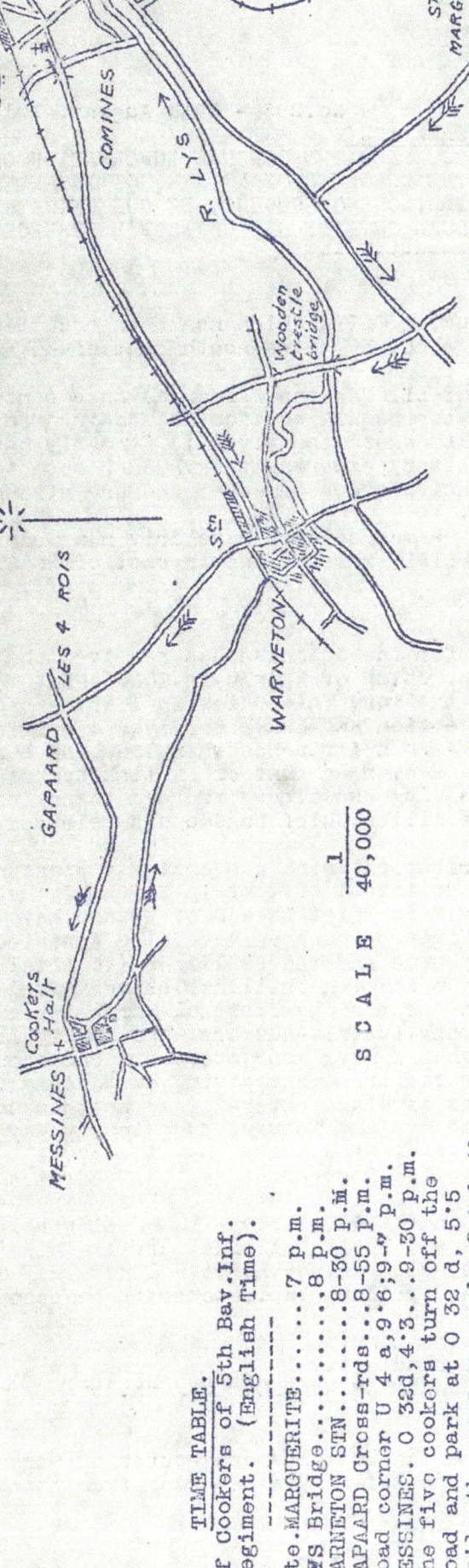

Sketch Map showing Route
(marked by arrows)

TIME TABLE.
of Cookers of 5th Bav.Inf.
Regiment. (English Time).

Ste.MARGUERITE........7 p.m.
LYS Bridge............8 p.m.
WARNETON STN.........8-30 p.m.
GAPAARD Cross-rds...8-55 p.m.
Road corner U 4 a,9 6;9-7 p.m.
MESSINES. O 32d,4-3...9-30 p.m.
The five cookers turn off the
road and park at O 32 d, 5·5
while the company cooks fetch the
supper.

Leave MESSINES..........10-0 p.m.
WARNETON STATION........10-40 ::
LYS Bridge..............11-10 ::

N.B. The LYS Bridge at V 8c 2·1 is a wooden
trestle bridge 350 yards long,
which bridges over the watermeadows
liable to flood on the left bank.

The Reliefs take place as a rule every third night; and
follow the same route as the cookers. The men in the
trenches always sing and shout and whistle on the evening
when they are going to be relieved.
From MESSINES cross-roads the reliefs enter the communication trench. The roads this side of MESSINES are never
used. The relief usually is over by midnight or 1 a.m.

29.8.1915.

31st Brigade Test

Times taken from giving order to operator in the trench to fall of shell.

battery	Trench	Time	
118th	How sap	15 sec.	
100th	G.3.	55 "	
100th	G.2.	14 "	
69th	F.3.	48 "	The battery report that the time would have been shorter had not a Staff Officer been in the line of fire.
103rd	F.4.	5m 15 sec.	Apparently fault of operator at battery
103rd	F.2.	25 "	
103rd	L.2.	25 "	
367th	L.1.	1m 35 "	Battery explains that trench operator did not state whether it was L.1.R. or L.L. which required fire.
367th	15	37 "	
367th	14	42 "	

28th Divisional Artillery

Items of Interest for 24 hours ending 6.0 a.m. 30th August 1915

1. Working parties seen and fired on by -
   - 365th Bty   at   W. edge of PETIT BOIS
   - 367th Bty   ..   N.36.a.7.7. Work stopped
   - 149th Bty   ..   N.36.b.7.9.
   - 366th Bty   ..   O.36.c.7.5. Party dispersed

2. Fire in retaliation, or by request, opened by -
   - 18th Bty on N.18.b.4.4. and 2.5. to stop shelling of trenches. Shelling stopped.
   - 62nd Bty .. Trench opposite H.2. and 3 to stop shelling of Via Gellia.

3. At 11.0 a.m. the enemy fired on LINDENHOEK Cross Roads with short range guns and 10.5 cm Howitzers. Fuze KZ11. Sp 15 and was set at 5.500 metres.

4. The 33rd Trench Howitzer battery fired three rounds into PETIT BOIS.

                                sd/ V.M. FERGUSSON Major.
                        Brigade Major R.A. 28th Division.

28th Divisional Artillery

Routine Orders

No. 232

30th August 1915

453

<u>Court Martial</u>. A Field General Court Martial composed as under will assemble at the Headquarters, 28th Divisional Ammunition Column at 10.0 a.m. on Wednesday, 1st September 1915, for the trial of the undermentioned man and such other accused persons as may be brought before it.

President. Major G.S. Hoare R.F.A. 28th Div.Am.Col.
Members. A Captain 3rd Brigade R.F.A.
         A Subaltern 146th Brigade R.F.A.

No. 389 Gunner W. Pyott, Trench Howitzer Brigade

The accused to be warned and all witnesses directed to attend.

C.R. Burkhardt
Captain.
Staff Captain R.A. 28th Division.

28th Divisional Artillery
-o-o-o-o-o-o-o-o-o-o-o-

Items of Interest for 24 hours ending 6.0 a.m. 31st August 1915.
-o-o-o-o-o-o-o-o-o-o-o-o-o-o-o-o-o-o-o-o-o-o-o-o-o-o-o-

1. Working parties seen and fired on by -
    - 18th Bty at N.24.d.4.5. TOEDELSTEDE work stopped.
    - 18th Bty .. N.18.b.9.2. direct hit. Work stopped
    - 69th Bty .. N.30.a.4.2. work stopped
    - 149th Bty .. O.19.d.5.7. party dispersed

2. Fire in retaliation, or by request opened by - hostile
    - 18th Bty on N.18.b.2.5. by request to stop/shelling
    - 75th Bty .. U.1.a.1.7. to stop shelling of O.2.
    - 75th Bty .. Opposite O.4. to stop shelling of that trench

3. Flashes seen at -
    8.55 pm on bearing 97° magnetic from HILULL Tower (Several flashes)

4. A field gun was reported by the infantry to have been brought up and placed in hedge near the cottage at N.36.d.10.5. from which position it had fired on the night 29th/30th. 365th Bty. registered this point and got a direct hit on the cottage.

5. 18th Battery yesterday fired on what appeared to be two embrasures in trench at N.18.b.8.2. The openings appear to be covered with sacking or boards.

6. A new communication trench is reported by 69th Battery at O.31.b.4.4.

7. 149th Battery report considerable movement about the house in O.19.d.5.7. where fresh works have recently been constructed in front of the building itself.

8. Enemy shelled PLOEGSTEERT area yesterday morning with 4.2" Howitzer, some of which fell on farm T.24.a.5.9.
It was remarked that the shell had practically no effect at all. They scarcely made even a hole in the ground though all exploded.

9. Heavy firing heard in the evening from the direction of STEENSTRAAT.

10. A certain amount of movement was observed during the day near the house O.32.c.2.3. by the 75th Battery. Brick
This battery also reports that some kind of/work is being carried out in the hedge which runs from LONE TREE Farm about O.31.d.9.5. It is suggested that a well is being sunk there.

11. 33rd Trench Howitzer Battery, at the request of the Infantry, at various times during the evening, fired 23 bombs to silence rifle grenadiers.

sd / V.M. FERGUSSON Major.

Brigade Major R.A. 28th Division.

NOMINAL ROLL OF OFFICERS.

Headquarters, 28th Divisional Artillery

Rank	Name		Date of Joining	Class of Commission	Date of Promotion to present rank	Remarks.
Brig.Gen.	Arbuthnot C.M.G.	D.	H.Q.R.A. 9.5.15	Regular	9.5.1915.	Commanding 28th Div.Arty.
Major	Fergusson	V.M.	" 16.12.14	"	30.10.14	Brigade Major R.A.
Captain	Burkhardt	V.R.	" 26.12.14	"	26.10.14	Staff Captain R.A.
Lieut.	Brooke	J.R.I.	" 14.5.15	Territorial	21.4.15	Aide-de-camp.

3rd Brigade R.F.A.

Rank	Name	Battery	Date of Joining	Date of promotion to present rank.	Class of Commission	Remarks.
Lt.Col.	Bruce T.	Bde.H.Q.	21.5.15	18.2.15	Regular	Commanding Brigade
Capt.	Adam R.F.	"	8.7.15	30.10.14	"	Adjutant
2/Lt.	Franey J.B.	"	4.1.15	15.8.14	Special Reserve	Orderly Officer.
Maj. Capt.	Lewin J.S. L.O.	18.16. 18th	12.1.15	17.10.14	Capt Sp. Res. Regular Regular	
Capt.	MacGregor J.St.C.	"	23.7.15 22.12.14	30.10.14 9.2.15	Special Reserve	
Lieut.	Maxwell J.L.	"	24.12.14	22.5.15	Regular	
2/Lt.	Woodgate F.C.I.	"	8.4.15	5.2.15	Special Reserve	
2/Lt.	Russell P.H.W.	"	21.6.15	22.4.15	Regular	
2/Lt.	Giles		26.8.15			
Major	Scarlett J.A.	62nd	23.3.15	30.10.14	Regular	(Sick 16.8.15)
2/Lt.	Cressey R.L.	"	28.12.14	24.9.14	Temporary	
2/Lt.	Finch M.B.I.	"	19.3.15	12.1.15	Temporary	
2/Lt.	Wheeton J.C.	"	17.5.15	6.5.15	Temporary	
Capt.	Farrant M.	22nd	12.2.15	30.10.14	Regular	
Lieut.	Bether E.J.	"	12.2.15	23.7.13	Regular	Absent sick Struck off 28.8.15 RA 700/6/8
2/Lt.	Backhouse H.W.	"	3.3.15	12.4.15	Special Reserve	
2/Lt.	Rex A.M.	"	29.5.15	27.2.15	Temporary	
Capt.	Yorke P.G.	365th	21.2.15	21.12.13	Regular	
2/Lt.	Collingwood A.H.	"	17.12.14	12.8.14	Regular	
2/Lt.	Pierce H.L.	"	5.8.14	15.8.14	Special Reserve	
2/Lt.	Pitt-Brown W.	"	29.5.15	2.2.15	Temporary	
2/Lt.	Pitt J.W.	"	2.4.15	1.5.15	From Ranks	
Capt.	Clarken G.	A.G.	11.1.15	28.8.14	Reserve of Officers	
2/Lt.	Harris W.G.	"	14.1.15	9.1.15	From Ranks	
2/Lt.	Dickens E.G.	"	22.7.15	6.5.15	From Ranks.	

31st Brigade R.F.A.

Rank	Name	Battery	Date of Joining	Date of promotion to present rank	Class of Commission	Remarks
Major	Bond H.H.	Bde.H.Q.	22.7.15	10.10.09	Regular	Cmdg. Bde.
Lieut.	Ireland K.G.	"	22.12.14	10.10.09		Adjutant
				23.7.13	Regular	
2/Lt.	Hollwey J.E.	"	2.5.15	10.6.14	Regular	Orderly Officer
Major	Willis J.G.L.	69th	1.3.15	1.10.14	Regular	
2/Lt.	Mackenzie D.F.	"	24.12.14	15.8.14	Special Reserve	
2/Lt.	Short P.V.	"	9.5.15	13.12.14	From Ranks	
2/Lt.	Nodin E.A.	"	2.6.15	21.12.14	Temporary	
Major	Ramsden R.L.	100th	22.12.14	15.5.12	Regular	
Capt.	Sandeman T.F.	"	5.5.15	30.10.14	Regular	Sick 20.8.15
Lieut.	Hawkins A.L.	"	22.12.14	22.5.15	Regular	
2/Lt.	Brown C.F.	"	27.5.15	27.4.15	From Ranks	
Major	Mortimore C.A.	103rd	16.6.15	21.11.14	Regular	posted to R.C. (sick 21.8.15)
2/Lt.	Poer H.L.B.	"	15.5.15	15.8.14	Special Reserve	
2/Lt.	Gretton W.E.	"	22.12.14	20.12.14	From Ranks	
2/Lt.	Welby G.	"	9.5.15	4.4.15	From Ranks	
Major	Ross Hudson	118th	5.2.15	5.9.13	Regular	
2/Lt.	Smith S.R.T.	"	27.5.15		Temporary	
2/Lt.	Russell G.A.	"	5.2.15		Regular	
2/Lt.	Chase A.G.	"	24.7.15	24.3.15	Temporary	
Major	Cope J.S.	A.C.	12.1.15	17.10.14	(Captain) Special Reserve	
2/Lt.	Johnson P.E.	"	22.12.14	20.12.12	Regular	posted to 103rd Bdy
2/Lt.	Braddick J.B.	"	8.4.15	15.8.14	Temporary	
2/Lt.	Cunliffe T.	"	29.7.15	29.3.15	Special Reserve	
Lieut.	Lomax R.H.W.	"		12.9.14	Special Reserve	Struck off 25.8.15
2/Lt.	Brink J.H.	"	2.3.15	15.8.14	Special Reserve	(Cmdg 33rd Trench How Bdy)

146th Brigade R.F.A.

Rank	Name	Battery	Date of Joining	Date of promotion to present rank	Class of Commission	Remarks.
Major	de Berry P.P.L.	Bde.H.Q.	22.7.15	15.10.09	Regular	Cmdg. Brigade
Lieut.	Graham S.D.	"	17.12.14	23.7.13	Regular	Adjutant
2/Lt.	Hossack H.V.	"	29.7.15	3.4.15	Special Reserve	Orderly Officer
Major	Jervis N.G.M.	75th	21.12.14	30.10.14	Regular	
2/Lt.	Coed E.H.	"	21.12.14	16.9.14	Regular	
2/Lt.	Renny G.H.	"	21.12.14	16.9.14	Regular	Struck off. (Auth. 2nd Army RO20/4/5)
2/Lt.	Strachan A.C.	"	20.6.15	22.4.15	Regular	
2/Lt.	Hossack P.M.O'F.	"	22.7.15	5.8.14	Special Reserve	
Capt.	Parbury K.	149th	7.2.15	30.10.14	Regular	
2/Lt.	Russell G.C.	"	3.1.15	15.8.14	Special Reserve	
2/Lt.	Cooper Smith L.J.	"	27.3.15	4.1.15	From Canadian Ranks	
2/Lt.	Wood J.L.	"	16.5.15	11.3.15	From Ranks	
2/Lt.	Gage H.J.	"	12.2.15	12.9.14	Regular	Wounded 26.4.15 Struck off. RO20/6/5
2/Lt.	Coles T.W.	"	21.12.14	1.10.14	Absent sick (3 months) Struck off 28.5.15	
2/Lt.	Yearsley H.Q.	"	22.7.15	27.2.15	Temporary	Attached.
Capt.	Shaw G.D.A.	366th	25.7.15	30.10.14	Regular	
Lieut.	Scott F.V.	"	25.5.15	15.4.15	Special Reserve	
Lieut.	French E.W.	"	12.2.15	31.8.14	Reserve of Officers	Wounded 30.4 Struck off RO20/6/5
2/Lt.	Wood E.J.W.	"	9.5.15	20.6.15	From Ranks	
2/Lt.	Meyrick-Weites A.S.	"	22.7.15		From Ranks	
Major	Carlyon T.	367th	31.3.15	13.2.15	Regular	
2/Lt.	Johnson F.J.C.	"	17.12.14	17.11.14	Temporary	
2/Lt.	Stansfield E.J.	"	17.12.14	8.2.15	Regular	
2/Lt.	Herbert L.W.	"	9.5.15		From Ranks	
Capt.	Allen J.	A.C.	16.6.15	14.12.14	District Officer	
2/Lt.	Jackson F.	"	8.4.15	16.1.15	Temporary	
2/Lt.	Brown S.G.	"	25.5.15	11.12.14	Temporary	
Lieut.	Foster D.S.	"	29.12.14	5.12.14	Territorial	

A/73rd Battery

Rank	Name	Battery	Date of Joining	Date of Promotion to present rank	Class of Commission	Remarks
Major	Edwards	A/73rd	8.8.15	13.5.10	Regular	
Lieut.	Messervy	"	8.8.15	12.12.14	Temporary	
2/Lt.	Burbridge	"	8.8.15	19.9.14	Temporary	
2/Lt.	Morgan	"	8.8.15	22.10.14	Special Reserve	

B/89th Howitzer Battery

Rank	Name	Battery	Date of Joining	Date of Promotion to present rank	Class of Commission	Remarks
Capt.	Darrell	B/89th	7.8.1915	14.11.14	Temporary	
Lieut	Rudio	"	7.8.1915	22.4.15	Temporary	
2/Lt.	O'Donovan	"	7.8.1915	1910.15	Temporary	
2/Lt.	Lumsden	"	7.8.1915	23.4.15	Regular	
2/Lt.	Harper	R.H.B.		3.10.14	Temporary	

A/49th Howitzer Battery.

Rank	Name		Battery	Date of Joining	Class of Commission	Date of promotion to present Rank	Remarks
Major	Bridges	A.H.	A/49th	19.6.15	Regular	30.10.14	Commanding Battery
Lieut.	Campbell-Johnston	P.S.C.	"	19.6.15	Temporary	26.11.14	
2/Lt.	Hughes	F.E.	"	19.6.15	Temporary	5.11.14	
2/Lt.	Groom	S.A.H.	"	19.6.15	Temporary	7.12.14	
2/Lt.	Penny	G.H.L.	"	19.6.15	Temporary	24.12.14	
2/Lt.	Culpin	H.		29.12.14	From Ranks	20.12.14	

28th Divisional Ammunition Column

Rank	Name	Section	Date of Joining	Date of promotion to present rank	Class of Commission	Remarks
Lt.Col.	Kerrich	H.Q.	29.12.14	22.8.14	Reserve of Officers	Cmdg. D.A.C.
Capt.	Stevens	"	29.12.14	21.12.13	Adjutant	
Lieut.	King		29.12.14	29.8.14	Territorial	
Major	Hoare		29.12.14	5.7.13	Territorial	
Lieut.	Schuster		29.12.14	17.11.12 1.12.14	Regular Territorial	
2/Lt.	Maitland	A.	29.12.14	11.9.14	Territorial	
2/Lt.	Trim	B.	4.6.15	30.9.14	Temporary	
2/Lt.	Oakley	D.A.	31.5.15	21.10.14	Territorial	
2/Lt.	Allen	F.A.	22.7.15	12.6.15	From Ranks.	

Trench Howitzer Battery.

Rank	Name	Battery	Date of Joining	Date of promotion to present rank	Class of Commission	Remarks
Capt.	Gilpin B.B.	25th		5.8.14	Reserve of Officers	
2/Lt.	Felton R.E.	"	4.8.15	9.10.14	Temporary	
2/Lt.	Brink J.H.	33rd		15.8.14	Special Reserve (Attached)	
2/Lt.	Harvey W.G.	"	4.8.15	9.14	Temporary	

9th Anti Aircraft Section.

Rank	Name	Battery	Date of Joining	Date of Promotion to present rank	Class of Commission	Remarks.
Capt.	Worsley H.G.	9th AAC	1.8.1915	30.10.14	Regular	
Lieut.	Oldham E.C.	"	1.8.1915	30.1.15	Temporary	

12th Anti Aircraft Section

Rank	Name	Battery	Date of Joining	Date of promotion to present rank	Class of Commission	Remarks
Capt.	Wright	H.E.Fitz.H. 12th AAS	8.8.15	29.8.14	Territorial	

121/6993

28th Division

Hd Qrs R.A. 28th Division

Vol IX
Sept. 15

Army Form C. 2118.

WAR DIARY
or
INTELLIGENCE SUMMARY.
(Erase heading not required.)

28th Div Arty

123

Hour, Date, Place	Summary of Events and Information	Remarks and references to Appendices

LOCRE CHATEAU 1st Sept. — Improvement of present positions & preparation of back positions continued as material becomes available. WF

2nd " — Nothing to report. WF Kean from to North in command

3rd " — BGRA 1st Corps to visit close defence gun positions with CRA, but not turned. Received GHQ3 dividing line from 2nd Corps. The situation apparent for 146 B. can now be proceeded with. Kean from trench during the evening. Shelled PECKHAM.

4th " — BGRA 1st Corps visited close defence gun positions with CRA. CRA also visited GHQ3 positions of 3rd Bde.

5th " — Nothing to report. Battalion daily fire at working parties in retaliation.

6th " — Line for a communication on KEMMEL selected. DAC will commence work on it tomorrow. SCHERPENBERG received about 10 & 2 in howitzer batteries ordered to fire half 3 HE + 38 shrapnel at 16 BLACK REDOUBT.

7th " — Corps allot 30 rounds HE for 18 pdr, 20 for BLACK REDOUBT, 110 for an experimental shoot at some cement works erected by the GE.

8th " — Position for 110th Battery selected by CRA for WULVERGHEM Switch. Arrangements made for a series of 18 hr HE 14.5in Hm on BLACK REDOUBT tomorrow. WF

WAR DIARY
or
INTELLIGENCE SUMMARY. 124   28th Div Arty.

Army Form C. 2118.

Hour, Date, Place	Summary of Events and Information	Remarks and references to Appendices
LOCRE CHATEAU 8th (Cont)	Hostile aeroplane dropped hookup containing information of Capt W.C. Alderman RFC this observer, who were brought down on 5th inst. also the private effects of Lieut Meier. WF	
9th Sept	Some 18hr HE being here allotted by 11th Corps a new was fired at the BLACK REDOUBT. Two field batteries and howitzer fired the while a third field battery but one shrapnel. The hookup was considerably damaged. WF	
10th Sept	Nothing to record. WF	
11th Sept	Several troops inflicted with hollow straw stems. WF	
12th Sept 4AM	Bombardment of BLACK REDOUBT resumed. In addition to the batteries which fired on the 9th, a mountain gun fired from the trenches opposite, at the same time the gun of the 2 Lyst Section of No 2 M.L. Battery + the 25 T.M. Battery engaged some house at M30 c. The mountain gun entrance having been damaged by a shell in the early afternoon, fell in after the 3rd round. One house was cut in two. WF	
13 Sept.	D5 + D4 trenches worried by rifle grenades most of the day. In envoy Common retaliated to fire with mortar mortar after it D3 with starting guns 4.2" How +5.9" How. 2nd Campbell Johnston of M/Bo Battery was wounded	

Army Form C. 2118.

WAR DIARY
INTELLIGENCE SUMMARY.
(Erase heading not required.)

125 28th Div Arty

Hour, Date, Place	Summary of Events and Information	Remarks and references to Appendices

LOCRE CHATEAU 14th Sept — Nothing to report.

15" — Capt DEVITT. 130th B'AC to command B/130 Bty vice EDWARDS to LRCA in 37th Divn.

16" — Maj Edwards landed our Battery. Divnl Cmdr visited 3rd r part of 31st Bty Bm positions. Short 9.2 in throne postponed. Arrangements made for use of trench or OP wires to between 6.9.2" Seige tomorrow.

7 - 4 PM — 12 round 9.2 on BLACK REDOUBT & 8 on SPANBROEK MOLEN. 15hm confirmed with Seaforth spherical attributed points in Comms' & support trenches aft first 4 rounds spectacular. Three 4.5in BDe bombarded by 25th TM Battery & 4.5in How Battery. Orders received for relief 9Div Arty by 2nd Canadian & 21st Div AF.

18" — Orders received that 4 CFA + 54 would relieve 146th By — start on Bty 17th Divn would relieve 3rd r 37th Bdes, namely 80th Bdy. Arrangements made accordingly.

19" — Orders issued for relief. Night 19/20 following units took place — first Section relieved
D 80 — 18 pdr Battery   A 80 — 100th Battery } 13 CFA Bde — 149
B 80 — 22" "   C 80 — 103" "   — 75
                                                                        — 366
                                                                   14" —
                                                                   15" —
                                                                   16" —
                                                                        — 297

Army Form C. 2118.

WAR DIARY
or
INTELLIGENCE SUMMARY.

(Erase heading not required.)

126.   28th Div Arty

Hour, Date, Place	Summary of Events and Information	Remarks and references to Appendices
LOCRE Chateau 20th Sept	Registration carried out by 4th CFA Bde & 80th Fd Bty.	
1.40 P.M.	with 18hr Section of 4 CFABde relieves Left 18hr Section 146th BAC. 28th Div wired that the howitzer Batty 1st Canadian Div would relieve 130th B.M. Instructions received from Corps Artillery that the Section 18 hrs from 1st Canadian Div would relieve 26th H. By	
6.35 P.M.	Afternoon cancelled. Only one howitzer section coming to relieve C/1 Bde. Necessary alteration in orders made. Orders for hour to break area issued.	
21st Sept	Registration continued. S.A.A. Section + Remainder of 18 pr Sect 146 BAC relieved. First half of 31st BAC 18 pr Section relieved.	
8.30 P.M.	Relief of 146th BA Completed.	
22nd Sept	Relief of remainder 18pr Section completed. Registration continued. 31st B.A.C Gtd retired line. Landed wire. Telephone system struck mine. Some through renewals made to connect Trenches with this Corner batteries.	
10 A.M.	14th (E.) Bde marched under Divnl Orders X 26 d 3.2 [Sheet 27] 95th Bty to Bty area on Section D.A.C. to Sq BOESE in B4 Bty Area.	
9.30 P.M.	Relief of 18th 22nd B.AC in (31st BA) and 100th No 3 (31st BA) by 80th B3 M. Complete. Remaining batteries of these B as withdrawn.	

Army Form C. 2118.

WAR DIARY
or
INTELLIGENCE SUMMARY.
(Erase heading not required.)

127

28th Div. Art.

Instructions regarding War Diaries and Intelligence Summaries are contained in F.S. Regs., Part II and the Staff Manual respectively. Title pages will be prepared in manuscript.

Hour, Date, Place	Summary of Events and Information	Remarks and references to Appendices
MERRIS. 23rd Sept.	CRA handed over command at 9 AM to Br. Gen. Shut. M. Cmdg. Lumsden commanding RA 2nd Canadian Div.	
9 AM	Remainder M.D.A.C. marched to S. of BORRE.	
10 AM	HQ RA. 2nd - 130 - 3rd Bde marched from Station front to back area - 31st in B4 area with 130 - Bde MDAC. The 3rd Bde to OULTERSTEENE in B3 & B4 area.	
3.45 PM	Ordered to be ready to move at one hour notice.	
24th Sept.	Squadron not out. Kit-exercise carried out by all Bde. Wind S. Low. Transport kept stand as much as possible.	
25th Sept.	Divl Cavalry exercised. Stood by ready for a move.	
8.30 PM	Order from Div. that is was unlikely we should move before daylight.	Appendix 20.
26th Sept.		
2.45 AM	Divl Op Order No 54 received. 18 Bde. wanted. They would receive orders from comdg B. Cmdr.	
3.15 AM	Orders for DAC received. Communicated	
7.30 AM	RA HQ moved off. CRA moved by motor to MERVILLE.	
11.30 AM	Orders received for continuation of march towards BETHUNE. 3rd - Bde to billets to & 3 Bde about ROBEQUE. 31st - 130 r DAC " " 84 " - PARADIS. 146 " Bde " " " 85 " - BETHUNE. HQ 31 Rue GAMBETTA BETHUNE.	

Army Form C. 2118.

WAR DIARY
or
INTELLIGENCE SUMMARY.
(Erase heading not required.)

28th Divn Arty

Hour, Date, Place	Summary of Events and Information	Remarks and references to Appendices
BETHUNE. 27th Sept.	7.15 AM orders received for concentration of Divl Arty in area Oyeschi Sy. Oblinghem – Pont L'Hinges – Les Choqueaux – Essars. Divl Arty billeted as under 3rd Bde. about Le Vertannoy. 31st " " Hingette. 130 " " Pont L'Hinges. 146 " " Essars. DAC about Fouquereuil, 1 mile S.W. Bethune.	Appendix 21 amended by G.H.Q.R
12 midnight	Orders received for the batteries 26th Divl Arty to replace 105th Battn at Vermelles. B5 Cmdr to report to OC 2nd Bde RFA at Fosse No 9.	
28th Sept. 10 AM	at Bethune. Annequin, 18th Battery, attached to 3rd Bde Cmdr, moved thro Bethune at 9 AM en route to take over.	
3.15 PM	31st Bde. Moved at disposal of the 2nd Divl Arty Cmdr. B4 + B5 Cmdr ordered to report at Le Quesnoy at 6 AM tom mng. First set'n Bde into action tomorrow night (29/30 in).	
29th Sept.	B4 Cmdr. Battery Cmdrs – new officers for Battn 3rd + 146. FA Bdys at 30th H4 Bdy attached to 9th Divl Arty for instruction with a view to taking over batteries. Detached to Vendin Les Bethune. 62nd TMB Battery – Lt. G. Webster - 9.3 two inch mortars ordered to 105th Bty. Only one mortar arrived. all in store. Rifles ammn were found in the trenches. 9th T.M.B Battery – Lt Caerie – one 15 in mortar ordered by D's staff	

Army Form C. 2118.

WAR DIARY
or
INTELLIGENCE SUMMARY.
(Erase heading not required.)

12a   28th Div Arty.

Hour, Date, Place	Summary of Events and Information	Remarks and references to Appendices
BETHUNE. 29th Contd.	10/om 83rd Bty.— A Stokes T.M. Battery. Throwing smoke bombs und.— was handed over by the 9th Divn Lt MURRAY, commanding, to actions of the B.I.R - Suffolks - who had installed an officer in the rear of the mortars. LT WEBSTER reported that more of his mortars were fit for action so took etc. were wired for to ft. army, T.M. School. W/E Relief Feb.	
30 Sept. 2.0 PM	First section 93rd - 12th 0746 — B— ashed up in relief.	
6.0 PM	Completed by 6.0 PM. Relief completed by first section. B— HB5 Garden handed to be ready to assume command at 1.10.15	WmF

28th Divisional Artillery

Items of Interest for 24 hours ending 6.0 a.m. 2nd September 1915

1. Working parties seen and fired on by -
    - 18th Bty at N.18.b.2.6. work stopped on two occasions
    - 18th Bty " N.18.b.9.1. work stopped
    - 69th Bty " N.30.a.4.5. " "
    - 69th Bty " N.26.c.2.1. " "
    - 100th Bty " N.30.a.5.8. PECKHAM work stopped

2. Fire in retaliation, or by request, opened by -
    - 18th Bty on N.30.c.3.8. SPANBROEK MOLEN to stop whizbang on F. trenches. 2 direct hits.
    - 22nd Bty " N.18.d.0.0. by request
    - 62nd Bty " Opposite H.2. to stop shelling of that trench
    - 62nd Bty " O.19.d.2.5. House in WYTSCHAETE. To stop shelling of H. trenches
    - 365th Bty " PETIT BOIS by request to stop shelling. shelling ceased
    - 103rd Bty " N.30.a.3.2.
    - 118th Bty " N.30.a.7.7. PECKHAM to stop shelling of G.1
    - 367th Bty " Fire trench N.30.c.5.0. and 5.2. to stop shelling of communication trench
    - 367th Bty " Support trench N.36.a.5.9.
    - 149th Bty " Fire trench T.6j.b.9.9.

3. The 18th Battery report that work continues at N.18.b.4.0. Earth is continually being thrown over the parapet and a glacis is gradually being formed.

4. In rear of the houses at N.36.a.9.5. a tumulus has been made into a dugout. The actual position of this dugout is reported by 149th Battery to be N.36.b.1.5½ and it is suggested that it is used as a Battalion Headquarters. The point was registered.

5. A large flash and a cloud of smoke were seen at 6.0 p.m. yesterday behind the screen mentioned in item 3 of yesterday.

6. 33rd Trench Howitzer Battery fired series at trench opposite J.3. left in reply to whizbang, on PETIT BOIS with good effect, and after dark on working party in PETIT BOIS.

7. A working party near HAMMART Farm drew fire of 8inch howitzer on N.27.b. B/89th Battery at once replied on SPANBROEK MOLEN, and the enemy replied with 6 more rounds. B/89th battery then put 6 lyddite into SPANBROEK MOLEN and closed the argument.

8. Four rounds of 5.9 inch shrapnel were burst over the N.E. end of KEMMEL Hill. Two burst near the Tower.

9. At 5.15 p.m. the Heavy Howitzers, according to arrangement, opened fire on PECKHAM, the 31st Brigade standing by to cooperate. After the 4th round, which was very effective, a party of Germans were seen strenuously digging in the debris. The opportunity was at once seized by the field batteries and several men were seen to fall. Six rounds from the Heavy Howitzer are reported to have hit the farm.

10. The enemy retaliated by firing on the support trenches behind F.5. with 6 inch and 8 inch shell, but no damage was done.

sd/ V.M. FERGUSSON Major.
Brigade Major R.A. 28th Division.

28th Divisional Artillery

Items of Interest for 24 hours ending 6.0 a.m. 3rd September 1915

1. Working parties seen and fired on by -
   118th Bty   at   O.19.c.10.4.   party dispersed

2. Fire in retaliation, or by request, opened by -
   18th Bty   on   N.30.c.1.9. fire trench
   22nd Bty   ..   N.18.c.   Fire trench
   62nd Bty   ..   O.19.a.1.5. House in WYTSCHAETE. to stop shelling of KEMMEL
   69th Bty   ..   N.30.a.4.4. Black Redoubt in return for explosion of mine
   100th Bty ..   N.30.a.5.8. PECKHAM by request, on explosion of mine
   118th Bty ..   N.24.c.8.5. to stop shelling of trenches
   367th Bty ..   N.36.a.7.7. to stop shelling behind trench No. 15.   Frenchman's
   B/89th Bty ..   SPANBROEK MOLEN in return for/ farm in N.34.b. being set on fire by H.E. shell
   366th Bty ..   O.32.b.3.6. to stop whizbang on D.3.
   367th Bty ..   N.30.c.4.5. To stop shelling of supports

3. Flashes seen -
   6.44 pm on bearing 90° magnetic from N.26.b.4.8.
   6.48 pm ..   .. 92°   ..   ..   ..
   7.17 pm ..   .. 82°   ..   ..   ..
   6.10 pm ..   .. 93°.30 ..   .. N.26.b.2.7.
   6.45 p.m..   .. 94°.30 ..   .. N.30.c.9.1.
   7.2. pm ..   .. 89°   ..   ..   N.26.b.1.9.
   7.9. pm ..   .. 97°   ..   ..   ..
   6.55 pm ..   .. 99°.30 ..   .. N.26.c.1.9.
   7.5. pm ..   .. 94°   ..   ..   ..
   7.7. pm ..   .. 97°.30 ..   .. ..
   6.45 pm ..   .. 91°   ..   ..   N.26.c.4.8.

4. A/73rd Battery fired a short series at the observing station in the brickstack, and obtained a direct hit with lyddite. 103rd Battery scored 3 direct hits on house at O.19.c.1.1. which is used as an observing station, and set it on fire.

5. German observation balloon was up on a bearing of 99° magnetic from N.26.c.2.8. between noon and 1.30 pm.

6. From 5.30 pm onwards enemy shelled KEMMEL Hill, at first with 8-inch on lower slopes, and later with 5.9-inch and 4.2-inch below the Tower. No damage was done. It is suggested that this 8-inch Howitzer occupies a position about GARDELILU.

7. 100th Battery notes that our aeroplanes are no longer fired on by any anti-aircraft guns on the WYTSCHAETE ridge. During the day only rifle fire was directed against them, possibly, it is suggested to entice the wily pilots to fly lower.

8. 367th Battery reports the short range battery which was firing over the F. trenches last night at 9.12 pm, is on a bearing of 102° magnetic from N.26.c.1.9. There appears to be four guns and the time between the report of the gun and the burst of the shell was about ½ a second.

9. 149th Battery reports that German guns were very active. PLOEGSTEERT area was shelled with H.E. and Shrapnel from 3.0 pm onwards, Hill 63 also shelled with 4.2-inch shell.

10. The trench opposite D.4. is being deepened and the parapet appears to have been lowered.

11. At 6.45 pm the 100th Battery received a call from the trenches as a mine had been exploded near G.2. Both the 69th and 100th Batteries opened fire at once and B/89th Battery was ordered to put lyddite into PECKHAM. The trench reporting shortly afterwards that all was quiet, the Howitzers did not open fire. The batteries stood by and kept in constant touch with the trenches. The explosion of the mine was preceeded by one heavy shell and followed by several.

12. The reason for the heavy firing from the North yesterday evening has not yet come to light.
It appears to have commenced at 3.30 p.m., at which time an observer saw shell bursting about HOOGE and North of YPRES. The firing became very heavy about 5.0 p.m. and about 5.30 pm the French 75 mm could be heard joining in.

sd/ V.M. FERGUSSON Major.

Brigade Major R.A. 28th Division.

28th Divisional Artillery
.o.o.o.o.o.o.o.o.o.o.o.o.o.

Items of Interest for 24 hours ending 6.0 a.m. 4th September 1915
.o.o.o.o.o.o.o.o.o.o.o.o.o.o.o.o.o.o.o.o.o.o.o.o.o.o.o.o.o.o.o.

1. The light was extremely bad all day and practically no movement was discernable in the German lines. There was practically no hostile fire during the 24 hours. On our side some registration was carried out and some Battery and trench tests.

2. O.C. A/73rd Battery has found a position in L.2. from which the support trench from N.24.b.7.10. to N.24.b.7.1. can be seen. From the same place the newly turned earth and the many fresh sandbags which can be seen at N.18.b.1.8., in the second line trench, show that a great deal of work is being done at that place.

3. 75th Battery observer reports that opposite D.4. trench the enemy were seen putting rectangular metal frames over the parapet. These frames measure 4 feet each way, and their object is not known. The Infantry are of opinion they may possibly be connected with some liquid fire or gas machine. (See sketch below).

4. 7.10 p.m. on 2nd September flash of heavy gun, which was shelling G.2., was seen on bearing 98° 30' from N.26.b.2.7.

sd/ V.M. FERGUSSON Major.
Brigade Major R.A. 28th Division.

28th Divisional Artillery

Items of Interest for 24 hours ending 6.0 a.m. 5th September 1915

1. Working parties seen and fired on by -
   366th Bty   at N.36.b.0.6.   Two rounds effective
   149th Bty   ,, N.36.b.7.9.   Party dispersed
   118th Bty   ,, N.31.d.10.5. ,,   ,,

2. Fire in retaliation, or by request, opened by -
   365th Bty   on N.W. corner of PETIT BOIS to stop shelling
                                            of J.4.
   365th Bty   ,, Opposite K.1. and J.3.L. to stop trench
                                    mortar and 5.9" shell on K.1.
   62nd Bty   ,, Opposite G.4. and H.2. to stop shelling of
                                            those trenches
   367th Bty   ,, L'ENFER Wood heavy shell on F. trenches
                                            stopped.
   367th Bty   ,, N.30.c.5.1. to stop trench mortar
   B/89th Bty ,, SPANBROEK MOLEN to stop heavy shell on F.6
   B/89th Bty ,, PECKHAM in retaliation for heavy shell on
                                            F.5 and 4.
   B/89th Bty ,, MADDELSTEDE in retaliation for heavy shell
                                            on H.2.

3. Flashes seen at -
   7.30 pm on bearing 99° magnetic from N.20.d.1.1.
   7.30 pm ,,   ,, 98°   ,,   ,, N.26.c.2.8.
   6.47 pm ,,   ,, 102°   ,,   ,, N.26.b.2.8.
   7.25 pm)
   7.26 pm)
   7.27 pm)
   7.28 pm)..   ,, 99°   ,,   ,, KEMMEL Tower
   7.33 pm)
   7.35 pm)
   7.37 pm)

4. A/73rd Battery fired a series on the German second line trench behind PETIT BOIS from N.24.b.7.10. to N.24.b.7.1. Several direct hits were made in the trench. See item 2 of 4th inst.

5. German observation balloon was up on bearing of 99° magnetic from N.26.c.2.8.

6. B/89th Battery reports that it has been noticed more or less every day that pigeons - a cross between "blue rocks" and "homing" pigeons - fly towards enemy positions about 8.45 a.m. and return about 4.30 p.m.

7. A white flag, with a black design in the centre of it, was observed by the A/49th battery in a communication trench behind SPANBROEK MOLEN throughout the day.

8. About 7.10 to 7.30 p.m. a number of 4.2" and 8-inch shell fell in N.9.b.3.6. and 7.
   This was probably in retaliation for the bursts of rapid fire in which the Batteries of the 17th Division were indulging at intervals between 2.55 and 7.0 p.m.

9. About 1.15 pm the heavy Howitzer fired a series on the Black Redoubt. Probably considerable damage was done as the enemy retaliated on the trenches opposite with 4.2' and 5.9'. This fire which is reported to have come from the direction of WYTSCHAETE was however ineffective.

10. 33rd Trench Howitzer Battery made use of his 1½-inch mortar for the first time yesterday.
At 4.0 p.m. 2 rounds were fired into fire trench opposite J.3. which was suspected of containing a trench mortar.
Again at 5.0 p.m. two more rounds of 1½-inch and several of 3.7-inch were fired at same trench. On each occasion the enemy stopped shooting.

sd/ V.M. FERGUSSON Major.

Brigade Major R.A. 28th Division.

28th Divisional Artillery

Items of Interest for 24 hours ending 6.0 a.m. 6th September 1915.

1. Working parties seen and fired on by -
   69th Bty   at O.25.a.9.2.   party disappeared
   100th Bty   .. O.25.a.7.8.   ..   ..
   A/49th Bty   .. O.32.c.7.5.   ..   dispersed
   366th Bty   .. O.31.d.9.9.   good bursts. movement stopped

2. Fire in retaliation, or by request, opened by -
   103rd Bty   on N.30.c.2.6. on fire trench in retaliation
   367th Bty   .. N.30.c.4.6. to stop whizbang on L.1.
   367th Bty   .. N.36.a.6.5. to stop rifle grenades on 14 trench.

3. Flashes seen -
   6.37 pm on bearing 111°30' magnetic from N.26.b.2.8.
   8.46 om ..   ..   84°   ..   ..   N.26.c.2.8.

4. The 100th Battery registered a target - cross roads O.20.a.3.9.- with balloon observation. The balloon also put the 103rd Bty on to road junction O.32.c.5.1. and the B/89th Howitzer Battery on to O.25.d.8.8. L'ENFER.

5. B/89th Battery put some H.L. into the Black Redoubt yesterday evening while the 118th Battery fired shrapnel.

6. About 5.30 pm the Heavy Howitzer fired a series on SPANBROEK MOLEN, the 118th Battery following up each explosion with a burst of shrapnel. The Heavy Howitzer series is reported to have been very effective.
   Enemy retaliated by putting about 7 4-inch shell behind F.2. trench.

7. 100th Battery reports that a lot of work has been done in the digging line, about the S.W. corner of PETIT BOIS. The freshly turned earth showed up very clearly in the evening light.

8. 367th Battery report that the communication trench at N.30.c.4.7 has been deepened and improved.
   At N.30.c.5.7½. what appears to be a rectangular wooden box about 6' x 8' x 6' was seen.
   It is suggested that it may be a framework for a dugout.

9. The 103rd Battery fired a series at enemy trench at N.30.c.2.8. where some fresh sandbags have made their appearance.
   The infantry are of opinion that a machine gun fires at night from this position.

10. German observation balloon up on a bearing of 64° magnetic from N.26.b.3.7.

11. A/49th Battery fired a series at the screen behind SPANBROEK MOLEN, said to cover some engine. The screen was hit by shrapnel bullets but not direct by H.L. shell.

12. 149th Battery has noticed that a lot of work has been done opposite D.4. on a communication trench which runs from fire trench to KRUISSTRAAT Road.

13. One of our aeroplanes was observed to have been brought down in the German lines somewhere opposite D.2. trench about 6.0 pm.

sd/ V.M. FERGUSSON Major.
Brigade Major R.A. 28th Division.

28th Divisional Artillery

Items of Interest for 24 hours ending 6.0 a.m. 7th September 1915

1. Working parties seen and fired on by -
    62nd Bty   at   N.24.d.7.8. in WYTSCHAETE Wood. party dispersed
    69th Bty   ..   O.25.b.6.2. work stopped
    103rd Bty   ..   O.25.b.8.6. work stopped
    366th Bty   ..   N.36.d.5.3. on 3 occasions by request

2. Fire in retaliation, or by request, opened by -
    A/73rd Bty on   N.18.b.3.5. front trench in retaliation
    18th Bty   ..   N.18.b.2.5.   ..   ..   by request
    18th Bty   ..   N.18.b.4.8. M.G. emplacement firing stopped
    75th Bty   ..   U.1.a.1.9. opposite C.2. to stop shelling of
                                            that trench
    75th Bty   ..   T.6.b.9.9. opposite C.3. to stop shelling of
                                            that trench

3. Reference item 3 of yesterday the 1st flash reported should read
   6.39 p.m. on bearing 112° from KEMMEL Tower and not as stated

4. O.C. 18th Battery reports that about 4.30 p.m. while carrying out
   communication tests from the L. trenches, a British aeroplane flew
   over, well within rifle range, with the result that at least three
   machine guns as well as many rifles were turned on to it.
   During the fusilade two Machine Gun emplacements were spotted at
   N.18.b.4.8. and N.18.b.5.5.
   Guns were turned on these spots and the machine guns stopped
   firing.
   Another machine gun emplacement is suspected at N.18.b.2.2.

5. B/89th Battery, in cooperation with 118th Battery fired an effective
   series on the Black Redoubt.
   In retaliation the enemy put some 6-inch H.E. over F.4. and F.5.
   which appeared ineffective.
   A/49th Battery fired a series later at the Redoubt.

6. 149th Battery reports that a new communication trench has been
   dug west of the house in N.36.b.7.9.

7. Some H.E. and shrapnel fell in the vicinity of the 366th Battery.
   The bearing of a scoope was taken from N.33.b.2.5. and read 104°
   magnetic.

8. Some 10 shell, percussion shrapnel, fell about 1.0 p.m. yesterday
   on SCHERPENBERG. A fuze which was picked up indicates that the
   shell was fired from a 5.1-inch or 6-inch gun. The scoops show that
   the shell came from the direction of WYTSCHAETE. The only battery,
   the position of which is known to be on that line is in O.21.d.5.4.

                                sd/ V.M. FERGUSSON Major.
                        Brigade Major R.A. 28th Division.

28th Divisional Artillery

Items of Interest for 24 hours ending 6.0 a.m. 8th September 1915

1. Working parties seen and fired on by -
    - 18th Bty   at   N.18.b.3.6. work stopped on two occasions
    - 118th Bty   ..   Black Redoubt. Work stopped (see item 5)

2. Fire in retaliation, or by request, opened by -
    - 18th Bty   on   N.18.b.5.5. Machine gun emplacement Fire ceased
    - 365th Bty   ..   Trench opposite K.1. by request on two occasions
    - 365th Bty   ..   "   "   J.3.d. and K.1. in retaliation for shelling
    - 367th Bty   ..   N.36.a.9.4. to stop whizbang on trench 14
    - 75th Bty   ..   T.6.b.5.2. opposite trench C.4. to stop shelling
    - 366th Bty   ..   O.32.b.3.8. to stop shelling of D. trenches and R.E. Farm

3. WULVERGHEM was shelled by 5.9-inch and 8-inch Howitzers between 10.0 a.m. and 11.30 a.m.
    R.E. Farm, KEMMEL and LINDENHOEK villages and the C. and D. trenches all came in for some attention.

4. Some enemy heavy guns were active about 8.0 a.m. yesterday. A considerable number of heavy shell were heard coming from the OOSTAVERNE direction, of which a large percentage was blind. They passed over to the left near the 69th Battery, but the objective could not be seen.

5. The Black Redoubt was fired at during the day by the three Howitzer Batteries in co-operation with 18-pdrs firing shrapnel. After one series a working party commenced repairing the parapet but stopped work when a shrapnel burst amongst them.

6. Two German aeroplanes crossed well behind our lines yesterday, in the morning and evening. A light was fired over one of the batteries and shortly afterwards two 5.9-inch and one 4.2-inch shell fell in the neighbourhood.

7. The O.C. 100th Battery verified from the balloon a point which had been previously registered by one of the balloon observation officers. The registration was found completely successful.

8. Between 8.0 and 10.0 a.m. C. and D. trenches were subjected to a bombardment from 77 mm, 10.5 cm, and 15 cm Howitzers. A hostile aeroplane was up at the time. Two field batteries, one field Howitzer and the Heavies replied. A/49th Battery observer, from the trenches, calculated that the 10.5 cm shell came from the direction of O.33.c., and the 15 cm came from O.34.b. The magnetic bearing of a 10.5 cm shell scoop at N.36.c.2½.9½. was 102.

9. 149th Battery reports that more work has been done on the trenches on Southern slopes of hill 73 in N.24.d.

10. A/49th Battery reports an undue amount of smoke was seen issuing in puffs and clouds, from the communication trench West of KWISTRADT Cabaret.

                sd/ V.M. FERGUSSON Major
        Brigade Major R.A. 28th Division.

28th Divisional Artillery

Items of Interest for 24 hours ending 6.0 a.m. 10th September 1915

1. Working parties seen and fired on by -
    - 18th Bty at O.7.d.8.3. party dispersed
    - 18th Bty .. O.13.c.4.9. work stopped
    - 62nd Bty .. N.24.d.7.8. working party in open. Dispersed
    - 100th Bty .. O.25.a.9.8. ruins which men were seen to enter
    - A/130th " .. O.31.d.10.5. Men moving along communication trench.

2. Fire in retaliation, or by request, opened by -
    - 18th Bty on N.18.b.3.1. and 4.4. by request of Infantry
    - 365th Bty .. opposite K.1. to stop enemy mortars on several occasions.
    - 365th Bty .. N.W. corner of Petit Bois to stop shelling of J.3.L. shelling ceased.
    - 103rd Bty .. M.G. emplacement N.30.c.1.10. by request
    - 366th Bty .. N.36.d.1.8. to stop rifle grenading of D.2.
    - 366th Bty .. O.32.b.3.6. to stop mortar on D.3. on 3 occasions.

3. Flashes seen at -
    - 10.20 pm on bearing 105° magnetic from N.26.b.4.2.
    - 10.44 pm .. .. 63° .. .. ..
    - 6.30 pm .. .. 99° .. .. N.26.b.3.8.

4. 5.15 pm the 69th and 100th Batteries and the B/130th Howitzer Battery each fired 5 rounds of H.E. at the BLACK REDOUBT. Each round was followed by shrapnel, the 118th Battery firing after the Howitzers.
   The firing appeared very effective, and observers report considerable damage was done to the parapet.
   The enemy retaliated by putting 3 heavy shell behind F.4.

5. 75th Battery reports that the work which has been going on behind the German trench at N.36.b.1.1½. has resulted in the erection of a mound 4 feet higher than the parapet. This can be seen from D.3. bay 17.
   The mound, it is said, commands L.1. support trench.
   The O.C. 25th Trench Howitzer Battery reports that this mound affords a most suitable target for his 1½ inch Howitzers.

6. The shell which fell in and round the D. trenches on the 7th inst. were 8-inch Armour piercing shell with a base fuze. The markings on the base are Kz Bd Z 10. Sp 14 c 8502, also the word, BORSIGTEGEL 4/3.

7. 365th Battery observer saw a flash at 12.15 pm about 100 yards East of the N.W. corner of Petit Bois, which he took to be that of a trench mortar.
   K.1. trench reported immediately afterwards that a trench mortar was firing on them, but no other flash was seen.

8. At 4.30 pm an enemy aeroplane passed over and dropped copies of the GAZETTE des ARDENNES dated 19th August 1915. A copy has been forwarded to 28th Division.

9. The window frames of the two Northern windows on West side of House in O.19.c.9.10. appear to have been removed during the night 8th/9th.

10. 33rd Trench Howitzer Battery fired 10 rounds on a registered point in Petit Bois to stop the enemy mortar shelling our trenches. Mortar stopped.

11. At about 7.0 pm our miners exploded a mine near J.3. right and drew a burst of – rapid fire and mortar bombs. 25th Trench Howitzer Battery replied by putting 17 rounds into the German trenches.

12. A new kind of bomb has been discovered, blind, in D.3. trench and has been made the subject of a separate report.

                              sd/ V.M. FERGUSSON Major.
                              Brigade Major R.A. 28th Division.

28th Divisional Artillery

Items of Interest for 24 hours ending 6.0 a.m. 17th September 1915.

1. Working parties seen and fired on by -
   - 62nd Bty   at   O.19.c.10.4.   work stopped
   - 62nd Bty   ..   N.24.d.3.6.   ..   ..
   - 149th Bty   ..   Reserve trench behind SPANBROEK MOLEN.
                                                work stopped
   - A/130th Bty..   N.36.a.9.5.   party dispersed
   - A/130th Bty..   O.32.o.2.3½.   house (see item 6)

2. Fire in retaliation, or by request, opened by -
   - 22nd Bty   on   N.18.d.1½.2. to stop hand grenading of K.2.
   - 366th Bty   ..   N.36.d.5.6.) repeatedly as L.2, 3 and 4
                      O.32.b.3.6.) were continuously troubled
                      N.36.d.1.8.) by rifle grenades
   - 100th Bty   ..   N.30.a.5.8. whizbang on G.1. and G.2.
                                   stopped.
   - 367th Bty   ..   N.36.a.8.7. by request, to stop bombing of
                                        Trench 15.

3. Flashes seen -
   7.39 pm on bearing 120° magnetic from KEMMEL TOWER.
   The mist was very thick last night and the flash observing officer was unable to locate any flashes.

4. 18th Battery reports that a small screen has been erected across a communication trench which runs North and South behind HOLLANDSCHESCHUUR Farm about N.18.b.6.6.

5. The central "pit" of the mound behind the German trenches opposite D.3. appears to have been slightly deepened during the night.

6. A large working party was busy on the house O.32.o.2.3½. 4 people, apparently officers, inspected the building and walked up the road. It is evident that the house is being prepared for some special purpose.

7. Some white sandbags, having made their appearance in front parapet opposite trench 15, show that some alteration and improvement is being carried on at that place.

                                                          sd/ V.H. FERGUSSON Major.
                                              Brigade Major R.A. 28th Division.

28th Divisional Artillery

Items of Interest for 24 hours ending 6.0 a.m. 19th September 1915.

1. Working parties seen and fired on by -
    149th Bty   at N.36.b.7.9. work stopped

2. Fire in retaliation, or by request, opened by -
    149th Bty   on opposite D. trenches to stop rifle grenading
    366th Bty   .. O.32.b.3.6.) enemy very persistent last night
                    N.36.d.5.6.) in rifle grenading and mortaring
                                 the D. trenches
    69th Bty   .. BLACK REDOUBT to stop shelling of F trenches
                    SPANBROEK MOLEN   ..   ..
                    L'ENFER WOOD   ..   ..
    100th Bty   .. N.24.c.6.1.   ..   ..   .. G   ..
    103rd Bty   .. N.30.c.2.6.) to stop whizbangs on F.4
                    N.30.c.7.9.)
    118th Bty   .. N.24.c.8.4. to stop shelling G.4
    367th Bty   .. to stop rifle grenades N.36.a.7.7.
    B/130th Bty .. SPANBROEK MOLEN to stop shelling of F.4.
                    shelling stopped
    B/130th Bty .. MADDELSTEDE to stop shelling of H.1. and H.2
    62nd Bty   .. O.19.c. fire trench to stop shelling of H.
                    trenches
    365th Bty   .. Fire trench opposite K.1. to stop rifle
                    grenades

3. Flashes seen from N.26.b.1½.6½.
    Time   Magnetic bearing   True bearing   Remarks
    8.7 pm   91° 15'   77° 30'   Field gun
    8.15 pm   87° 15'   73° 30'   ..   ..
    9.3 pm   99° 15'   85° 30'   ..   ..
    9.22 pm   106° 15'   92° 30'   )   Thought to be a
    9.24 pm   106° 15'   92° 30'   )   5.9 Howr.
    9.35 pm   101° 15'   87° 30'   Field gun
    10.57 pm   98° 15'   84° 30'   Heavy gun 2 flashes
    11.5 pm   86° 15'   72° 30'   Field gun
    11.15 pm   84° 15'   70° 30'   ..   ..
    11.30 pm   92° 15'   78° 30'   ..   .. 2 flashes
    11.46 pm   98° 15'   84° 30'   Heavy gun 2 ..
    12.4 am   111° 15'   97° 30'   Field gun
    12.47 pm   93° 15'   79° 30'   Field gun

4. 149th Battery reports that men were observed in the morning in
   the neighbourhood of the steam engine. Some work has been done
   there and the screen has been moved from the east of the
   emplacement to the west, altering the whole appearance of the
   place.
   Several clouds of steam were observed rising from behind
   SPANBROEK MOLEN between 5 and 6.0 pm

5. Probably in retaliation for the series by the 9.2-inch Howr.
   on SPANBROEK MOLEN and BLACK REDOUBT on the 17th instant the
   F. trenches were subjected to a severe bombardment yesterday
   afternoon.
   The whole of the 31st Brigade batteries and B/130th Howr. Bty.
   retaliated but the shelling continued till about 4.45 pm.
   In all probably 60 shell from 8-inch, 5.9-inch and 4.1-inch
   Howitzers fell about the F. and H. trenches.
   During the afternoon the 10th Heavy Brigade did all they could
   to stop the bombardment by engaging several enemy gun positions
   whence the fire might have come. Fire eventually ceased after
   some H.E. had been put into trenches near MADDELSTEDE Farm.

6. The 33rd Trench Mortar Battery fired some bombs to stop hostile
   fire.

                                    sd/ V... FERGUSSON Major
                                    Brigade Major R.A. 28th Division

SECRET.

Appendix 20

Copy No. 3

28th DIVISION OPERATION ORDER NO. 53.

September 26th 1915.

1. 28th Division will march to MERVILLE today.

2. The troops in the 83rd Brigade Area, under Orders of G.O.C. 83rd Infantry Brigade will march at 6 a.m. by VIEUX BERQUIN and NEUF BERQUIN to MERVILLE.

Div H.Q.
Cyclists.
Yeomanry.
Div. Signal Co.
H.Q.R.A.
H.Q.R.E.
86 Field Amb.

3. The troops in the Divisional Headquarter Area, order as in the margin, will move via VIEUX BERQUIN - NEUF BERQUIN - to MERVILLE. Head to pass starting point cross roads one mile South of MERRIS at 7.30. a.m.

4. The troops in the 84th Brigade Area less Divisional Ammunition Column under orders of G.O.C. 84th Infantry Brigade, will march at 8.a.m. by PETIT SEC BOIS - VIEUX BERQUIN - NEUF BERQUIN to MERVILLE.

5. The troops in the 85th Brigade Area under orders of G.O.C. 85th Infantry Brigade will march at 9.40 a.m. by VIEUX BERQUIN - NEUF BERQUIN - to MERVILLE.

6. Special instructions will be given to the Divisional Ammunition Column.

7. Staff Captains will meet Divisional Billetting Officer at road junction due West of B in LA BRIANNE (¾ mile N.E. of MERVILLE). at 7.30 a.m.

8. Reports to Hotel de Ville MERVILLE after 7 a.m. September 26th.

R. H. Hare.
Lieut-Colonel.
General Staff. 28th Divn.

Issued at :- 1.0 a.m.
Copies to :-
 Surrey Yeomanry.   Signals.
 Cyclists.   A.D.M.S.
 C.R.A.   Train.
 C.R.E.   A.P.M.
 83rd Infantry Brigade.
 84th Infantry Brigade.
 85th Infantry Brigade.

80
250
125
100

555

"A" Form.   Army Form C. 2121.
MESSAGES AND SIGNALS.

TO: CRA

Sender's Number: Aa2   Day of Month: 27th   AAA

Ref Operation Order attached Div Am Col will probably be march about 1 pm aaa instructions will be issued in the morning aaa it will march to FOUQUEREUIL 1½ miles S.W. of BETHUNE

From Place: 28th Div

Time: 12.20 pm

R Henvey Lt Col

"A" Form.
MESSAGES AND SIGNALS.

Army Form C. 2121.

TO 85th Bde,   CRE,   ADMS.

Sender's Number: GH 972   Day of Month: 24   AAA

Para one of of Order No 54 is cancelled AAA The Brigadier 85th Bde will go forward as soon as possible to 9th Div. HQ at CHATEAU DES PRES at SAILLY LABOURSE to arrange to relieve that Division on the front of a general line the QUARRIES trench map G.6.c and G.12.a FOSSE No 8 the left resting on VERMELLES - AUCHY road AAA The Brigade will march via BEUVRY and ANNEQUIN whence the road to the front will be shewn by 9th Div AAA The ADMS will arrange in conjunction with ADMS 9th Div to make the necessary medical arrangements AAA The CRE will arrange to

"A" Form.
MESSAGES AND SIGNALS.
Army Form C. 2121.

TO **Sheet 2.**

and forward with the 85 Bde such portions of the 38° Field Coy RE as may be necessary tht. the move of the Bde will probably take place about 10 am and the relief this afternoon. tht Addressed 85 Inf Bde, ADMS & CRE acknowledge

From 28° Div.
Place
Time 9.25 am

SECRET.

Appendix 81

Copy No. 5.

28th Division Operation Order No. 54.

Reference Map 1/40,000   27th September 1915.

1. On the 27th September the 85th Infantry Brigade will march at 11 a.m. from BETHUNE to VERMELLES, route BEUVRY - cross roads F.29.c. - VERMELLES and relieve the 7th Division in the trenches on the night 27th/28th September. The 38th Field Co R.E. will accompany the 85th Infantry Brigade.
   Officers of the 85th Infantry Brigade will go forward and meet guides of the 7th Division at 1 p.m. at VERMELLES CHURCH. The details of the relief to be arranged direct between the G.O.C. 85th Infantry Brigade and the 7th Division.

2. The 84th Infantry Brigade will leave PARADIS at 10 a.m. on the 27th, in motor busses, for BETHUNE, route LOCON to GRAND PLACE, BETHUNE, where they will debus and march via BEUVRY to the area SAILLY LABOURSE - NOYELLES where they will halt for the night. Busses will arrive at PARADIS at 10 a.m.

3. The 83rd Infantry Brigade will leave ROBECQ at 1 p.m. in motor busses and proceed to BETHUNE, route MONT BERNECHON to GRAND PLACE, BETHUNE where they will debus and march to BEUVRY and halt for the night. Busses will arrive at ROBECQ at 12 noon.

4. The 2/1st Northumbrian Field Co will join the 84th Infantry Brigade tomorrow afternoon in the area SAILLY LABOURSE by march route.

5. The Divisional Artillery will move and be billeted under the orders of the G.O.C., R.A., in the area PONT D'HINGES - AVALETTE) LES CHOQUAUX - ESSARS - OBLINGHEM - LE CAUROY. Times of departure to be wired to 28th Division Headquarters.

6. The transport of 83rd and 84th Infantry Brigades will join their Brigades before nightfall 27th September.

7. Special instructions will be issued later for Train Companies and Divisional Ammunition Column which will remain in their present billets.

8. The A.D.M.S., will make the necessary arrangements for Field Ambulances to accompany the Infantry Brigades.

R. H. Hare
Lieut Colonel.
General Staff, 28th Division.

Issued at 6.0 a.m.
Surrey Yeomanry.
Cyclists.   Signals.
C.R.A.   A.D.M.S.
C.R.E.   Train.
83rd Infantry Brigade.   A.P.M.
84th Infantry Brigade.   7th Division.
85th Infantry Brigade.

On His Majesty's Service.

121/7140

28th Division

HdQrs R.A. 28th Division

Vol X

a2/a56

October 15

WAR DIARY
or
INTELLIGENCE SUMMARY.
(Erase heading not required.)

Army Form C. 2118.

28th Divn Arty.

130.

Hour, Date, Place	Summary of Events and Information	Remarks and references to Appendices
CHATEAU DES PRES SAILLY LA BOURSE 1st Oct 15 12. noon 2.45 P.M. 3.10 P.M. 6.0 P.M. 8.0 P.M. night 1/2nd	During the morning HdQrs CRA - Bdes & Batteries moved up to SAILLY LA BOURSE. CRA assumed command of the artillery covering 28th Divl Front. viz 3rd B.A.C, the 130th How Bde, 146" R.A. (heavy batteries under 2nd A.S. R.F.A. having a country battery) & 50th B.A, 9th S.A.A.F. The front allotted by 1st Corps Artillery runs from G5c8.5 in QUARRY TRENCH to P3 (A28c 3.4). It was decided that at 8.0 P.M. the inf. tooth should silently raid LITTLE WILLIE. Orders been issued to O.C. 7th Siege Group. (Orders attached - Appendix 123) Orders issued to Field Artillery. (Orders attached - Appendix 124) Relief of Second Section completed except for 50th Bde which is ordered to be relieved tonight. The attack is however reported to have failed at first its him succeeded ultimately its two lines which were recaptured by the C.Bs. Batteries laid on their night lines which were intermittent fire all night. SLAG ALLEY was kept under intermittent fire all night. Communications satisfactory, but were 84th Bdy & 3rd M.46. B.A. by direct wire with So. Bs. Through F.O.O. By night of Brigadier learns that it was engaged in early morning	Appendix 123. " 124.

WAR DIARY
or
INTELLIGENCE SUMMARY.
(Erase heading not required.)

Army Form C. 2118.

131

28th Div. Arty.

Hour, Date, Place	Summary of Events and Information	Remarks and references to Appendices
SAILLY LA BOURSE 2nd October.	Situation 6.30 A.M. We hold LITTLE WILLIE – WEST FACE – Chord running through pt 33 + BIG WILLIE. The junction of NEW TRENCH + LITTLE WILLIE is not in our hands. Various patrols of Germans appear to be in its spread amongst our Trenches.	
8.45 A.M.	Orders issued for PEKIN + FOSSE ALLEYS to be fired on intermittently throughout the day by 3" + 5.0" B.Ls. respectively. (Inf. art. orders) An attack on hive similar to last night was arranged + orders issued.	
	The attack was to be at 9 P.M. Fire was opened by Divnl Arty at 8 P.M. to continue till 9.30 speeding up at 9.10 P.M.	
9 P.M.	at attack. Fire host opened till 10 P.M. + later till 12 midnight. Orders for midnight attack were that there should be no artillery support but batteries were to stand by in case of a bombardment help from 84th Bde Crchk.	
3rd Oct. 5. A.M.	46th Bde. Fired on FOSSE TRENCH to new gOC 84th B.A. on a Division.	
	Station.	
7.15 P.M.	German counter attacked from LITTLE WILLIE across the open. All batteries were at once turned on to LITTLE WILLIE, the rear + DUMP TRENCHES.	
7.55 P.M. 8.5 A.M.	Manners reported Germans had been driven back. 1st Cnf. Artillery fired 6" How. on LITTLE WILLIE	

WAR DIARY
or
INTELLIGENCE SUMMARY.
(Erase heading not required.)

Army Form C. 2118.

132

28th Div A...

Hour, Date, Place	Summary of Events and Information	Remarks and references to Appendices
SAILLY LA BOURSE (Contd.)		
8.20 AM	O.C. B.4 B.H. ordered Artillery fire to cease. 3rd Bn 146th B.Gs stopped from — 50th B.H ordered to continue enfilading FOSSE TRENCH. 1st Cpl. asked to mow. fire off 6 in How into FOSSE TRENCH & FOSSE COTTAGES.	
8.30 AM	1st Cpl. had turned on 6in. to FOSSE COTTAGES - while 6" howitzers Cottages + FOSSE TRENCH. 146th asked to fire on North Face parapets to counter attack on the HOHENZOLLERN CHORD.	
8.50 AM	Fire on LITTLE WILLIE turned again 1st Cpl. asked to drop onto that trench again. 3rd B.H. ordered to bombard the trench also. Cpl. Commanders asked how artillery bombardment shd. afford.	
10.0 AM	Sq. I.M. informed 146 - of this intention to renew HOHENZOLLERN Redoubt Sd. B.M. ... reported cut our objective to that B.M. 28.X.R.mad... bombarded second HOSSE TRENCHES. 3rd B.M. ... standing by. 146 B.M 3 M.Bn from on LITTLE WILLIE.	
10.30 AM	1st Cpl. Artillery asked for fire of heavy guns on LITTLE WILLIE + front 33 in the Redoubt. Latter considered too risky. So rel... ... engaged by "Sing" front about 11. AM	
2.15 PM	The heavy Artillery fire on LITTLE WILLIE has stopped + a second Battery of 3" Bd. put on in substitution.	

WAR DIARY or INTELLIGENCE SUMMARY

Army Form C. 2118.

133   28 Div AK

Hour, Date, Place	Summary of Events and Information	Remarks and references to Appendices
SAILLY LA BOURSE	Oct.	
3rd 1.10 PM	Infantry Brigadiers reported all quiet on the front relief in progress. An reported him my 1st cease. Orders given accordingly.	
2.30 PM	An observer of 146th Bn saw German bombing HOHENZOLLERN from LITTLE WILLIE. Our men opened slow rate of fire.	
4.50 PM	Suppt. Brigadiers in moved + significant approval. 7th Divn reported Germans massing opposite Gun Trench. 1st Corps instructed FOSSE ALLEY Annual.	
5.10 PM	3rd BdeBdy ordered to bombard on point 42. Suggested projected attack into f. Trench. Bombard went by 9m Trench. Batteries 86, 73 to be covered. Batteries 3 MB + but in fire Battery 146 "B" on Trench junction G.6.d.4.2. Trench junction G.6.A.2.4. On Battery 146 "B" on Trench junction.	
5.30 PM	Divnl Staff said it was expected that BIG WILLIE might be attacked from SOUTH FACE. To meet this the Battery 146th Bn on junction 35 + 42 m DUMP TRENCH. The Battery to open slow fire down SOUTH FACE from point 35 half way down to point 60. No artillery SA Bde to fire slowly on DUMP TRENCH in enfilade as far South as point 60. 2 Bde Batteries 3, 73, 87 + 2 Howitzers to stand by to shoot on South Face	
8.57 PM	Heavy firing broke out on divisional front + our 83rd Bde ordered the 3rd ¼ of 4th Bn to open on return of German trenches. by Wire.	

Army Form C. 2118.

WAR DIARY
or
INTELLIGENCE SUMMARY.
(Erase heading not required.)

134   28th Div Arty

Hour, Date, Place	Summary of Events and Information	Remarks and references to Appendices
SAILLY LA BOURSE (3rd Cmte) 8.25 PM	1st Cmte turned on Letters of 2nd Div to MADAGASCAR & CEMETERY TRENCH, first as a burst. Shortly afterwards the infantry slackened 18.3"B & crushed asken batteries to renew intermit. rifle fire.	Appendix 125.
8.50 PM	The conduct of batteries during the night laid down in Operation order No. 50 - appendix 125.	
4th Oct 15 At 1.20 AM	the rate of fire was increased from 4.15 AM to 4.45 AM. Instructions were allotted to the Bty 38"B & to 9/14+6". To fire for half an hour from 4.45 AM, at which time all other fire was to cease.	
4.45 AM	Fire on front line ceased & rate of batting each of 86" 14+6"B" interfered as prior 97+35 in FOSSE TRENCH.	
6.30 AM	Tasks were allotted to different Btys by Sec. 83rd Subft. Bde. Throughout the morning fire maintained in accordance with the wishes of the Subft Infy Cmdrs.	
12.15 PM	Arrangements made with Rifle for reputation of Hindgen on front maned by the 1st Cmte Artillery.	
1.55 PM	In accordance with 1st Cmte G 514. BM 507 (appendix 126) issued to Batteries ordering fire accordingly.	Appendix 126.
2.0 PM	Cmte Arty opened fire on Hohenzollern Redoubt. So c/1.20 ordered & fire 10 rounds HE & continue at rate of 10 rounds per minute with HE.	

WAR DIARY or INTELLIGENCE SUMMARY.
(Erase heading not required.)

Army Form C. 2118.

135   **28th Div Arty.**

Hour, Date, Place	Summary of Events and Information	Remarks and references to Appendices
SAILLY LA BOURSE (4th Corps)		
4.10 PM	Information from a F.O.O. that Panorama could be seen manning ham- let from G4 b 69, 65 4 b & w. 36th De Battery on that portion of FOSSE Trench ordered to fire 10 rounds y/HE with shift. Programme carried out during the night, which, otherwise, passed quietly. Wind	
5th Octb. 6.40 AM	Arranged to registration of C/130 R.F.A. with Aeroplane observation.	
9.25 AM	146. B.A. Observer reported a howitzer at work on BIG WILLIE. Position of howitzer suspected to be between points 97 + 35 on DUMP TRENCH a howitzer battery put on to fire 20 rounds H.E.	
9.30 PM	Minenwerfer located by a F.O.O. at about pt 35 on SOUTH FACE. 1st Corps Arty informed so heavy howitzer put onto shoot it in addition to the 4.5 in howitzer already engaging it. after about 8 rounds from the 71 Siege Brock the minenwerfer stopped firing.	
10.30 PM	minenwerfer still silent	
12.45 PM	Rate of fire of Rifle Batteries reduced from 30 per hour to 15 per hour in orders of 1st Corps Artillery. Enemy after our information received that the Division would remain in action & but move out with the division but would remain in action & came the Grenade div. in. Following instruction from XI Corps orders forwarded from 1st Corps. The first of the Grenade Division in which comes on the artillery of the 28th Division the brigade of the 7 Div Artillery under orders of	

Army Form C. 2118.

WAR DIARY
or
INTELLIGENCE SUMMARY.
(Erase heading not required.)

28th Div Arty.

136.

Hour, Date, Place	Summary of Events and Information	Remarks and references to Appendices
SAILLY LA BOURSE (5 Cents)		Under Command of CRA 2nd.
6. Octr	G.O. CRA. 2nd Division.	3rd Bde } 28th Div Arty
	Cable Company sent out to lay wire to 35th Bde which is the Bde in	130th " }
	the 7th Div placed under CRA 28th. United wire is laid commn:	146th " 2nd Div Arty
	been through 7th Div Arty H.Q.	25th " " " "
10 AM	1st Corps cut off communication. Grenade Division took over.	35th " " " "
	Commns: established with 11th Corps.	Both BM of 2nd & 28th Div Arty still
10.30 AM	About 11 AM Germans started shelling our trenches. Retaliated on	attached to 2nd Div.
	LITTLE WILLIE with 146th Bde. 7 Siege & Grant put some rounds into	
	LITTLE WILLIE also	
4.35 PM	A number of S.O.S. shell reports falling about CENTRAL BOYAU.	
	Retaliated on trenches with addition of the 3rd Bde on WEST FACE.	
	Night passed quietly. huF	
7. Octr.		
	At 30 AM German shells fall in a field from which we were shelling our support trenches	
	with great occurance. N. Corps Artillery informed needed to turn on	
	a heavy battery.	
2.30 PM	Conference Mitchelmode at R.A.H.Q.	
	Night passed quietly. huF	

WAR DIARY
or
INTELLIGENCE SUMMARY.

Army Form C. 2118.

137.

28th Div^n in Corps.

Hour, Date, Place	Summary of Events and Information	Remarks and references to Appendices
SAILLY LA BOURSE 8th Oct		
11.30 AM	Garden alley shelled with 5"g'n Howr. 35th B^n retaliated + 7th Siege Bomb. also retaliated.	
12.30 PM	Enemy party fired on in SLAG ALLEY by 35th B^n. German shelled the trenches about Central Boyau. Retaliated with the Batteries & each of 2 Boy cell.	
1.15 PM	9/30" Howr Battery had 15 observing stations knocked out. 7th Div Arty reports their front line heavily shelled, No casualties but Aeroplanes immediately. Bombardt most methodical continued through the afternoon.	
3.40 PM	Rifle fire broke out from HOHENZOLLERN T at	
3.50 PM	The spread down the front after Guards Division.	
4.15 PM	19th Battn observing officer reports enemy bombing in G5.D8.7 where to Thumbs Communicn were using for. Rate 4/m in DUMP TRENCH & SLAG ALLEY increased.	
4.30 PM	Aeroplane reported German attack from HULLUCH and in cover of same. Reported at moment mentioned. 7 th Div Arty asked if they inform own lines - replied the attack - as far as could be made out, was South of LOOS.	35th B^n - SLAG ALLEY Dump Trench 97-35
5.45 PM	News received that Coldstream Guards had repulsed the bomb attack and had taken some prisoners. Distribution officer as in margin.	5th B^n - South face of Gubior^s. West face. 146 B^n - LITTLE WILLIE. 36th - FOSSE TRENCH. 13 co - Trustym - A2q & S.3 Trench joints G5a.S.7 Trench in between.

WAR DIARY
or
INTELLIGENCE SUMMARY.
(Erase heading not required.)

Army Form C. 2118.
138.
28th - Divnl Arty.

Hour, Date, Place	Summary of Events and Information	Remarks and references to Appendices
SAILLY LA BOURSE (9th cont)	Trench distorted 100° E & to W. Prisoners reported reinforcements from 6am MG fire. Front Divnl Cmdr thanked CRA 2d for the support of the 9am.	
9th Oct.	Conference ref. shttle. Programme of distribution of fire submitted to Corps. 22 MGs by 6–9am in stud of 3"–MGs by 12"–15 Divnl Arty. Quiet day – nothing to report.	Skenker note No 51 & phone note September 125
10th Oct.	Quiet day, no form except artil aircraft fire on Divnl front till about 5 PM when a fine battery fire on BIG WILLIE + DUMP TRENCH. QUARRY TRENCH down KIPPER HEAD. Probably in retaliation for our trench fire of recent Heavy Batteries on BIG WILLIE. 35th B'de Still covers front M. Fund. Reln. until relieved in night 10/13.	Barrage attached.
7 PM	About 7 PM news received from 5th — Bde with RFB Bfl 2nd fund Bn that attack on BIG WILLIE was expected. Batteries a barrage Stand manner was maintained.	
11 PM	Rnrd Divn reported having gained position at G 5 a 7,2 Communication trench at G 5 a 7,2. It was attacked with that trench. Batteries stood by for a Counter attack. Same as for 7 P.M. attack.	

Army Form C. 2118.

2g D ind Arty.

139

WAR DIARY
or
INTELLIGENCE SUMMARY.
(Erase heading not required.)

Instructions regarding War Diaries and Intelligence Summaries are contained in F. S. Regs., Part II and the Staff Manual respectively. Title pages will be prepared in manuscript.

Hour, Date, Place	Summary of Events and Information	Remarks and references to Appendices
SAILLY LA BOURSE 11th Oct	Early afternoon Germans reported Germans were using gas South of LOOS. Shortly afterwards liquid fire was heard from the South East which continued.	
5.40 PM	Information received that our trench opposite HOHENZOLLERN & SPURN HEAD. Retaliated with Field brigade worked Scrip point to engage DUMP TRENCH G7 C.N.W. also the Quarries. Quiet night. Nothing else to report. huF	
12 Oct	SPURN HEAD Communication Trench & ELLIS Avenue came in for considerable attention from German heavy batteries. The trench was considerably damaged about G5d41. Retaliated with 6in Hows (Seig group) on Quarries & STONE ALLEY with Trupnen Sueras during morning & early afternoon. Big Willie was attacked by bombs at either end. In enemy bar at N.E. was established at 6.15 PM Spinach reported troops had been put forward. Three were minutes to & horned artillery answered. The German attack was repulsed. Quick relieved 46° recaptured front. 3rd B Lantern 67 D; aF. Night huF huF	Orders & Spme Jan 15th OD 51.

Army Form C. 2118.

WAR DIARY
or
INTELLIGENCE SUMMARY.

(Erase heading not required.)

40.

28th Div Arty.

Hour, Date, Place	Summary of Events and Information	Remarks and references to Appendices
SAILLY LA BOURSE 13th Oct	Wire cutting on DUMP undertaken by battery 6" B.G mine in hinterland of G.5a 46-72 undertaken by 9.2" Battery. The in trenches, in armoured vault with the 9.6" Divns, were moved back to line G.5c 57-87.	
11.30 AM noon	Hostiges fired incediary shell at AVONT LA-BASSÉE. Reported being set fire to several houses. Bombardment commenced.	
12.45 PM	Heavy shelling of our support trenches from W. eye of LA BASSÉE.	
1.0 PM	Smoke liberated & blew in right direction with the wind.	
2.0 PM	Assault delivered with little opposition on troops left the trenches.	
2.15 PM	All Bty's informed that 2nd Inf phase to extend till 2.30 PM.	
2.20 PM	2nd Inf phase extended to 2.30 PM.	
2.27 PM	Bdr lifted off G.5a and left on A 26d. till 2.45 PM.	
3. PM	Fire lifted off whole of 2nd Inf phase except at NE end of SLAG ALLEY & PENTAGON.	
3.8 PM	All down in 3rd Inf phase target.	
3.15 PM	Divisional Flag seen in N end of HOHENZOLLERN REDOUBT & Rd Mullen flags all over the redoubt.	
3.30 PM	Continuous trustful information sent in by all brigades. 3 PSA reports that their third the attack is held up by bombers in LITTLE WILLIE. 137 Inf Bde report themselves being established on their first objective. Situation on right obscure.	

WAR DIARY or INTELLIGENCE SUMMARY

Army Form C. 2118.

141

28th Divl AK

Hour, Date, Place	Summary of Events and Information	Remarks and references to Appendices

SAILLY LA BOURSE

3.0 PM — 22nd Bn. at request of Capt 137th Bde brought the barrage this night Northw forward from PEKIN TRENCH to FOSSE ALLEY. Then gradually lengthened again.

3.45 PM — Divisional sitrep report Bombing in LITTLE WILLIE.

4.30 PM — 3 M.Bde the battery by 4 Bde ordered to fire rapid rate of fire on Dump for 15 minutes.

4.35 PM — Arty cancelled. Battn — both laid but not to open fire.

5.5 PM — 3 M.Bde notify 64th Bde resume barrage — phase 3.

5.27 PM — All Bdes informed that barrage will be carried out further as shown in the programme.

7.15 PM — hot stuff at 5.30 PM as ordered in the programme. Barrage established on MAD POINT, MADAGASCAR Support Trench A.28.d.47-63 by 36 Bde. Support trench A28.d 63-91 by 148 Bdr. Commn Trench A28d 15 — A.29.c.1.6.

7.45 PM — 3rd Bde ordered retaliation barrage between a North Face between junction with Dump Trench A.29.d.77 to G.4.B.6.5. A Smith Face from junction with Dump Trench about 35 N.point G.4.B.8.2. down Dump trench between pts 42-35. All Bdes retaliated.

7.35 PM — Arty retaliated efficiently on targets for phase 2, with exception of trench Artillery of a little & falling on battery mad Point + Madagascar, the battery Retaliation three times to GSA57 Coy His with reasonable amount on FOSSE COTTAGES REAR ALLEY. On battery Commn. trench parallel to FOSSE TRENCH.

WAR DIARY
or
INTELLIGENCE SUMMARY.
(Erase heading not required.)

Army Form C. 2118.

142   28th Div Arty

Hour, Date, Place	Summary of Events and Information	Remarks and references to Appendices
SAILLY LABOURSE (13 Cont)	Rate f/m 18 hrs 2 rounds per battery per hour. Increase in hours to rounds per battery per hour. 7th G. informed of closing of gun turrets & the arrange to continue harass from MAD POINT. B/gun called up telephone & harass in the night fixed up. 9.22 TFB Lt asked to shunt down the New Trench which runs from ALLET G.5 a 8.5 to G.5 d 8.5, a fire on G.5 823 from Sugar 9.50PM OC 94 TFB ordered to withdraw his section to a position further back - where the Germans can shoot in the ordinary way tomorrow. O.C. his subjects ordered - Though 3rd TFB S - to remain where is his South TFB S are. 10.10PM The lifted Off Fosse Trench from 9.7 hrs on to Suffer trench in here. Fire sustained at these hrs throughout night 13/14. WF.	Plan map of 14th art appendix 126
14 Oct		
12.25AM	One battery 146th Bde on N end of LITTLE WILLIE, between Junction of NEW TRENCH & Junction with FOSSE TRENCH.	
5.30AM	137 Bde ask for fire on North & South Face also on DUMP TRENCH.	
5.45PM	3rd Brigade rate of fire doubled.	

Army Form C. 2118.

WAR DIARY
or
INTELLIGENCE SUMMARY.
(Erase heading not required.)

143   28th Div Art.

Hour, Date, Place	Summary of Events and Information	Remarks and references to Appendices
SAILLY LA BOURSE (14th Cnt) 5.50 AM	Hearing that 137th Bde were about to attack about front G.W. fire of all Batteries increased to Section Fire 1 minute. (less 3rd Bde)	
7.25 AM	Rain in accordance that trophies for attack signalled on North South Face run the DUMP TRENCH, the following alterations were made in the distribution After the 36th Bde from junction of New Trench HOTTIE WILLIE Northwards up LITTLE WILLIE. 18th Map Point to A28d1.5 146 Bde all batteries on FOSSE TRENCH between 15+97. 3rd Bde 18th M. Face, 18th S. Face, 18th DUMP TRENCH between Pt 97 + 35. 18th on DUMP TRENCH between 35 +42. Remainder as before, except How Battery in Fosse Support to fire on A29 c 16 down Corons ALLEY thence A22 & 86. Rate of fire Section Fire 30 seconds.	
7.58 AM	137th Bde reported enemy running his wire from in front of South Face - Howitzers, with a view to stopping this WILLIE.	
9 AM	Cx permission to reduce fire to Section Fire 1 minute.	
9.25 AM	Fire reduced to Section Fire 2 minutes.	

WAR DIARY
or
INTELLIGENCE SUMMARY.
(Erase heading not required.)

Army Form C. 2118.

144   28th Div Arty

Hour, Date, Place	Summary of Events and Information	Remarks and references to Appendices
SANCT LABOURSE 10.15 AM	Fire reduced to 30 rds per battery per hour. Except on LITTLE WILLIE wh is Free.	
10.25 AM	Hrs 8 mmty batteries. Rate of fire of batteries on N & S Faces reduced to 30 rds per battery per hour. Battn on LITTLE WILLIE unrestricted.	
11.35 AM	Heavy from NEW TRENCH Junction. All Field Batteries (except Littleton on LITTLE WILLIE) fire at 15 rds per battery per hour. LITTLE WILLIE to fire 30 rds per hour. Batteries ordered to fire occasionally one round between the two lines & between Fosse Trench & LITTLE WILLIE in case enemy are forming advantageously. This not to exceed the amount allowed for batteries.	
1.10 PM	22nd Bn not a battery on any support advanced from front line SE of 6aW to assist Bombing party. In British bombers marched to front line with Kirk. Without short known of all.	
2.30 PM	To pretty against bombers fire in LITTLE WILLIE. North & South Faces Quickened. Another batten (the two coys 'B' 'A') put into former bombers in LITTLE WILLIE.	
3.50 PM	For 75's (32 rds pp) ordered to stop firing by CRA.	
6.0 PM	Night lines a fire at afternoon — at 30 rds.	
6.54 PM	3rd FB. orders for increased fire on South Face as Infantry reported a front attack from there. Barrage established.	

Army Form C. 2118.

WAR DIARY
or
INTELLIGENCE SUMMARY.
(Erase heading not required.)

145   28 Div Arty

Hour, Date, Place	Summary of Events and Information	Remarks and references to Appendices

SAILLY LA BOURSE (14th Gnft)

7.5PM C-in-C asked to turn some heavy shell on South Face. 6 in How turned on.
Night passed quietly. 3rd Brand Bde relieved 137th Bde. WF

15th Oct. Quiet day. Light hostile artillery activity with heavier movement occasion from the shelling of our old front line trenches opposite the Redoubt

8.45PM An observer reported rifle + machine gun fire - bombs + Whizz bangs from South Face. Barrage at once established. Turned out to be a German attack which came to nothing. Night passed quietly. 2nd Grand Bde relieved the 72 Bde. WF

16 Oct. Very quiet. Quiet morning. Some retaliation for shelling your trenches reported in the afternoon.

7.10PM German attacked Big Willie with Bombs. Barrage at once established at increased rate of fire.

7.25PM Report received that attack was repulsed. Normal rate resumed.

Army Form C. 2118.

WAR DIARY
or
INTELLIGENCE SUMMARY.
(Erase heading not required.)

146.

28th Divi Arty

Hour, Date, Place	Summary of Events and Information	Remarks and references to Appendices
SAILLY LA BOURSE (16 Cant)		
8.25 PM	3rd Grenade Bn informed 22nd Bn that they have been attacked again by bombs asked for fire in DUMP TRENCH & AS ALLEY. Batteries reported. Instruction order No 52 for the support of frontal bombing attack at 5 AM issued. Night Quiet. HWF	
17 Oct 5 AM	Barrage established.	
6.35 AM	1st Grenadier Guards reported suffering from M.G. fire from DUMP. Scots Guards & 5th H.A.R. asked to fire on DUMP. No Scots in 22nd Bn hut in S.W. face.	
7.20 AM	M.G. fire held up progress of Bombers going towards LITTLE WILLIE. No battery 3 MG in hut on DUMP.	
7.35 PM	Chilsteans having much reached point 60 were obliged to with draw to original line by MS fire from DUMP.	
7.54 AM	Scots Guards reported suffering from M.S. from DUMP. Bomb HQrs Bn turned onto it.	
8.40 AM	Divl asks to make fort Montferins Rate of fire reduced to 5 rounds per Battery per hour.	
9.10 AM	Guards reported they expect an attack from FOSSE & SLAG ALLEYS. 7th Divn asked to barrage with mg. it 22nd Bn hut onto SLAG	

WAR DIARY or INTELLIGENCE SUMMARY

Army Form C. 2118.

28th Div. Arty.

Hour, Date, Place	Summary of Events and Information	Remarks and references to Appendices
SAILLY LA BOURSE (17 Cont:)		
10.10 AM	and FOSSE ALLEY for new trench which runs S.E. from G.5.a.85. Our artillery fire shelling all down our trenches rate of fire in crescendo to Section Fire 1 min: for 2 an hour & after much at 2 min.	
10.17 AM	Enemy artillery moving in DUMP TRENCH – from which found have retired to point G.5.c.6.9. 3rd Bde Battery on DUMP put in to DUMP TRENCH from point 17 to just S.E. of pt 35.	
10.25 AM	Siege group put on DUMP TRENCH from pt 35 N. wards. a request for fire on DUMP TRENCH on hard & smith on G.5.a.5.2 in attempt to Sp. it up decided that the front was too close to hunt on another battery 3rd Bde taken up a commn: trench. Its exit on which are already covered put on DUMP TRENCH. As fire from 3rd Bde heavy now 4 from minenwerfer in DUMP SUPPORT.	
11.30 AM	4 min: on Battery and DUMP TRENCH from point 97 to 35. not got in in	
12.30 PM	Rate of fire again increased in retaliation for heavy shelling gone old front line trenches.	
1.30 PM	Normal rate of fire now resumed. Nothing further to report. That 28th Div Art would be relieved by South African Arty moved that A/5 on nights 19/20 & 20/21 & moved in stern order over from Mount Dis. Art. on night 20/21 & 21/22.	

Army Form C. 2118.

148

28th Div Ark

WAR DIARY
or
INTELLIGENCE SUMMARY.
(Erase heading not required.)

Hour, Date, Place	Summary of Events and Information	Remarks and references to Appendices
SAILLY LA BOURSE 18th Octr	A.A officer ordered to retaliate vigorously for any German shelling of our line. To start with at section first 10 rounds for 5 minutes. Practically no German fire on our front.	
6PM	6" Hows searched DUMP support trench for minenwerfer. Batteries ordered to stop the enemies barrages, tend to fire in anticipation or when called upon.	
7.30 PM	Report received of heavy shelling of point 57. Heavies retaliated. Ops Staff asked for heavies in retaliation as they anticipated a counter attack.	
8.0 PM	Nothing happened. Fire stopped. My LP front Patrols to catch working party on our front E of LITTLE WILLIE a short distant front of fire ordered for 10.45 PM. hvF	
19-Octr	Orders received for 28th Divn Artillery to hull out in nights 19/20 & 20/21 & to proceed to area CANTRAINNE, L'ECLEME, BUSNETTES & BAS RIEUX prior to entrainment at LILLERS & CHOCQUES on 21st Octr & subsequent days.	
5.5PM	37th By - sent message through 3rd Inf Bde that Germans were heavier in the trenches. They were not spotted with our artillery	

Army Form C. 2118.

WAR DIARY
or
INTELLIGENCE SUMMARY.

(Erase heading not required.)

Instructions regarding War Diaries and Intelligence Summaries are contained in F.S. Regs., Part II and the Staff Manual respectively. Title pages will be prepared in manuscript.

149

28th Div Arty.

Hour, Date, Place	Summary of Events and Information	Remarks and references to Appendices
STILL LA BOURSE 19h Oct 6.5 P.M.	6nd wanted support. 12th Div Arty informed & Senior Group asked to start. Later infantry but free was being attacked - Barrage established but had to be cancelled. Some retaliation for German shelling.	

WAR DIARY
or
INTELLIGENCE SUMMARY.
(Erase heading not required.)

Army Form C. 2118.

Hour, Date, Place	Summary of Events and Information	Remarks and references to Appendices
SAILLY LA BOURSE 19th Octr.	During the night first section of 28th Div Arty were relieved and proceeded to billets not ann. next morning.	
BETHUNE 20th Octr	CRA Front. Div assumed Command at 4 P.M., CRA 28 Div moved to BETHUNE. At same hour Bde HQ's Cmdrs gathering Btts and Batteries assumed Command. Ammn Columns & first section moved back to following areas. 3rd Bde BUSNETTES. 3rd Bde CANTRAINNE. 130 Bde BAS RIEUX 146 Bde LECEME. Bde HAUT RIEUX. Remaining section relieved throughout by 7 A.M. next morning in accordance with instructions in appendix 127	Appendix 127
In train 21st Octr	146th Bde RFA entrained — in accordance appendix 127	
In train 22 Octr	20th Bde, 3rd Bde & part of 130 Bde entrained.	
MARSEILLES 23rd Octr	Remainder Div. Bde RFA entrained. 1st train 146 Bde & CRA reached MARSEILLES & camped at Parc BORELY	
25th Octr	all D.A. camped in Parc BORELY	
25-31st Octr	waiting for home transports.	

121/7439

Hd. Qrs. R.A. 28th Division

Compilation of Vol X

Oct 15

13.	(2886)	23rd Oct.	6.51	2/1st Northbn.Fd.Co. R.E.
14.	(2884) (2885)	do.	9.51	(H.Q. Divl.Engineers. (38th Field Coy.R.E.
15.	(2845)	do.	12.51	146th Bde.RFA.Amm.Col. (less 40 horses.)
16.	(2855)	do.	15.51	31st Bde. RFA. Amm.Col. (less 40 horses.)
17.	(2865)	do.	18.51	3rd Bde. RFA. Amm.Col. (less 40 horses.)
18.	(2892) (½2874)	do.	22.51	(84th Field Ambulance. (½ 130th Bde.RFA.Amm.Col.
19.	(½2874) (2893)	24th Oct.	2.51	(½ do. do. (85th Field Ambulance.
20.	(2894)	do.	6.51	(86th Field Ambulance. (Field Amb.Workshop Unit.

SECRET.

Appendix 127.

1. The 28th Division will entrain at FOUQUEREUIL and LILLERS in accordance with attached time tables.

2. In order to make more room for men in the closed trucks which have a maximum capacity of 40 men or 8 horses each, Infantry Brigades should arrange to divide the horses of 1st Line Transport of Battalions so as to have the full number of 8 horses per truck as nearly as possible. Thus each battalion is taken to have 81 horses and the total for the 4 battalions of a Brigade would thus be 324 horses for which 41 trucks are necessary, i.e. 10 trucks for each battalion except one which has 11 trucks, instead of 11 trucks for each battalion.

3. Transport and strong working parties (1 company) for Infantry battalions will arrive 3 hours and remainder of Battalion 1 hour before time of departure of train. All other units 3 hours before.

4. The flat sided trucks provided should take four pairs of wheels except in cases of large vehicles such as G.S. Wagons, motor ambulances, etc., and a small vehicle such as a water cart can be loaded with a G.S. Wagon.

5. Units will entrain with 3 days preserved rations, exclusive of the unexpired portion of the day's ration and the iron ration.

6. Straw for trucks will be available at the entraining station.

7. Blankets will be taken. They will be handed in at the detraining station.

8. A Divisional representative and an A.S.C. Officer will be present at the entrainment.

9. A statement showing number of Officers, N.C.O's and men, horses and vehicles entrained and the name of the Commanding Officer of the train will be handed to the Divl. representative.

10. The first halting place for tea and water is at LONGUEAU. Details as to others will be communicated en route.

R. HENVEY, Lieut. Colonel,
A.A. & Q.M.G., 28th Division.

20th October 1915.

SECRET.

28th DIVISION.
PROGRAMME OF ENTRAINING
FOUQUEREUIL STATION.

Number of Train.	Distinguishing No. of Unit.	Date.	Time	Units.
1.	2821.	21/10/15.	12.35	2/Northd. Fusiliers.
2.	2822.	21/10/15.	15.35	1st Suffolk Regt.
3.	2823.	21/10/15.	18.35	2nd Cheshire Regt.
4.	2824.	21/10/15.	22.35	1st Welsh Regiment.
5.	(2820. (2825. (2803.	22/10/15. --- ---	2.35 --- ---	H.Q. 84th Inf. Brigade. No.3 Sec: Div. Signal Co. "B" Sqdn. Surrey Yeom:
6.	2831.	22/10/15.	6.35.	2nd East Kent R.
7.	2832.	22/10/15.	9.35.	3rd Royal Fusrs.
8.	2833.	22/10/15.	12.35.	2nd East Surrey Regt.
9.	2834.	22/10/15.	15.35.	3rd Middlesex Regt.
10. 10.	(2830. (2835. (2810. (2815. (2895. (2896.	22/10/15. --- --- --- --- ---	18.35. -- -- -- -- --	85th Bde. Hd. Qrs. No.4 Sect: Div. Signal Co. 83rd Bde. Hd. Qrs. No.2 Sect: Div. Signal Co. 15th Sanitary Section. No.17 Mob: Vet. Sect, and Salvage Co.
11.	2811.	22/10/15.	22.35.	2nd K.O. R. Lancs.
12.	2812.	23/10/15.	2.35.	2nd East Yorks.
13.	2813.	23/10/15.	6.35.	1st K.O.Y.L.I.
14.	2814.	23/10/15.	9.35.	1st York & Lancs.
15.	2880.	23/10/15.	12.35.	H.Q. Div. Ammn. Column.
16.	2881.	23/10/15.	15.35.	No.1 Sect. D.A. Col.
17.	2882.	23/10/15.	18.35.	No.2 Sect. D.A. Col.
18.	2883.	23/10/15.	22.35.	No.3 Sect. D.A. Col.
19.		(24/10/15.	2.35.	(Surplus Vehicles D.A.C. (and 40 horses from each (18 pr. Bde. Ammn. Col. (and 2 closed trucks for (D.A.D.O.S. stores.

SECRET.

28th Division.

PROGRAMME OF ENTRAINING.

LILLERS STATION.

No. of Train.	Distinguishing No. of Unit.	DATE.	TIME.	UNITS.	REMARKS.
1.	(2841) (½2842)	21st Oct.	12.51	(75th Bty. RFA. (½149th Bty. RFA.	
2.	(½2842) (2843)	do.	15.51	(½149th Bty. RFA. (366th Bty. RFA.	
3.	(2801) (2802) (2804) (2805)	do.	18.51	(Divl. Headquarters) (H.Q. Divl. Artillery) (Divl. Cyclist Coy. (H.Q. & No.1 Sec. Div. Sig. Co.	
4.	(2840) (2844)	do.	22.51	(H.Q. 146th Bde. RFA. (367th Bty. RFA.	
5.	(2851) (½2852)	22nd Oct.	2.51	(69th Bty. RFA. (½ 100th Bty. RFA.	
6.	(½2852) (2853)	do.	6.51	(½ 100th Bty. RFA. (103rd Bty. RFA.	
7.	(2850) (2854)	do.	9.51	(H.Q. 31st Bde. RFA. (118th Bty. RFA.	
8.	(2861) (½2862)	do.	12.51	(18th Bty. RFA. (½ 22nd Bty. RFA.	
9.	(½2862) (2863)	do.	15.51	(½ 22nd Bty. RFA. (62nd Bty. RFA.	
10.	(2860) (2864)	do.	18.51	(H.Q. 3rd Bde. RFA. (365th Bty. RFA.	
11.	(2870) (2871) (½2872)	do.	22.51	(H.Q. 130th (How) Bde. RFA. ('A' Bty do. (½ 'B' Bty do.	
12.	(½2872) (2873)	23rd Oct.	2.51	(½ 'B' Bty do. ('C' Bty do.	

2.-

Appendix 123

O.C. Seige Group.

SECRET

BM 481

1st Oct-15

(1). The 84th Infty Brigade is to assault LITTLE WILLIE trench tonight at 8.0 P.M.

(2) Will you please arrange for Heavy Artillery support as under :-
(a) Slow rate of fire on LITTLE WILLIE as far South as G4 b 2.5 from 5.0 PM to 8.0 P.M.

(b). A slow rate of fire on MAD POINT and MADEGASCAR from 5 PM to 9.0 P.M.

(3). At 8.0 P.M. precisely, the fire will be lifted from LITTLE WILLIE directed on to FOSSE TRENCH, Junctions of NORTH FACE with DUMP TRENCH, and DUMP TRENCH not further South than G5 a 2.6. Also on South end of FOSSE Cottages and NORTH FACE TRENCH from G4 b 9.7 to G4 b 6.5.

(4) Fire should be maintained at a slow rate till 9.0 AM.

(5) Acknowledge.
2.45 P.M.

WFergusson
Maj BMRA
28

Appendix 124

3rd Bde
OC 130 Bde
146 "
50 "

SECRET
BM 482.

1-10-15

(1). At 8.0 P.M precisely - the 84th Infty Bde will assault LITTLE WILLIE.

(2). A programme for heavy artillery support has been arranged.

(3). The Divisional Artillery will open fire at 8.0 P.M. as under:—
One Battery 146th Bde on MAD POINT & MADAGASCAR.
Two batteries 146th " on FOSSE TRENCH.
3rd Brigade on DUMP TRENCH as far South as G5a2.6.
50th Brigade on PEKIN ALLEY
Send FO

(4). Batteries will maintain a rate of fire of Battery fire 30 seconds until 8.30 P.M.

(5). Acknowledge.

3.10 P.M.

[signature]
Maj BMRA
28.

It must be understood that the preparation for the assault is to be carried out by the Heavy Artillery. The Divnl Artillery opens fire - on points in rear, at the moment the assault is delivered.

Copy No. 5.

28th DIVL ARTY O.O No. 50
3rd Oct. 1915

1. The 83rd Infantry Bde will assault WEST FACE from point 60 to junction of Communicating Trench at G 4 b 1.2 at 4.30 a.m. tomorrow.

2. Artillery fire will be maintained all night as follows.
 146 Bde   One Battery Northern half of LITTLE WILLIE; but 100 yards North and South from the junction of NEW TRENCH will be avoided.
  One Battery NORTH FACE TRENCH and to search open ground, included in triangle FOSSE TRENCH – LITTLE WILLIE – NORTH FACE.
 3rd BRIGADE   One Battery SOUTH half of LITTLE WILLIE and WEST FACE down to G 4 b 1.2
  One Battery WEST FACE to G 4 b 3.0, and not EAST of that point.
  One Battery DUMP TRENCH between points 42 and 60 and to search open ground between North and South face, but not to shoot within 250 yards of point 60.

C BATTERY /130th BDE to fire 10 rounds an hour (spread out) into HOHENZOL-LERN Redoubt, searching about.

3. Rate of fire for 18pr Batteries 40 rounds an hour, but rate at no time to be faster than one round a minute.

4 Acknowledge

8.50 pm A.R. Burkhardt Capt
for Bde Major R.A.
28th Division

Copy No 1   28th DIVISION
Copy No 2   1st CORPS
Copy No 3   3rd BDE R.F.A
Copy No 4   146 Bde R.F.A
Copy No 5   R.A (File)

"A" Form.
Army Form C. 2121.
MESSAGES AND SIGNALS.

TO: all Bdes

Sender's Number: BM 507 Day of Month: 4 In reply to Number: — AAA

Corps directs that the trenches and areas mentioned below be kept under intermittent artillery fire day and night aaa Parapets should be destroyed especially on WEST FACE aaa Objectives are allotted as under aaa 3 Batteries 3rd Brigade WEST NORTH and SOUTH FACES and area between two last named aaa fire should not be brought beyond G4b40 on WEST FACE aaa Two batteries 36th Brigade FOSSE TRENCH and DUMP TRENCH as far South as point 60 also ground in triangle FOSSE TRENCH — LITTLE WILLIE — NORTH

"A" Form. — MESSAGES AND SIGNALS. — Army Form C. 2121.

FACE aaa Two batteries 146th Brigade LITTLE WILLIE and triangle LITTLE WILLIE — FOSSE TRENCH — NORTH FACE aaa shell should not be dropped within 100 yards of NEW TRENCH which our troops hold aaa Occasional rounds from 130th Brigade will be put into FOSSE COTTAGES and CORONS DE MARON and PEKIN aaa 18pr Batteries will fire at the rate of 30 rounds an hour aaa Shooting will commence on receipt of this order aaa HE will be used aaa acknowledge.

From POMRA
Time 1.25PM

(Z) signed Ferguson Maj RFA

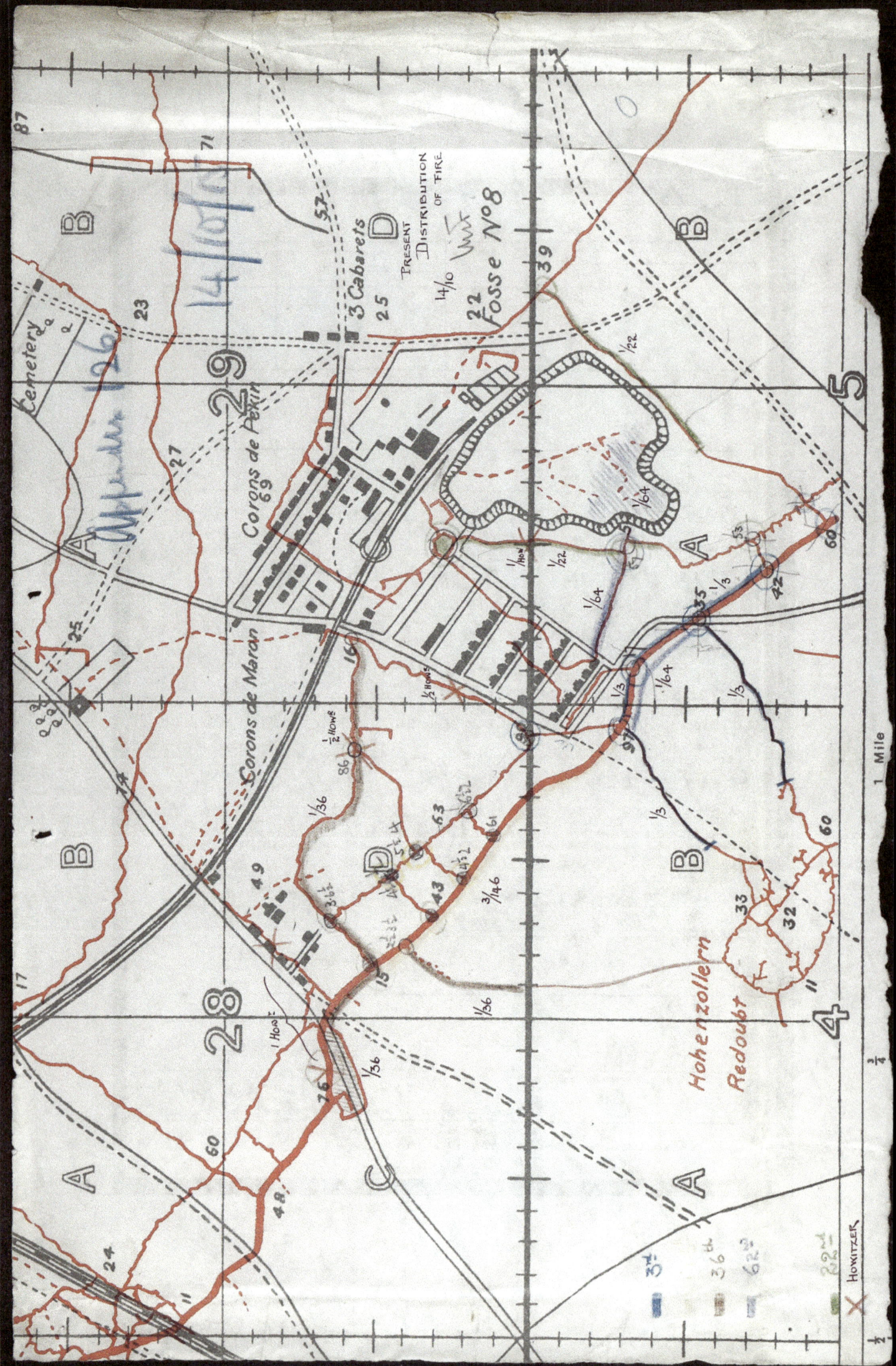

SECRET   C.R.A.   B.M. 532

11th October 1915.

The following table shows rates of fire to be employed in carrying out the programme on the 13th instant.

1.   18-pounder Batteries.

       From   12 noon to 1.0 p.m.   Section fire 30 seconds
               1.0 p.m. to 2.0 p.m.   ..   .. 2 minutes
               2.0 p.m. to 4.0 p.m.   ..   .. 1½ minutes
    x   4.0 p.m. to 5.30 p.m.   ..   .. 2 minutes

x During this period equal proportions of H.E. and Shrapnel will be used.

2.   4.5" (Howitzer) Batteries.

A.B. & C. From 12 noon to 1.45 p.m.   Section fire 1 minute
A&B (Lachry-) 1.45 pm to 2.30 p.m.   ..   .. 1 minute
     (matory   )
  C (shell   ) 1.45 p.m. to 2.0 p.m.   ..   .. 15 seconds
A and B   2.30 pm to 5.30 p.m.)
)   ..   .. 1 minute
  C   2.0 pm to 5.30 p.m.   )

3.   In the event of the wind being unfavourable and the gas not being employed the amount of ammunition to be expended - as authorised in above table - will be increased by 20% of the whole amount during the first two hours. Under present arrangements 18-pounders will fire 200 rounds per gun, and 4.5" Howitzers 150 rounds per Howitzer exclusive of Lachrymatory shell.

                                                      Major.

                           Brigade Major R.A. 28th Division.

28th Divisional Artillery
Operation Order No. 51

Copy No. 10

SECRET

Reference Map 1/10,000

9th October 1915.

1.   The XIth Corps will, on the 13th instant, attack and capture the QUARRIES and FOSSE No. 8.

The line which will be established runs from G 12 d 3.9 G 12 b 2.2 - G 6 c 8.2 and 4.5 - G 6 a 4.2 - A 29 d 2.5 N.W. corner of CORONS DE MARON A 29 c 1.6 - A 28 d 4.9 and along AUCHY - LEZ - LA - BASSEE - VERMELLES Road to present front trench A 28 c 3.3

2.   Point of junction between 46th and 12th Divisions is G 5 b 6.8

3.   28th Divisional Artillery will support the attack of the 46th Division which will be launched at 2.0 p.m.

4.   46th Division will deliver a LEFT and RIGHT attack, the dividing line between them will be G 4 b 6.0 - right edge of FOSSE COTTAGES and the PENTAGON.

5.   FIRST OBJECTIVE LEFT ATTACK

PENTAGON (exclusive) A 29 c 1.6, A 28 d 6.3 and 4.3, to present front trench at A 28 c 5.1

6.   SECOND OBJECTIVE.

Railway A 29 c 1.6 (inclusive) A 28 d 6.9 - MAD POINT to front trench A 28 c 3.3

7.   RIGHT ATTACK FIRST OBJECTIVE.

TRACK crossing FOSSE ALLEY at G 5 b 6.8 - G 5 b 3.9 and 2.2 PENTAGON (inclusive)

8.   SECOND OBJECTIVE.

A 29 d 2.5, 3 cabarets, N.E. edge of CORON de PEKIN - West edge of CORONS DE MARON Railway A 29 c 1.6 (exclusive)

9.   The Peliminary bombardment will commence at 12.0 noon and will continue until 2.0 p.m.

H.E. will be fired up to 1.0 p.m. at which hour smoke and gas will be launched and shrapnel only will be fired for the remainder of that phase and the succeeding ones.

Separate orders have been given to the 4.5" Howitzers.

Secret.

CRA appendix 125

Amendment to Tables of Rates and Distribution of Fire.

1. The Infantry will now be withdrawn from BIG WILLIE to a point G 5 a 2.0 prior to the bombardment.

2. The 3rd Brigade Battery which fires on WEST FACE will extend its zone to cover the whole of WEST FACE to POINT 60 where it joins BIG WILLIE.

3. The battery 64th Brigade will in addition to bombarding points 32 and 33 bombard also trench running from points 32 to point 1.1 and 33 - 2.4 in WEST FACE.

4. At commencement of bombardment from noon to 12.20 p.m. the rate of fire will be Section Fire 15 seconds. The order for increased rate of fire for 10 minutes before the assult is cancelled. From 12.20 p.m. till 2.0 p.m. the rate will be as ordered in Table of rates of fire with the following exception.

5. The rate of fire of batteries shooting on HOHENZOLLERN REDOUBT and SOUTH FACE i.e. One battery 3rd Brigade on SOUTH FACE, one battery 3rd Brigade on WEST FACE [one battery North Face] and one battery 64th Brigade on points 32 33 and 1.1 and 2.4, will be maintained at section fire 15 seconds during the whole of the first phase - noon till 2.0 p.m.

MF

Major.

12th October 1915.   Brigade Major. R.A. 28th Division.

(2)

10.   The F.O.Officers of the 146th and 3rd Brigades now with the LEFT and RIGHT Battalions of the 2nd Guards Brigade and the F.O. Officers of the 22nd Brigade, hitherto found by the 35th Brigade now with the RIGHT and LEFT Battalions of the 1st Guards Brigade will accompany the Battalions Commanders of the assulting Battalions in the attack.   The F.O.O. of the 36th Brigade and of the 22nd Brigade now with the 2nd and 1st Guards Brigade H.Q. will remain with Headquarters of LEFT and RIGHT attack, namely the Headquarters of the 138th and 137th Brigades respectively.

11.   The F.O.O. of the single gun of the 64th Brigade near WELLS will establish a visual signalling station on the DUMP at the first opportunity. He will also run out wires to connect him with his gun.

12.   A visual signalling station will be established by the 3rd Brigade near the WELLS.

13.   The programme for the distribution of fire for the 28th Divisional Artillery and the affiliated Brigades is forwarded herewith.

14.   Acknowledge.

Major.
Brigade Major R.A. 28th Division.

Copy No. 1 filed
Copy No. 2 3rd Brigade
Copy No. 3 146th Brigade
Copy No. 4 138th Brigade
Copy No. 5 36th Brigade
Copy No. 6 22nd Brigade
Copy No. 7 46th Division
Copy No. 8 XIth Corps

DISTRIBUTION OF FIRE OF 28th DIVISIONAL ARTILLERY.

First phase.

    Bombardment   -   Noon till 2 p.m.

    Gas   -   1 p.m. till 1.50 p.m.

    Smoke   -   1 p.m. till 2 p.m.

3rd Brigade.

    1 battery - WEST FACE as far South as G 4 b 5.0

    1 battery - NORTH FACE.

    1 battery - DUMP Trench between points 97 and 35

    1 battery - SOUTH FACE from point 35 to G 4 b 7.2

146th Brigade.

    1 battery - LITTLE WILLIE Northern half.

    1 battery - LITTLE WILLIE Southern half.

    1 battery - FOSSE Trench 43 - 97

22nd Brigade.

    1 battery - SLAG ALLEY not further South than G 5 a 8.4

    1 battery - PENTAGON (A 29 c 5.3) to G 5 a 5.5

    1 gun   SLAG ALLEY from G 5 a 8.4 (enfilade)

36th Brigade.

    1 battery - FOSSE TRENCH. MAD POINT TO point A 28 d 5.2

    1 battery - A 28 d 5.2 to G 4 b 9.7

    1 battery - Communication Trenches N.E. of FOSSE TRENCH in A 28 d especially CORONS ALLEY and Trench A 28 d 4.8 to A 29 c 2.6

64th Brigade.

    1 battery - HOHENZOLLERN 32 - 33

    1 battery - Trench G 5 a 5½.7 to G 5 a 1½.7½

    1 battery - S.W. face of DUMP.

Howitzers - 130th Brigade.

    1 battery - Communication Trench A 28 d 4½.2 to 8½.6) From 12 noon till 1 p.m. firing lyddite. From 1 p.m. till 1.45 p.m. lyddite on MAD POINT and MALAGASCAR.

    1 battery - LITTLE WILLIE Northern half.

    1 battery - LITTLE WILLIE Southern half   12 noon till 1 p.m. At 1 p.m. fire on AUCHY LA BASSEE slow rate lyddite till 1.45 p.m.

Second Phase.   2 p.m. till 2.10 p.m.

3rd Brigade.

- 1 battery — DUMP TRENCH
- 1 battery — Raise fire off WEST FACE on to A 28 d 9.0 to G 4 b 9.7
- 1 battery — Raise fire off SOUTH FACE on to DUMP TRENCH 97-35

146th Brigade.

- 1 battery — Lift off Northern Half of LITTLE WILLIE on to Trench from A 28 d 4½.7 – 9.0 Then from 2.10 p.m. to 2.30 p.m. on Trench A 28 d 1.5 – A 28 d 4.8
- 1 battery — COMMONS ALLEY
- 1 battery — FOSSE TRENCH

36th Brigade.

As for first phase

22nd Brigade.

As for first phase

Howitzers. 130th Brigade.

- 1 battery — MAD POINT) From 1.45 pm to 2.30 pm 200 rounds of
- 1 battery — MADAGASCAR) lachrymatory shell then continue with) lyddite till 4.0 pm

- 1 battery — AUCHY LA BASSEE at 1.0 pm at slow rate till 1.45 pm at 1.45 pm on front row of FOSSE COTTAGES with 100 rounds Lachrymatory shell till 2.0 pm then back on AUCHY LA BASSEE with lyddite till 5.30 pm

64th Brigade.

As for first phase except one battery (lift off HOHENZOLLERN REDOUBT on to FOSSE TRENCH 15 to 97)

Third Phase.   From 2.10 pm to 4.10 pm after 4.10 pm continued at
                    Section fire 1 minute, till 5.30 p.m.

146th Brigade.

    3 batteries - A 28 c 4.8 to A 22 d 8.4 (1 battery from 2.30)

36th Brigade.

    1 battery   - A 28 b 1.7 to A 28 b 7.4

    2 batteries - A 29 b 4.2 to A 30 a 7.4

22nd Brigade.

    2 batteries - on PEKIN Trench A 30 a 8.8 - A 30 a 7.4 -

                    A 30 a 7.1 - A 30 c 10.6

3rd Brigade.

    3 batteries - Barrage A 29 b 7.1 across open to A 30 c 7.2

    1 battery   - A 29 a 7.2 to A 29 b 4.2

Howitzers. 130th Brigade.

    The batteries on MAD POINT and MADAGASCAR at 4.0 p.m. will fire on
trench A 28 c 4.8 to railway at A 28 a 9.8

64th Brigade.

    1 battery   - A 28 b 7.4 through LONE FARM along trench A 29 a 5.6

    1 battery   - A 29 b 2.4 to A 29 b 4.8

    1 battery   - A 29 a 5.6 to A 29 b 2.4

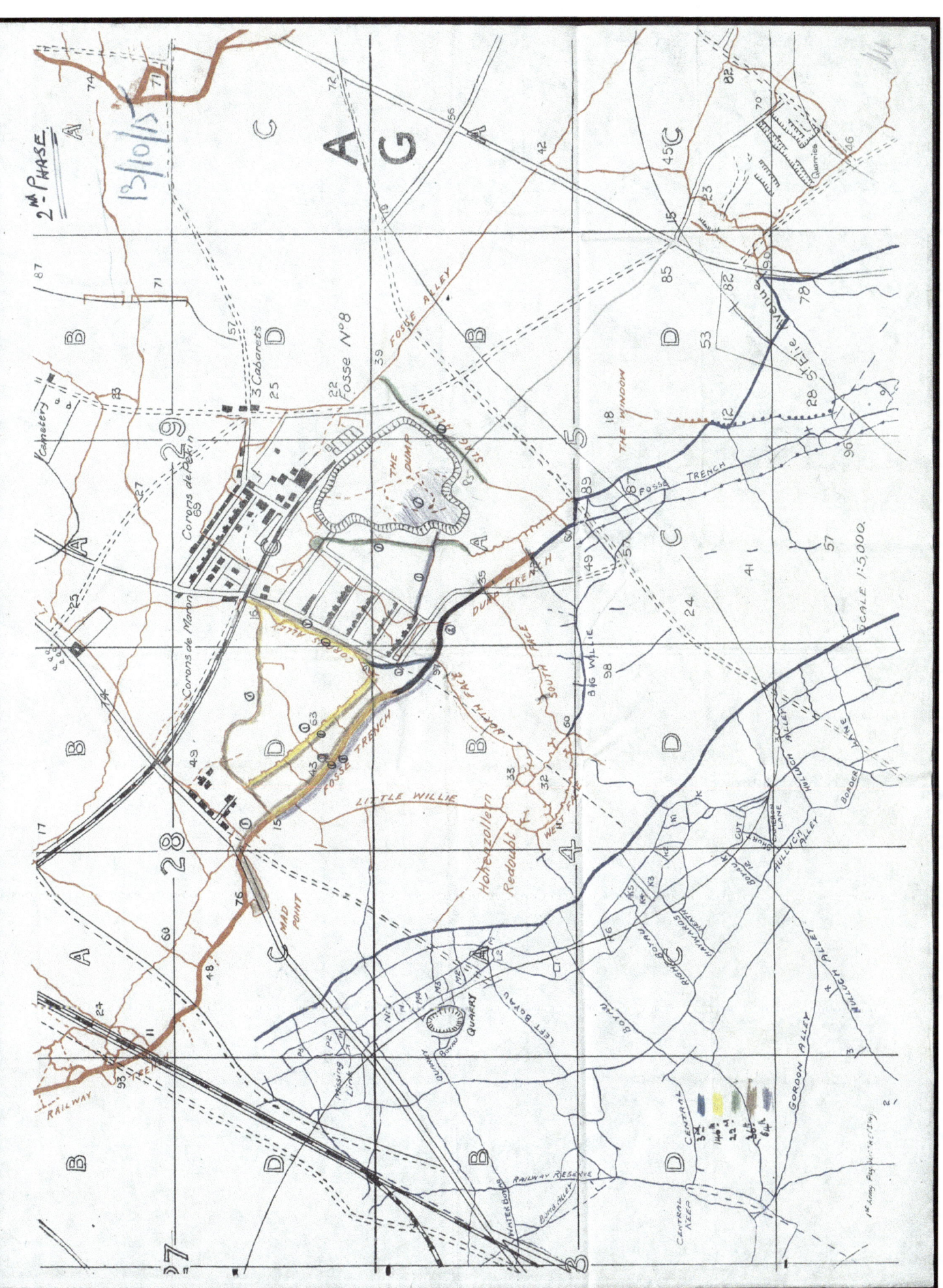

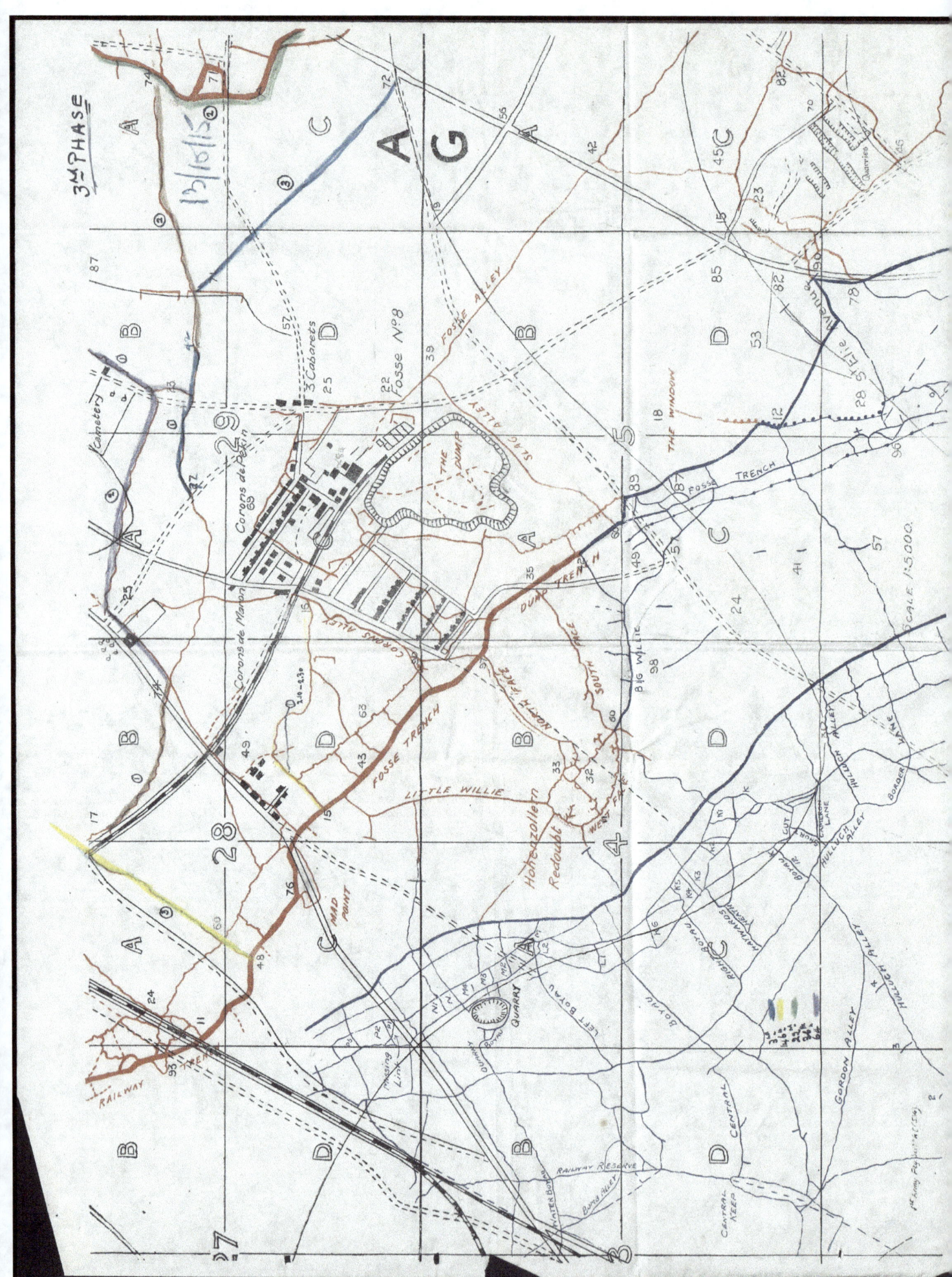

www.ingramcontent.com/pod-product-compliance
Lightning Source LLC
Chambersburg PA
CBHW080851010526
44117CB00014B/2233